THE WEST
62,

WM(
The Grais
Pool
Wolverl
WV2

WEST MIDLANDS EDUCATION AUTHORITIES

BOOK No. ....

Please return this book to the Library from which it was
borrowed on or before the last date stamped. Fines will
be charged on overdue books.

For information about the Library Service please ring
Wolverhampton 764287.

The Constitutions and Laws of the American Indian Tribes — Volume XII

CONSTITUTION

AND

LAWS

OF

THE CHOCTAW NATION.

TOGETHER WITH THE

TREATIES

OF

1837, 1855, 1865 and 1866.

PUBLISHED BY AUTHORITY OF THE GENERAL COUNCIL

BY

A. R. DURANT,

Commissioned for the Purpose,

AND

DAVIS HOMER AND BEN WATKINS, *Assistant Compilers.*

SR *Scholarly Resources Inc.*
Wilmington, Delaware • London

SCHOLARLY RESOURCES, INC.
Wilmington, Delaware • London

Reprint edition published in 1973
First published in 1894 by John F. Worley
    Dallas, Texas

Library of Congress Catalog Card Number: 73-88765
ISBN: 0-8420-1706-2

Manufactured in the United States of America

CONSTITUTION

AND

LAWS

OF

THE CHOCTAW NATION.

TOGETHER WITH THE

TREATIES

OF

1837, 1855, 1865 and 1866.

PUBLISHED BY AUTHORITY OF THE GENERAL COUNCIL

BY

A. R. DURANT,

Commissioned for the Purpose,

AND

DAVIS HOMER AND BEN WATKINS, *Assistant Compilers.*

DALLAS, TEXAS:
JOHN F. WORLEY, PRINTER AND PUBLISHER,
1894.

PREFACE.

The Choctaws have for many years urgently demanded that the laws of the Nation be printed in both English and Choctaw ; then each language bound in one volume.

We have earnestly endeavored to comply with their request, and also with the law passed on the 27th of October, 1893, ordering this compilation.

We find some laws in the Code compiled by Hon. J. P. Folsom, 1869, not embraced in the Code compiled by Hon. J. H. Standley, and as they have never been repealed we thought best to give them a place in this volume and leave the question of validity to be decided by the proper tribunal.

We have given the translation of the English into Choctaw our careful and undivided attention, and trust our earnest work will be appreciated and universally accepted, as our honest effort has been to give you a volume which shall comprise all the laws of the Choctaw Nation now in force.

A. R. DURANT,
Commissioned for the purpose.

DAVIS HOMER,
BEN WATKINS,
Assistant Compilers.

CONSTITUTION

OF THE

CHOCTAW NATION.

We, the representatives of the people inhabitating
the Choctaw nation, contained within the following
limits, to wit: Beginning at a point on the Arkansas
river, one hundred paces east of old Fort Smith, where
the western boundary line of the State of Arkansas
crosses the said river, and running thence due south to
Red river; thence up Red river to the point where the
meridian of one hundred degrees west longitude crosses
the same; thence north along said meridian to the main
Canadian river; thence down said river to its junction
with the Arkansas river; thence down said river to the
place of beginning, except the territory bounded as follows, to-wit: Beginning on the north bank of Red river,
at the mouth of Island Bayou, where it empties into Red
river, about twenty-six miles on a straight line below
the mouth of False Washita; thence running a northwesterly course along the main channel of said bayou,
to the junction of the three prongs of said bayou, nearest the dividing ridge between Washita and Low Blue
rivers, as laid down on Capt. R. L. Hunter's map; thence
northerly along the eastern prong of Island Bayou to
its source; thence due north to the Canadian river;
thence west along the main Canadian to the ninety-eighth

degree of west longitude; thence south to Red river, and thence down Red river to the place of beginning; *Provided, however,* if the line running due north from the eastern source of Island Bayou, to the main Canadian shall not include Allen's or Wa-pa-nacka Academy within the Chickasaw district; then an offset shall be made from said line, so as to leave said academy two miles within the Chickasaw district, north, west and south from the lines of boundary, said boundaries being the limits of the Chickasaw district—assembled 'in con- vention at the town of Doaksville, on Wednesday, the eleventh day of January, one thousand eight hundred and sixty, in pursuance of an act of the general council, approved October 24, 1859, in order to secure to the cit- izens thereof the right of life, liberty and property, do ordain and establish the following constitution and form of government, and do mutually agree with each other to form ourselves into a free and independent nation, not inconsistent with the constitution, treaties and laws of the United States, by the name of the Choctaw Nation.

DISTRICT BOUNDARIES.

For the convenience and good government of the people of the Choctaw nation, we do make, ordain and establish four districts in this nation, to be known by the following names and boundaries, viz: Mosholatubbee district, Pushamataha district, Apuckshunnubbee district and Hotubbee district.

The boundary line of Mosholatubbee district shall begin near old Fort Smith, where the Arkansas boundary line crosses the Arkansas river; thence up said river to the Canadian fork; thence up said Canadian to where the Chickasaw district boundary strikes the same, as de- fined by the treaty of 1855; thence along the said boun- dary to where it strikes the dividing ridge between the

Canadian and Red rivers; thence easterly along said dividing ridge to the western boundary of the state of Arkansas ; thence along said Arkansas line to the beginning.

The boundary of Apuckshunnubbee district shall begin on Red river, where the Arkansas state line strikes the same; thence running up said river to the mouth of Kiamichi; thence up said river to the mouth of Jack's fork ; thence up said Jack's fork to the old military road; thence along said road to the boundary line of Mosholatubbee district, on the top of the dividing ridge, between the Arkansas and Red rivers ; thence easterly along said boundary to the western boundary line of the state of Arkansas; thence along the said state line to the beginning.

The boundary of Pushamataha district shall begin on Red river at the mouth of Kiamichi : thence running up said Red river to the mouth of Island Bayou, to where the eastern boundary line of the Chickasaw district strikes said river, as defined by the treaty of 1855 ; thence along said boundary line to the dividing ridge between the Canadian and Red rivers ; thence easterly along said ridge to the line of Mosholatubbee district, on the top of the dividing ridge, to where the district line of Apuckshunnubbee district intersects Mosholatubbee disirict; thence southerly along said line to the beginning.

The boundaries of Hotubbee district shall be embraced within the limits of the ninety-eighth and one hundredth degree of west longitude, and between Red river and Canadian river, known as the "Lease Land."

ARTICLE I.

DECLARATION OF RIGHTS.

That the general, great and essential principles of

liberty and free government may be recognized and established, we declare:

SECTION 1. That all free men, when they form a social compact, are equal in rights, and that no man or set of men are entitled to exclusive, separate public emolument or privileges from the community, but in consideration of public services.

SEC. 2. That all political power is inherent in the people, and all free governments are founded on their authority and established for their benefit, and therefore they have at all times an inalienable and indefeasible right to alter, reform or abolish their form of government in such manner as they may think proper or expedient.

SEC. 3. There shall be no establishment of religion by law. No preference shall ever be given by law to any religious sects, society, denomination or mode of worship, and no religious test shall ever be allowed as a qualification to any public trust under this government.

SEC. 4. No human authority ought in any case whatever to control or interfere with the rights of conscience in matters of religion.

SEC. 5. No person shall for the same offence be twice put in jeopardy of life or limb, nor shall any person's property be taken or applied to public use without the consent of the general council, and without just compensation being first made therefor.

SEC. 6. No person shall ever be appointed or elected to any office in this nation for life or during good behavior, but the tenure of all offices shall be for some limited period of time, if the person appointed or elected thereto so long behave well.

SEC. 7. The right of trial by jury shall remain inviolate.

SEC. 8. Every citizen has a right to bear arms in defence of himself and his country.

SEC. 9. That the printing-press shall be free to every person, and no law shall ever be made to restrain the rights thereof. The free communication of opinion is one of the inviolable rights of man, and every citizen may freely speak, write and print on any subject, being responsible for abuse of that liberty.

SEC. 10. That the people shall be secure in their persons, houses, papers and possessions from unreasonable seizures and searches, and that no warrant to search any place or to seize any person or thing shall issue, without describing the place to be searched and the person or thing to be siezed as nearly as may be, nor without probable cause supported by oath or affirmation. But in all cases where suspicion rests on any person or persons of conveying or secreting whisky or other intoxicating liquors, the same shall be liable to search or seizure as may be hereafter provided by law.

SEC. 11. That no free man shall be taken, or imprisoned, or disseized of his freehold liberties or privileges, or outlawed, or exiled, or in any manner destroyed or deprived of his life, liberty, and property, but by the judgment of his peers or the law of the land.

SEC. 12. No person shall ever be imprisoned for debt.

SEC. 13. That excessive bail shall not be required, nor excessive fines imposed, nor cruel or unusual punishments inflicted.

SEC. 14. That all courts shall be open and every person for an injury done him in his lands, goods, person or reputation, shall have remedy by due course of law, and right and justice administered without sale, denial or delay.

SEC. 15. That the citizens have a right in a peaceable manner, to assemble together for their common good, to instruct their representatives, and apply to those invested with the powers of the government for redress of grievances, or other proper purposes, by petition, address or remonstrance.

SEC. 16. That no power of suspending laws shall be exercised except by the general council or its authority.

SEC. 17. That in all criminal prosecutions, the accused hath a right to be heard by himself or counsel, or both, to demand the nature and cause of the accusation, to be confronted by the witnesses against him, to have a compulsory process for obtaining witnesses in his favor; and in all prosecutions by indictment or information, a speedy and public trial by an impartial jury of the county or district where the offence was committed; that he cannot be compelled to give evidence against himself, nor can he be deprived of his life, liberty, or property, but by due course of law.

SEC. 18. That all prisoners shall, before conviction, be bailable by sufficient securities, except for capital offenses, where the proof is evident or the presumption great, and the privilege of the writ of *habeas corpus* shall not be suspended, unless when in case of rebellion or invasion, the public safety may require it.

SEC. 19. That the general council shall have power to pass general laws in regard to the collection of fines, bonds, forfeitures, and court fees, and direct the manner of such collection.

SEC. 20. No property qualification for eligibility to office, or for the right of suffrage, shall ever be required by law in this nation.

SEC. 21. No conviction for any offense shall work

corruption of blood and forfeiture of estate. The general council shall pass no bill of attainder, retrospective law, nor law impairing the obligation of contracts.

ARTICLE II.

DISTRIBUTION OF POWER.

SECTION 1. The powers of government of the Choctaw nation shall be divided into three distinct departments, and each of them confined to a separate body of magistracy, to wit: Those which are legislative to one, those which are executive to another, and those which are judicial to another.

SEC. 2. No person or collection of persons, being of one of those departments, shall exercise any power properly belonging to either of the others, except in the instances hereafter expressly directed or permitted by the general council.

ARTICLE III.

LEGISLATIVE DEPARTMENT.

SECTION 1. The legislative power of this nation shall be vested in a general council which shall consist of a senate and house of representatives, and the style of their laws shall be, "Be it enacted by the general council of the Choctaw nation assembled."

SEC. 2. The senate of the Choctaw nation shall be composed of four senators from each district, chosen by the qualified electors thereof, for the term of two years.

SEC. 3. No person shall be a senator who shall not have attained the age of thirty years and been one year a citizen of this nation, and who shall not, when elected, be an inhabitant of that district at least six months preceding his election for which he shall be chosen.

SEC. 4. The house of representatives shall be composed of members chosen every year by the qualified electors in the several counties of each district, at the ratio of one representative to every one thousand citizens; nevertheless when there is a fractional number of five hundred or more citizens in any county, they shall be entitled to one additional representative; but when the population of any one of the counties shall not reach the ratio of one thousand, they shall still be allowed one representative.

SEC. 5. In case of death, resignation, or inability of any of the senators or representatives, the principal chief shall have the power to make temporary appointments and fill vacancies that may occur in any of the counties.

SEC. 6. No person shall be a representative, unless he be a citizen of this nation, and shall have been an inhabitant thereof six months next preceding his election, and the last month thereof a resident of the county for which he shall be chosen, and shall have attained the age of twenty-one years.

SEC. 7. The house of representatives, when assembled shall choose a speaker and its other officers, and the senate shall choose a president and its officers, and each shall judge of the qualifications and elections of its own members, but a contested election shall be determined in such manner as shall be directed by law. A majority of each house shall constitute a quorum to do business, but a smaller number may adjourn from day to day and may compel the attendance of absent members in such manner and under such penalties as each house may provide.

SEC. 8. Every bill which shall have passed both houses of the legislature shall be presented to the principal chief; if he approve he shall sign it, but if not he shall return it, with his objections, to the house in which it shall have originated, who shall enter the objections at large upon the journal and proceed to reconsider it; if, after such reconsideration, two-thirds of the members present shall agree to pass the bill, it shall be sent with the objections to the other house, by which it shall likewise be reconsidered; if approved by two-thirds of the members present of that house it shall become a law, but in such case the vote of both houses shall be determined by the yeas and nays, and the names of the members voting for and against the bill be entered on the journals of each house respectively ; if any bill shall not be returned by the principal chief within three days (Sundays excepted) after it shall have been presented to him, the same shall become a law in like manner as if he had signed it. Every bill presented to the principal chief one day previous to the adjournment of the legislature, and not returned to the house in which it originated before its adjournment, shall become a law and have the same force and effect as if signed by the principal chief.

SEC. 9. Each house may determine the rules of its own proceedings, punish members for disorderly behavior, and with the consent of two-thirds, expel a member, but not a second time for the same cause.

SEC. 10. Each house shall keep a journal of its proceedings and publish the same, and the yeas and nays of the members of either house, on any question, shall, at the desire of any three members present, be entered on the journal.

SEC. 11. Each house may punish by imprisonment, during the session, any person not a member, for disrespectful or disorderly behavior in its presence, or for obstructing any of its proceedings, provided such imprisonment shall not at any one time exceed forty-eight hours.

SEC. 12. Neither house shall, without the consent of the other, adjourn for more than three days, nor to any other place than that in which they may be sitting.

SEC. 13. Each member of the general council shall receive from the public treasury a compensation for his services, which may be increased or diminished by law; but no increase of compensation shall take effect during the session at which such increase shall have been made.

SEC. 14. No person who hath heretofore been, or hereafter may be a collector or holder of public moneys, shall have a seat in either house of the general council, until such person shall have accounted for, and paid into the treasury, all sums for which he may be accountable.

SEC. 15. The first election for senators and representatives shall be general throughout the nation, and shall be held on the first Wednesday in August, 1860, and thereafter there shall be biennial elections for senators.

SEC. 16. Senators and representatives shall, in all cases except of treason, felony, or breach of the peace, be privileged from arrest during the session of the general council, and in going to and returning from the same.

ARTICLE IV.

JUDICIAL DEPARTMENT.

SECTION 1. The judicial power of this nation shall be vested in one supreme court, in circuit and county courts.

SEC. 2. Until Hotubbee district shall be duly organized, and officers elected therein under this constitution, the supreme court shall be composed of three supreme judges, one to be chosen from Apuckshunnubbee district, one from Pushamataha district, and one from Mosholatubbee district, one of whom shall be styled chief justice, and two of whom shall constitute a quorum to do business.

SEC. 3. The supreme court shall have no jurisdiction but such as properly belongs to a court of errors and appeals.

SEC. 4. The supreme judges shall have power to issue writs and other process necessary to the exercise of their appellate jurisdiction, and shall have original jurisdiction only in such cases as may hereafter be provided by law, and shall be conservators of the peace throughout the nation.

SEC. 5. The circuit courts shall be composed of one circuit judge in each district, and shall have original jurisdiction in all criminal cases which shall not be otherwise provided for by law, and exclusive original jurisdiction in all crimes amounting to felony, and original jurisdiction of all civil cases which shall not be cognizable before the judges of the county, until otherwise directed by law, and original jurisdiction in all matters of contracts, and in all matters of controversy where the same is over fifty dollars. It shall hold its term at such times and places in each district as are now specified by law or may hereafter be provided.

SEC. 6. The circuit courts shall exercise a superintending control over the county courts, and shall have power to issue all necessary writs and process to carry into effect their general and specific powers under such regulations and restrictions as may be provided by law.

SEC. 7. The circuit judge in each district shall be elected by the qualified voters of their respective districts, and the general council by a joint vote of both houses shall elect the supreme judges. Any person receiving the highest number of votes cast shall be elected.

SEC. 8. The judges of the supreme court shall be at least thirty years of age, and the circuit judge of the circuit courts shall be at least twenty-five years of age before they shall be eligible to hold the office, and when elected they shall serve for the term of four years from the date of their commission; they shall appoint their own clerks under such provisions as the law may prescribe.

SEC. 9. The judges of the supreme court and circuit courts shall at stated times receive such compensation for their services, which shall not be increased or diminished during the term for which they are elected, as may be determined by law. They shall not be allowed any fees or perquisites of office.

SEC. 10. There shall be a court established in each county of this nation, to be called county courts, which shall have jurisdiction in all matters relative to disbursement of money for county purpose, and in every other case that may be necessary to the internal improvements and local concerns of their respective counties.

SEC. 11. The judges of the county court shall in no case have jurisdiction to try and determine any criminal case or penal offense against this nation, but may sit as examining courts, and commit, discharge, or recognize to the court having jurisdiction for further trial of all offenses against the peace and dignity of this nation; for the foregoing purposes, they shall have power to issue all necessary writs and process, to bind any person to keep the peace, or to give security for his good behavior.

SEC. 12. The county judges shall be elected by the qualified electors of their respective counties, and shall be commissioned by the principal chief, and shall hold their office for the term of two years.

SEC. 13. No judge shall preside on the trial of any cause in the event of which he may be interested, or where either of the parties shall be connected to him by affinity or consanguinity within such degrees as may be prescribed by law, or in which he may have been of council, or have presided in any circuit or county courts, except by consent of all parties. In case any or all of the judges of the supreme court shall be thus disqualified from presiding on any cause, or causes, the court or judges thereof shall certify the same to the principal chief of the nation, who shall immediately commission the requisite number of men learned in the law for the trial and determination thereof. But in case such disqualification should take place in any of the circuit or county judges, the circuit or county judge shall have the power to appoint a substitute for that particular case for which he may be disqualified.

SEC. 14. Judges shall not charge juries with regard to matter of fact, but may state the testimony and declare the law.

SEC. 15. There shall be a prosecuting attorney elected in each district by the qualified electors of their respective districts, whose compensation and term of service shall be prescribed by law.

SEC. 16. The general council shall have power by law to prescribe the manner of holding and determining suits in the circuit and county courts and the manner of granting appeals.

SEC. 17. The county judges in addition to their respective duties that may be required of them by law, shall be judges of the courts of probate and have such jurisdiction in matters relative to the estate of deceased persons,

2

executors, administrators and guardians as may be prescribed by law, until otherwise directed by the general council.

SEC. 18.   Writs and other process shall run in the name of the Choctaw nation and bear test and be signed by the clerks of their respective courts from which they issue, and all indictments shall conclude against the peace and dignity of the Choctaw nation.

SEC. 19.   The general council shall provide by law for determining contested elections of county judges.

SEC. 20.   The supreme court shall be held twice in each year at the seat of government of the Choctaw nation.

SEC. 21.   The county judges shall appoint their own clerks, who shall act as treasurer of the county.

ARTICLE V.

EXECUTIVE DEPARTMENT.

SECTION 1.   The supreme executive power of the Choctaw nation shall be vested in one principal chief, assisted by three subordinate district chiefs, who shall hold their respective offices for the term of two years from the time of their installation. But they shall not be eligible for the same office for more than two terms in succession.

SEC. 2.   The principal chief of the Choctaw nation shall be elected by the qualified electors of the Choctaw nation, and the subordinate chiefs of the Choctaw nation shall be elected by the qualified electors of their respective districts on the first Wednesday in August, eighteen hundred and sixty, and every two years thereafter.

SEC. 3. The returns of every election for principal chief shall be made out, sealed up and transmitted to the supreme judges of each district, to be forwarded by him to the national secretary who shall deliver them to the speaker of the house of representatives during the first week of its organization, who shall proceed to open and count the votes in the presence of both houses of the general council, and the person having the highest number of votes shall be declared principal chief by the speaker. But if two or more shall be equal or highest in votes, then one of them shall be chosen principal chief by the joint ballot of both houses of the general council; but the returns of every election for district and county officers shall be made out, sealed and transmitted to the supreme judge of each district who shall proceed to open, take an abstract, and declare what candidates for district and county offices are elected, and forward a true copy of the same to the national secretary who shall file them in his office for safe keeping.

SEC. 4. In case of death, resignation or removal of the principal chief, the president of the senate shall exercise the duties of principal chief until the next regular election for that office; but should the vacancy be on account of the inability of the principal chief to discharge his duties, the president of the senate shall exercise the said duties until such inability shall be removed.

SEC, 5. In case of any vacancy occurring in the office of district chiefs, the principal chief shall have the power to appoint a chief *pro tem.* in the district where such vacancy may occur until the next regular election for that office.

SEC. 6. No person shall be eligible to the office of principal or district chief unless he shall have attained the age of thirty years, and have been an inhabitant of the Choctaw nation at least five years next preceding his election.

SEC. 7.   The principal chief shall from time to time give to the general council information of the state of the government, and recommend to their consideration such measures as he may deem expedient.

SEC. 8.   The principal chief shall take care that the laws be faithfully executed.

SEC. 9.   The principal chief may, by proclamation, on extraordinary occasions, convene the general council at the seat of government, or at a different place if that have become, since their last adjournment, dangerous from an enemy or from contagious disease.

SEC. 10.   In case of disagreement between the two houses with respect to the time of adjournment, the principal chief may adjourn them to such a time as he shall think best, not beyond the day of the next meeting of the general council.

SEC. 11.   All vacancies which may occur in offices that are elective by the people or general council, the principal chief shall have the power to fill such vacancies by appointment until the next regular election.

SEC. 12.   No person shall hold the office of principal or district chief, and any other office or commission, either in this nation, or under any state, or in the United States or any power, at one and the same time.

SEC. 13.   The district chiefs shall have such superintending control over the affairs of their respective districts as may be prescribed by the general council. It shall be their duty to have the laws properly enforced within their respective limits. They shall from time to time report to the principal chief such information respecting the affairs of their districts, and recommend for his consideration such measures as they may deem expedient.

Sec. 14. A sheriff and rangers shall be elected in each county by the qualified electors thereof, who shall hold their office for the term of two years unless sooner removed. And it shall be the duty of the district chiefs to appoint a competent number of light horsemen in their respective districts as may hereafter be provided by law, who shall hold their offices for the term of two years unless sooner removed.

Sec. 15. The principal chief, national secretary, national treasurer, national auditor, and national attorney, shall reside at or near the seat of government.

~~SMITH—8

Sec. 16. The principal chief shall be head commander of the militia of this nation.

ARTICLE VI.

IMPEACHMENTS.

Section 1. The house of representatives shall have the sole power of impeaching.

Sec. 2. All impeachments shall be tried by the senate. When sitting for that purpose, the senators shall be on oath or affirmation. No person shall be convicted without the concurrence of two-thirds of the members present.

Sec. 3. The chiefs and all civil officers shall be liable to impeachment for any misdemeanor in office, but judgment in such case shall not extend further than removal from office and disqualification to hold any office of honor, trust or profit under this nation, but the party convicted shall nevertheless be liable, and subject to indictment, trial, and punishment according to law as in other cases.

ARTICLE VII.

GENERAL PROVISIONS.

SECTION 1. Until Hotubbee district shall be duly organized, the principal chief of the Choctaw nation shall exercise such authority over the citizens of this nation, living in that district, as he may deem expedient for the protection of person, life and property.

SEC. 2. No person shall be principal chief, or subordinate chief, senator, or representative, unless he be a free male citizen of the Choctaw nation, and a lineal descendant of the Choctaw or Chickasaw race.

SEC. 3. The general council shall have the power to determine what county or counties shall be entitled to elect one or more senators in the several districts of this nation.

SEC. 4. Members of the general council and other officers, both executive and judicial, before they enter upon the duties of their respective offices shall take the following oath or affirmation, to-wit: "I do solmenly swear (or affirm, as the case may be,) that I will support the constitution of the Choctaw nation, and that I will faithfully and impartially discharge, to the best of my abilities, the duties of the office of ——— ——— according to law. So help me God."

SEC. 5. The general council shall have the power to determine the compensation of the principal chief, district chiefs and other officers of the nation, which compensation shall not be increased or diminished for the term of years they are elected or appointed.

SEC. 6. The general council shall have power by law to specify the manner in which offenders against the laws of this nation, who may escape into the United States or into any Indian nation, or from one district into another in this nation, shall be demanded, apprehended, and arraigned for trial in the several courts of this nation, having original jurisdiction thereof.

SEC. 7. Every free male citizen of this nation who shall have attained to the age of eighteen years, and who shall have been a citizen of the nation six months, shall be deemed a qualified elector, and shall be entitled to vote in the county or district where he may have actually resided at least one month preceding the election for each and every office made elective in this nation.

SEC. 8. All general elections shall be by ballot; and the electors in all cases, except in cases of treason, felony, and breach of the peace, shall be privileged from arrest during their attendance at elections and on going to and returning therefrom.

SEC. 9. The general council shall have the power by law to establish one or more precincts in each county in the several districts of this nation, and prescribe the mode and manner of holding and conducting elections.

SEC. 10. The oath of office may be administered by any of the judges of this nation until the general council shall otherwise direct.

SEC. 11. The general council shall have the power to pass such laws and measures as they shall deem expedient for the general good of the Choctaw people, provided no law be passed or adopted contrary to the provisions of this constitution.

SEC. 12. The mode of declaring war in this nation shall be by at least two-thirds of the members of the general council in full council, with the approval of the principal chief, unless in case of actual invasion by an enemy, in which case the people shall have the right to defend themselves until the council is convened by proclamation of the principal chief, and measures of defense prescribed.

SEC. 13. The principal chief shall have the power, by and with the advice and consent of the senate, to appoint commissioners, or delegates, to transact such business as may become expedient to the Choctaw nation, and all other officers whose appointments are not herein or otherwise provided for.

SEC. 14. The general council of the Choctaw nation shall have the power to pass such laws as they may deem expedient to punish rebellion, treason, and other high crimes against the nation.

SEC. 15. All contested elections for principal chief and other officers shall be determined as the law may prescribe.

SEC. 16. The general council shall have the power to create by law such regulations and commissions, and appoint superintendents and such other officers, as the case may be, required for the promotion and advancement of all the schools of this nation.

SEC. 17. Eighteen thousand dollars of the interest money arising from the Chickasaw fund, granted to the Choctaws by convention held and concluded at Doaksville, shall be set apart annually for educational purposes, and the remaining seven thousand dollars be set apart, annually, to be expended as the law may hereafter direct.

SEC. 18. Any citizen of this nation who may find any mine or mines, or mineral waters, shall have exclusive right and privilege to work the same, so long as he may choose, within one mile in any direction from his works or improvements; provided, however, he does not interfere with the rights of the former settler.

SEC. 19. No person who denies the being of a God, or a future state of rewards and punishments, shall hold any office in the civil department of this nation, nor shall he be allowed his oath in any court of justice.

SEC. 20. The treasurer of this nation, together with all other persons who may be intrusted with public money, shall be required to give such bond and security as may be prescribed by law.

SEC. 21. No laws of a general nature, unless otherwise provided for, shall be enforced until sixty days after the passage thereof,

SEC. 22. No money shall be drawn from the treasury but in consequence of an appropriation made by law; an accurate statement of the receipts and expenditures of public moneys shall be attached to and published with the laws, at every regular session of the general council.

SEC. 23. That all the provisions in the constitution, now in existence, and not revised or adopted by this constitution are hereby declared null and void; and that any law which may be passed contrary to the provisions herein specified shall be null and void; and all rights and powers not herein granted or expressed shall be reserved unto the people.

SEC. 24. Divorces from the bond of matrimony shall not be granted but in cases provided for by law.

ARTICLE VIII.

MILITIA.

SECTION 1. The general council shall provide by law for organizing and disciplining the militia of this nation, in such manner as they shall deem expedient, not incompatible with the constitution, treaties and laws of the United States, in relation thereto.

SEC. 2. Officers of the militia shall be elected or

appointed in such manner as the general council shall from time to time direct, and shall be commissioned by the principal chief.

SEC. 3. The principal chief shall have power to call forth the militia to execute the laws of the nation, to suppress insurrections and repel invasions.

ARTICLE IX.

MODE OF AMENDING AND REVISING THE CONSTITUTION.

SECTION 1. Whenever a majority of the members of the general council assembled shall deem it necessary, they may propose an amendment or amendments to this constitution; which amendment shall be submitted by the national secretary, at least four months preceding the next regular election, at which the qualified voters shall vote directly for and against such proposed amendment, or amendments; and if it shall appear that a majority of the qualified voters shall have voted in favor of such amendment, or amendments, then the same may be incorporated as a part of this constitution at the next succeeding general council.

SEC. 2. And if at any time two-thirds of the senate and the house of representatives shall think it necessary to revise and change this entire constitution, they shall recommend to the electors, at the next election for members of the general council, to vote for or against the convention, and it shall appear that a majority of the electors voting at such election, have voted in favor of calling a convention, the general council shall, at its next session, provide by law for calling a convention, to be holden within six months after the passage of such law; and such convention shall consist of delegates equal to the number of members in the house of representatives of the general council.

SCHEDULE.

SECTION 1. All matters now pending in the several courts of this nation shall be transferred to such courts as may have proper jurisdiction thereof under this constitution.

SEC. 2. All rights, prosecutions, claims on contracts, as well of individuals as bodies corporate, and laws now in force at the time of the adoption of this constitution, and not inconsistent therewith, until altered or repealed by the general council, shall remain in full force.

SEC. 3. Any special appointments or contracts heretofore made and approved under existing laws or resolutions of the general council, shall be approved by the principal chief of this nation, and the appointees commissioned, and contracts so made ratified by him.

SEC. 4. In order that no inconvenience may result to the public service, from the taking effect of this constitution, no office shall be suspended, nor any laws relative to the duties thereof be changed or abrogated, until the officers elected and appointed under this constitution shall be duly qualified and enter upon their respective duties.

SEC. 5. Immediately after the governor of this nation shall make proclamation that this constitution is ratified by the people, then it shall be the duty of the president of this convention to give notice forthwith to all the probate judges in this nation, directing them to hold an election on the first Wednesday in August A. D. 1860, for a principal chief and all other officers, district and county, provided for in this constitution, to be conducted in the manner prescribed by the existing election laws; should there be any vacancy, however, in the office of probate judge, then it shall be the duty of any of the county officers to order the said elections.

SEC. 6. The returns for the elections above directed shall be sent sealed to the president of this convention, who shall open and publish the same, giving certificates to those whom the returns show to be chosen for the various offices; the returns for principal chief shall be transmitted as the constitution directs.

SEC. 7. The president of this convention shall call to his assistance two or more competent persons to aid him in making out the returns of the said elections.

SEC. 8. In the event the president of this convention should die then the returns of the elections for principal chief and other officers, shall be transmitted to the national secretary, who shall proceed as in manner above directed.

SEC. 9. Until apportionment shall be made by law, in pursuance of this constitution, for the election of senators, the counties of three districts, singly and severally, shall elect a senator or senators for members to the general council as follows :

IN APUKSHANUBBEE DISTRICT.

Towson County, - - - -	One Senator.
Cedar County, ⎫ - - - - Wade County, ⎭	One Senator.
Red River County, ⎫ - - Boktucklo County, ⎭	One Senator.
Eagle County, ⎫ - - - - Nashoba County, ⎭	One Senator.

IN PUSHAMATAHA DISTRICT.

Kiamichi County, - - -	One Senator.
Blue County, - - - - -	One Senator.
Atoka County, - - - - -	One Senator.
Jack's Fork County, - - -	One Senator.

In Mosholatubbee District.

Sugar-Loaf County, - - -	One Senator.
Skullyville County, - - -	One Senator.
Sans Bois County - - - -	One Senator
Gaines County, } Tobucksy County, }	One Senator.

SEC. 10. The first election for members to the House of Representatives, under this constitution, shall consist of a number of members equal to the apportionment under the existing laws.

GEORGE HUDSON,

President of the Convention.

W. A. DIBRELL, Clerk.

___

DELEGATES OF THE CONVENTION:

FORBIS LEFLORE,
L. P. PITCHLYNN,
ELLIS W. FOLSOM,
WM. McCOY,
JOSEPH DUKES,
WM. S. PATTON,
EDMOND GARDNER,
JOSEPH P. FOLSOM,
JOHN PICKEN (his X mark),
STEPHEN HOLSON,
S. P. WILLIS,
ALFRED SHONG,
PLINY FISK,
SIMON CONKLIL,
PISTAMBEE,
PETER WATSON (his X mark),
DANIEL MILLER,
ADAM NAIL,
DAVIS KING.

AMENDMENTS

TO THE

CONSTITUTION

OF THE

CHOCTAW NATION.

SECTION 1. The national secretary, national treasurer, national auditor, and national attorney shall be elected by the qualified electors of this nation, who shall hold their offices for the term of two years and until their successor are elected and qualified, unless sooner removed; and they shall perform such duties as may be prescribed by law.

SEC. 2. The seat of government shall be permanently fixed at or about two and one half miles east of the old Nanih Waiya, and shall be called and known as Tushkahumma, and the first and all future sessions of the general council shall commence on the first Monday in October, 1884, and each and every year thereafter and shall be held at the Tushkahumma aforesaid.

TREATY OF 1830.

THE UNITED STATES OF AMERICA.

To all to whom these presents shall come, Greeting :

WHEREAS, By the second article of the treaty, be-
gan and held at Dancing Rabbit creek, on the fifteenth
day of September, in the year of our Lord One Thousand
eight hundred and thirty, (as ratified by the senate of
the United States, on the 24th of February, 1831) by the
commissioners on the part of the United States, and the
Mingoes, chiefs, captains, and warriors of the Choctaw
nation, on the part of said nation, it is provided that
"The United States, under a grant specially to be made
by the president of the United States, shall cause to be
conveyed to the Choctaw nation," a tract of country west
of the Mississippi river, in fee simple, to them and their
descendants, to inure to them while they shall exist as a
nation, and live on it: Beginning near Fort Smith,
where the Arkansas boundary crosses the Arkansas
river, running thence to the source of the Canadian fork,
if in the limits of the United States, or to those limits;
thence due south to Red river, and down Red river to
the west boundary of the territory of Arkansas; thence
north along that line to the beginning. The boundary
of the same to be agreeably to the treaty made and concluded at Washington City in the year 1825.

Now Know Ye, That the United States of America,
in consideration of the premises, and in execution of the
agreement and stipulation in the aforesaid treaty, have
given and granted, and by these presents do give, and

grant, unto the said Choctaw nation, the aforesaid "Tract of country west of the Mississippi;" to have and to hold the same, with all the rights, privileges, immunities, and appurtenances of whatsoever nature thereunto belonging, as intended "to be conveyed" by the aforesaid article, "in fee simple to them and their descendants, to inure to them, while they shall exist as a nation and live on it" liable to no transfer or alienation, except to the United States, or with their consent.

In testimony whereof, I, John Tyler, president of the United States of America, have caused these letters to be made patent, and seal of the General Land Office to be hereunto affixed. Given under my hand at the City of Washington, the twenty-third day of March, in the year of our Lord one thousand eight hundred and forty-two, and of the Independence of the United States the Sixty Sixth.

By the president—

JOHN TYLER.
DAN'L WEBSTER,
Secretary of State.

JOHN C. SPENCER,
Secretary of War.

T. HARTLEY CRAWFORD,
Commissioner of Indian Affairs.

Recorded.   Volume 1, Page 43.

J. WILLIAMSON,
Recorder of the General Land Office.

Executed in the Bureau of Typographical Engineers.

JOHN J. ALBERT,
Col. Corps T. Engineers.

Returned to the war department for the Choctaw nation March 24, 1842.

[L. S.]   E. M. HUNTINGTON,

Commissioner of the General Land Office.

I hereby certify that the foregoing and above trans-script is a true and correct copy from the original patent now on file in my office.

In witness hereto I have affixed the seal of the Choc-taw nation, this January 26th, 1886.

[L. S.]   THOMPSON McKINNEY,

National Secretary, Choctaw Nation.

TREATY OF 1837.

Articles of Convention and Agreement Made on the Seventeenth day of January, 1837, Between the Undersigned Chiefs and Commissioners duly Appointed and Empowered by the Choctaw Tribe of Red People, and John McLish, Pitman Colbert, James Brown and James Perry, Delegates of the Chickasaw Tribe of Indians, Duly Authorized by the Chiefs and Head Men of said People for that Purpose, at Doaksville, near Fort Towson, in the Choctaw Country.

ARTICLE I.

It is agreed by the Choctaws that the Chickasaws shall have the privilege of forming a district within the limits of their country, to be held on the same terms that the Choctaws now hold it, except the right of disposing of it, (which is held in common with the Choctaws and Chickasaws) to be called the Chickasaw district of the Choctaw nation ; to have an equal representation in their general council, and to be placed on an equal footing in every other respect with any of the other districts of said nation, except a voice in the management of the consideration which is given for these rights and privileges ; and the Chickasaw people to be entitled to all the rights and privileges of Choctaws, with the exception of participting in the Choctaw annuities and the consideration to be paid for these rights and privileges, and to be subject to the same laws to which the Choctaws are ; but the Chickasaws reserve to themselves the sole right and privilege of controlling and managing the residue of their funds as far as is consistent with the late treaty between the said people and the government of the United States, and of making such regulations and electing officers for that purpose as they may think proper.

ARTICLE II.

The Chickasaw district shall be bounded as follows, viz: Beginning on the north bank of Red river, at the mouth of Island Bayou, about eight or ten miles below the mouth of False Washita; thence running north along the main channel of said bayou to its source; thence along the dividing ridge between the Washita and Low Blue rivers to the road leading from Fort Gibson to Fort Washita; thence along said road to the line dividing Mosholatubbee and Pushamataha districts; thence eastwardly along said district line to the source of Brushy creek; thence down said creek to where it flows into the Canadian river, ten or twelve miles above the mouth of the south fork of the Canadian; thence west along the main Canadian river to its source, if in the limits of the United States, or to those limits; and thence due south to Red river, and down Red river to the beginning.

ARTICLE III.

The Chickasaws agree to pay to the Choctaws as a consideration for these rights and privileges, the sum of five hundred and thirty thousand dollars—thirty thousand of which shall be paid at the time and in the manner that the Choctaw annuity of 1837 is paid, and the remaining five hundred thousand dollars to be invested in some safe and secure stocks, under the direction of the government of the United States, redeemable within a period of not less than twenty years—and the government of the United States shall cause the interest arising therefrom to be paid annually to the Choctaws in the following manner: twenty thousand of which to be paid as the present Choctaw annuity is paid, for four years, and the residue to be subjected to the control of the general council of the Choctaws; and after the expiration of the four years the whole of said interest to be subject to the entire control of the said council.

ARTICLE IV

To provide for the future adjustment of all complaints or dissatisfaction which may arise to interrupt the peace and harmony which have so long and so happily existed between the Choctaws and Chickasaws, it is hereby agreed by the parties that all questions relative to the construction of this agreement shall be referred to the Choctaw agent to be by him decided; reserving, however, to either party, should it feel itself aggrieved thereby, the rights of appealing to the president of the United States, whose decision shall be final and binding. But as considerable time might elapse before the decision of the president could be had, *in the mean time* the decision of the said agent shall remain binding.

ARTICLE V.

It is hereby declared to be the intention of the parties hereto, that equal rights and privileges shall pertain to both Choctaws and Chickasaws to settle in whatever district they may think proper, and to be eligible to all the different offices of the Choctaw nation, and to vote on the same terms in whatever district they may settle, except that the Choctaws are not to vote *in anywise* for officers in relation to the residue of the Chickasaw fund.

Proclaimed March 24, 1837.

TREATY OF 1855.

Article of Agreement and Convention Between the United States and the Choctaw and Chickasaw Tribe of Indians, made and Concluded at the City of Washington, the twenty-second day of June, A. D. One Thousand Eight Hundred and Fifty-Five, by George W. Manypenny, Commissioner on the Part of the United States; Peter P. Pitchlynn, Israel Fulsom, Samuel Garland, and Dixon W. Lewis, Commissioners on the Part of the Choctaws; and Edmund Pickens and Sampson Folsom, Commissioners on the part of the Chickasaws.

WHEREAS, the political connection heretofore existing between the Choctaw and Chickasaw tribes of Indians has given rise to unhappy and injurious dissensions and controversies among them, which render necessary a readjustment of their relations to each other and to the United States; and, whereas, the United States desire that the Choctaw Indians shall relinquish all claim to any territory west of the one hundreth degree of west longitude, and also to make provision for the permanent settlement within the Choctaw country of the Wichita and certain other tribes or bands of Indians, for which purpose the Choctaws and Chickasaws are willing to lease, on reasonable terms, to the United States, that portion of their common territory which is west of the ninety-eighth degree of west longitude; and, whereas, the Choctaws contend that, by a just and fair construction of the treaty of September 27, 1830, they are, of right, en-

titled to the net proceeds of the land ceded by them to
the United States, under said treaty, and have proposed
that the question of their right to the same, together
with the whole subject-matter of their unsettled claims,
whether national or individual, against the United States,
arising under the various provisions of said treaty, shall
be referred to the senate of the United States for final
adjudication and adjustment; and, whereas, it is necessary for the simplification and better understanding of
the relations between the United States and the Choctaw
Indians, that all their subsisting treaty stipulations be
embodied in one comprehensive instrument:

Now, therefore, the United States of America, by
their commissioner, George W. Manypenny; the Choctaws by their commissioners, Peter P. Pitchlynn, Israel
Fulsom, Samuel Garland, and Dixon W. Lewis; and the
Chickasaws, by their commissioners, Edmund Pickens
and Sampson Folsom, do hereby agree and stipulate as
follows, viz:

ARTICLE I.

The following shall constitute and remain the boun
daries of the Choctaw and Chickasaw country, viz: Beginning at a point on the Arkansas river, one hundred
paces east of old Fort Smith, where the western boundary line of the state of Arkansas crosses the said river,
and running thence due south to Red river; thence up
Red river to the point where the meridian of one hundred degrees west longitude crosses the same; thence
north and along said meridian to the main Canadian
river; thence down said river to its junction with the
Arkansas river; thence down said river to the place of
beginning.

And pursuant to an act of congress, approved May
28, 1830, the United States do hereby forever secure and

guarantee the lands embraced within the said limits to the members of the Choctaw and Chickasaw tribes, their heirs and successors, to be held in common; so that each and every member of either tribe shall have an equal, undivided interest in the whole: *Provided, however*, no part thereof shall ever be sold without the consent of both tribes; and that said land shall revert to the United States if said Indians and their heirs become extinct or abandon the same.

ARTICLE II.

A district for the Chickasaws is hereby established, bounded as follows, to-wit : Beginning on the north bank of Red river, at the mouth of Island bayou, where it empties into Red river, about twenty-six miles on a straight line, below the mouth of False Washita; thence running a northwesterly course along the main channel of said bayou to the junction of the three prongs of said bayou, nearest the dividing ridge between Washita and Low Blue rivers, as laid down on Captain R. L. Hunter's map; thence northerly along the eastern prong of Island bayou to its source; thence due north to the Canadian river; thence west along the main Canadian to the ninety-eighth degree of west longitude ; thence south to Red river ; and thence down Red river to the beginning: *Provided, however,* if the line running due north from the eastern source of Island bayou, to the main ¦Canadian, shall not include Allen's or Wa-pa-nacka academy within the Chickasaw district, then an offset shall be made from said line, so as to leave said academy two miles within the Chickasaw district, north, west and south from the lines of boundary.

ARTICLE III.

The remainder of the country held in common by the Choctaws and Chickasaws, shall constitute the Choctaw district, and their officers and people shall at all times have the right of safe conduct and free passage through the Chickasaw district.

ARTICLE IV.

The government and laws now in operation and not incompatable with this instrument, shall be and remain in full force and effect within the limits of the Chickasaw district, until the Chickasaws shall adopt a constitution, and enact laws, superseding, abrogating or changing the same.   And all judicial proceedings within said district, commenced prior to the adoption of a constitution and laws by the Chickasaws, shall be conducted and determined according to existing laws.

ARTICLE V.

The members of either the Choctaw or Chickasaw tribe shall have the right, freely, to settle within the jurisdiction of the other, and shall thereupon be entitled to all the rights, privilege and immunities of citizens thereof; but no member of either tribe shall be entitled to participate in the funds belonging to any other tribe.   Citizens of both tribes shall have the right to institute and prosecute suits in the courts of either, under such regulations as may, from time to time, be prescribed by their respective legislatures.

ARTICLE VI.

Any person duly charged with a criminal offense against the laws of either the Choctaw or the Chickasaw tribes, and escaping into the jurisdiction of the other, shall be promptly surrendered, upon the demand of the proper authorities of the tribe within whose jurisdiction the offense shall be alleged to have been committed.

ARTICLE VII.

So far as may be compatible with the constitution of the United States and the laws made in pursuance thereof, regulating trade and intercourse with the Indian tribes, the Choctaws and the Chickasaws shall be secured in the unrestricted right of self-government and full jurisdiction over persons and property, within their respective limits; excepting, however, all persons with their property, who are not by birth, adoption or otherwise, citizens or members of either the Choctaw or Chickasaw tribe; and all persons not being citizens or members of either tribe, found within their limits, shall be considered intruders, and be removed from, and kept out of the same, by the United States agent, assisted if necessary by the military, with the following exceptions, viz: Such individuals as are now, or may be in the employment of the government and their families, those peacefully traveling, or temporarily sojourning in the country, or trading therein, under license from the proper authority of the United States; and such as may be permitted by the Choctaws or Chickasaws, with the assent of the United States agent, to reside within their limits, without becoming citizens or members of either of said tribes.

ARTICLE VIII.

In consideration of the foregoing stipulations, and immediately upon the ratification of this convention, there shall be paid to the Choctaws, in such manner as their national council shall direct, out of the national fund of the Chickasaws, held in trust by the United States, the sum of one hundred and fifty thousand dollars.

ARTICLE IX.

The Choctaw Indians do hereby absolutely and forever quit claim and relinquish to the United States all
their rights, title and interest in, and to any and all
lands, west of the one hundredth degree of west longitude, and the Choctaws and Chickasaws do hereby lease
to the United States all that portion of their common territory west of the ninety-eighth degree of west longitude
for the permanent settlement of the Wichita and such
other tribes or bands of Indians as the government may
desire to locate therein; excluding, however, all the
Indians of New Mexico, and also those whose usual
ranges at present are north of the Arkansas river, whose
permanent locations are north of the Canadian river, but
including those bands whose permanent ranges are south
of the Canadian, or between it and the Arkansas; which
Indians shall be subject to the exclusive control of the
United States, under such rules and regulations, not inconsistent with the rights and interests of the Choctaws
and Chickasaws, as may from time to time be prescribed
by the president for their government. *Provided, however,* the territory so leased shall remain open to settlement by Choctaws and Chickasaws as herebefore.

ARTICLE X.

In consideration of the foregoing relinquishment and
lease, and as soon as practicable after the ratification of
this convention, the United States will pay to the Choctaws the sum of six hundred thousand dollars, and to
the Chickasaws the sum of two hundred thousand dollars, in such manner as their general councils shall
respectively direct.

ARTICLE XI.

The government of the United States not being pre-

pared to assent to the claim set up under the treaty of
September the twenty-seventh, eighteen hundred and
thirty, and so earnestly contended for by the Choctaws
as a rule of settlement, but justly appreciating the sacri-
fices, faithful services, and general conduct of the Choc
taw people, and being desirous that their rights and
claims against the United States shall receive a just, fair
and liberal consideration ; it is therefore stipulated that
the following questions be submitted for adjudication to
the senate of the United States :

First—Whether the Choctaws are entitled to, or
shall be allowed, the proceeds of the sale of the lands
ceded by them to the United States, by the treaty of
September the twenty-seventh, eighteen hundred and
thirty, deducting therefrom the cost of their survey and
sale, and all just and proper expenditures and payments
under the provisions of said treaty ; and, if so, what
price per acre shall be allowed to the Choctaws to the
lands remaining unsold, in order that a final settlement
with them may be promptly effected. Or,

Second—Whether the Choctaws shall be allowed a
gross sum, in further and full satisfaction of all their
claims, national and individual, against the United
States ; and, if so, how much.

ARTICLE XII.

In case the senate shall award the Choctaws the net
proceeds of the lands, ceded as aforesaid, the same shall
be received by them in full satisfaction of all their claims
against the United States, whether national or individual, arising under any former treaty ; and the Choctaws
shall thereupon become liable and bound to pay all
such individual claims as may be adjudged by the
proper authorities of the tribe to be equitable and just—

the settlement and payment to be made with the advice
and under the direction of the United States agent for
the tribe ; and so much of the fund awarded by the senate to the Choctaws, as the proper authorities thereof
shall ascertain and determine to be necessary for the
payment of the just liabilities of the tribe, shall on
their requisition, be paid over to them by the United
States. But should the senate allow a gross sum, in further full satisfaction of all their claims, whether national or individual, against the United States, the same
shall be accepted by the Choctaws, and they shall thereupon become liable for, and bound to pay, all the indi-
ual claims as aforesaid ; it being expressly understood
that the adjudication and decision of the senate shall be
final.

ARTICLE XIII.

The amounts secured by existing treaty stipulations—viz: permanent annuity of three thousand dollars,
under the second article of the treaty of eighteen hundred and five; six hundred dollars per annum for the
support of light-horsemen, under the thirteenth article
of the treaty of eighteen hundred and twenty; permanent
annuity of six thousand dollars for education, under the
second article of the treaty of eighteen hundred and
twenty-five; six hundred dollars per annum permanent
provision for the support of a blacksmith, under the
sixth article of the treaty of eighteen hundred and twenty; and three hundred and twenty dollars permanent
provision for iron and steel, under the ninth article of
the treaty of eighteen hundred and twenty five, shall
continue to be paid to, or expended for the benefit of,
the Choctaws as heretofore; or the same may be applied
to such objects of general utility as may, from time to
time, be designated by the general council of the tribe,

with the approbation of the government of the United States. And the funds now held in trust by the United States for the benefit of the Choctaws under former treat-ies, or otherwise, shall continue to be so held; together with the sum of five hundred thousand dollars out of the amount payable to them under articles eighth and tenth of this agreement, and also whatever balance shall remain, if any, of the amount that shall be allowed the Choctaws, by the senate, under the twelfth article here-of, after satisfying the just liabilities of the tribe. The sums so to be held in trust shall constitute a general Choctaw fund, yielding an annual interest of not less than five per centum; no part of which shall be paid out as annuity, but shall be regularly and judiciously ap-plied, under the direction of the general council of the Choctaws, to the support of their government, for pur-poses of education, and such other objects as may be best calculated to promote and advance the improve-ment, welfare and happiness of the Choctaw people and their descendants.

ARTICLE XIV.

The United States shall protect the Choctaws and Chickasaws from domestic strife, from hostile invasion, and from aggression by other Indians and white persons not subject to their jurisdiction and laws; and from all injuries resulting from such invasion or aggression, full indemnity is hereby guaranteed to the party or parties injured, out of the treasury of the United States, upon the same principle and accord-ing to the same rules upon which white persons are en-titled to indemnity for injuries or aggressions upon them, committed by Indians.

ARTICLE XV.

The Choctaws and Chickasaws shall promptly apprehend and deliver up all persons accused of any crime or offense against the laws of the United States, or any state thereof, who may be found within their limits, on demand of any proper officer of a state or of the United States.

ARTICLE XVI.

All persons licensed by the United States to trade with the Choctaws and Chickasaws, shall be required to pay to the respective tribes a moderate annual compensation for the land and timber used by them; the amount of such compensation, in each case, to be assessed by the proper authorities of said tribe, subject to the approval of the United States agent.

ARTICLE XVII.

The United States shall have the right to establish and maintain such military posts, post roads and Indian agencies as may be deemed necessary within the Choctaw and Chickasaw country, but no greater quantity of land or timber shall be used for said purposes than shall be actually requisite, and if in the establishment or maintenance of such posts, post roads and agencies, the property of any Choctaw or Chickasaw shall be taken, injured or destroyed, just and adequate compensation shall be made by the United States. Only such persons as are, or may be, in the employment of the United States, or subject to the jurisdiction of the laws of the Choctaws or Chickasaws, shall be permitted to farm or raise stock within the limits of any of said military posts or Indian agencies. And no offender against the laws of either tribe shall be permitted to take refuge therein.

ARTICLE XVIII.

The United States, or any incorporated company shall have the right of way for railroads, or lines of telegraphy, through the Choctaw or Chickasaw country; but for any property taken or destroyed in the construc-tion thereof, full compensation shall be made to the party or parties injured, to be ascertained and determined in such manner as the president of the United States shall direct.

ARTICLE XIX.

The United States shall, as soon as practicable, cause the eastern and western boundary lines of the tract of country described in the first article of this convention, and the western boundary of the Chickasaw district, as herein defined, to be run and permanently marked.

ARTICLE XX.

That this convention may conduct, as far as possible, to the restoration and preservation of kind and friendly feeling among the Choctaws and Chickasaws, a general amnesty of all past offenses, committed within their country, is hereby declared. And in order that their relations to each other and to the United States may hereafter be conducted in a harmonious and satisfactory manner, there shall be but one agent for the two tribes.

ARTICLE XXI.

This convention shall supersede and take the place of all former treaties between the United States and the Choctaws, and, also, of all treaty stipulations between the United States and the Chickasaws, and between the Choctaws and Chickasaws, inconsistent with this agree-

ment, and shall take effect and be obligatory upon the
contracting parties, from the date hereof, whenever the
same shall be ratified by the respective councils of the
Choctaw and Chickasaw tribes, and by the president
and senate of the United States.

ARTICLE XXII.

It is understood and agreed that the expenses of the
respective commissioners of the two tribes, signing these
articles of agreement and convention, in coming to and
returning from this city, and while here, shall be paid
by the United States.

TREATY OF 1866.

CHOCTAWS AND CHICKASAWS.

Articles of Agreement and Convention Between the United States and the Choctaw and Chickasaw Nations of Indians, Made and Concluded at the City of Washington the 28th day of April, in the Year 1866, by Dennis N. Cooley, Elijah Sells, and E. S. Parker, Special Commissioners on the part of the United States, and Alfred Wade, Allen Wright, James Riley and John Page, Commissioners on the Part of the Choctaws, and Winchester Colbert, Edmund Pickens, Hoems Colbert, Colbert Carter and Robert H. Love, Commissioners on the Part of the Chickasaws.

ARTICLE I.

Permanent peace and friendship are hereby established between the United States and said nations; and the Choctaws and Chickasaws do hereby bind themselves respectively to use their influence and to make every exertion to induce Indians of the plains to maintain peaceful relations with each other, with other Indians, and with the United States.

ARTICLE II.

The Choctaws and Chickasaws hereby covenant and agree that henceforth neither slavery nor involuntary servitude, otherwise than in punishment of crime whereof the parties shall have been duly convicted in accordance

4

with laws applicable to all members of the particular
nation, shall ever exist in said nations.

ARTICLE III.

The Choctaws and Chickasaws, in consideration of
the sum of three hundred thousand dollars, hereby cede
to the United States the territory west of the ninety-
eighth degree west longitude, known as the leased district, provided that the said sum shall be invested and
held by the United States, at an interest not less than
five per cent., in trust for the said nations, until the legislatures of the Choctaw and Chickasaw nations respectively shall have made such laws, rules, and regulations
as may be necessary to give all persons of African descent, resident in the said nations at the date of the
treaty of Fort Smith, and their descendants, heretofore
held in slavery among said nations, all the rights, privileges, and immunities, including the right of suffrage,
of citizens of said nations, except in the annuities, moneys, and public domain claimed by, or belonging to, said
nations respectively; and also to give to such persons
who were residents as aforesaid, and their descendants,
forty acres each of the land of said nations on the same
terms as the Choctaws and Chickasaws, to be selected on
the survey of said land, after the Choctaws and Chickasaws and Kansas Indians have made their selections, as
herein provided; and immediately on the enactment of
such laws, rules, and regulations, the said sum of three
hundred thousand dollars shall be paid to the said Choctaw and Chickasaw nations in the proportion of three-
fourths to the former and one fourth to the latter—less
such sum, at the rate of one hundred dollars per capita,
as shall be sufficient to pay such persons of African descent before referred to as within ninety days after the
passage of such laws, rules, and regulations shall elect

to remove and actually remove from the said nations respectively. And should the said laws, rules, and regulations not be made by the legislatures of the said nations respectively, within two years from the ratification of this treaty, then the said sum of three hundred thousand dollars shall cease to be held in trust for the said Choctaw and Chickasaw nations, and be held for the use and benefit of such of said persons of African descent as the United States shall remove from the said territory in such manner as the United States shall deem proper —the United States agreeing, within ninety days from the expiration of said two years, to remove from said nations all such persons of African descent as may be willing to move; those remaining or returning after having been removed from said nations to have no benefit of said sum of three hundred thousand dollars, or any part thereof, but shall be upon the same footing as other citizens of the United States in the said nations.

ARTICLE IV.

The said nations further agree that all negroes, not otherwise disqualified or disabled, shall be competent witnesses in all civil and criminal suits and proceedings in the Choctaw and Chickasaw courts, any law to the contrary, notwithstanding, and they fully recognize the right of the freemen to a fair remuneration on reasonable and equitable contracts for their labor, which the law should aid them to enforce. And they agree, on the part of their respective nations, that all laws shall be equal in their operation upon Choctaws, Chickasaws and negroes, and that no distinction affecting the latter shall at any time be made, and that they shall be treated with kindness and be protected against injury; and they further agree, that while the said freemen, now in the Choctaw and Chickasaw nations, remain in said nations, respectively, they shall be entitled to as much land as they may cultivate for the support of themselves and families, in cases where they do not support themselves and families by hiring, not interfering with existing improvements without the consent of the occupant, it being understood that in the event of the making of the laws, rules and regulations aforesaid, the forty acres aforesaid shall stand in place of the land cultivated as last aforesaid.

ARTICLE V.

A general amnesty of all past offenses against the laws of the United States, committed before the signing of this treaty by any member of the Choctaw or Chickasaw nations, is hereby declared ; and the United States will especially request the States of Missouri, Kansas, Arkansas and Texas to grant the like amnesty as to all offenses committed by any member of the Choctaw or Chickasaw nation. And the Choctaws and Chickasaws, anxious for the restoration of kind and friendly feelings among themselves, do hereby declare an amnesty for all past offenses against their respective governments, and no Indian or Indians shall be prescribed, or any act of forfeiture or confiscation passed against those who may have remained friendly to the United States, but they shall enjoy equal privileges with other members of said tribes, and all laws heretofore passed inconsistent herewith are hereby declared inoperative. The people of the Choctaw and Chickasaw nations stipulate and agree to deliver up to any authorized agent of the United States all public property in their possesion which belong to the late "so-called Confederate States of America," or the United States, without any reservation whatever, particularly ordinance, ordinance stores and arms of all kinds.

ARTICLE VI.

The Choctaws and Chickasaws hereby grant a right of way through their lands to any company or companies which shall be duly authorized'by congress, or by the legislatures of said nations, respectively, and which shall, with the express consent and approbation of the secretary of the interior, undertake to construct a railroad through the Choctaw and Chickasaw nations from the north to the south thereof, and from the east to the west side thereof, in accordance with the provisions of the eighteenth article of the treaty of June twenty second, one thousand eight hundred and fifty-five, which provides that for any property taken or destroyed in the construction thereof, full compensation shall be made to the party or parties injured, to be ascertained and determined in such manner as the president of the United States shall direct. But such railroad company or companies, with all its or their agents and employes shall be subject to the laws of the United States relating to intercourse with Indian tribes, and also to such rules and regulations as may be prescribed by the secretary of the interior for that purpose. And it is also stipulated and agreed that the nation through which the road or roads aforesaid shall pass may subscribe to the stock of the particular company or companies such amount or amounts as they may be able to pay for in alternate sections of unoccupied lands for a space of six miles on each side of said road or roads, at a price per acre to be agreed upon between said Choctaw and Chickasaw nations and the said company or companies, subject to the approval of the president of the United States. *Provided, however*, that said land, thus subscribed, shall not be sold, or demised, or occupied by any one not a citizen of the Choctaw or Chickasaw nations, according to their laws and recognized usages: *Provided*, that the officers, servants, and employes of such companies necessary to the construction and management of said road or roads shall not be excluded from such occupancy as their respective functions may require, they being subject to the provisions of the Indian intercourse law and such rules and regulations as may be established by the secretary of the interior. *And provided also,* That the stock thus subscribed by either of said nations shall have the force and effect of a first mortgage bond on all that part of said road, appurtenances, and equipments situated and used within said nations respectively, and shall be a perpetual lien on the same, and the said nations shall have the right, from year to year, to elect to receive their equitable proportion of declared dividends of profits on their said stock, or interest on the par value at the rate of six per cent. per annum.

2. And it is further declared, in this connection, that as fast as sections of twenty miles in length are completed, with the rails laid ready for use, with all water and other stations necessary to the use thereof, as a first class road, the said company or companies shall become entitled to patents for the alternate sections aforesaid, and may proceed to dispose thereof in the manner herein provided for, subject to the approval of the secretary of the interior.

3. And it is further declared, also, in case of one or more of said alternate sections being occupied by any member or members of said nations respectively, so that the same cannot be transferred to the said company or companies, that the said nation or nations, respectively, may select any unoccupied section or sections, as near as circumstances will permit, to the said width of six miles on each side of said road or roads, and convey the same as an equivalent for the section or sections so occupied as aforesaid.

ARTICLE VII.

The Choctaws and Chickasaws agree to such legislation as congress and the president of the United States may deem necessary for the better administration of justice and the protection of the rights of person and property within the Indian territory: *Provided, however*, such legislation shall not in anywise interfere with or annul their present tribal organization, or their respective legislatures or judiciaries, or the rights, laws, privileges or customs of the Choctaw or Chickasaw nations respectively.

ARTICLE VIII.

The Choctaws and Chickasaws also agree that a council, consisting of delegates elected by each nation or tribe, lawfully resident within the Indian territory, may be annually convened in said territory, to be organized as follows:

1. After the ratification of this treaty, and as soon as may deemed practicable by the secretary of the interior, and prior to the first session of said assembly, a census of each tribe, lawfully resident in said territory, shall be taken, under the direction of the superintendent of Indian affairs, by competent persons, to be appointed by him, whose compensation shall be fixed by the secretary of the interior and paid by the United States.

2. The counsel shall consist of one member from each tribe or nation whose population shall exceed five hundred, and an additional member for each one thousand Indians, native or adopted, or each fraction of a thousand greater than five hundred being members of any tribe lawfully resident in said territory, and shall be selected by the tribes or nations respectively who may assent to the establishment of said general assembly:

and if none should be thus formally selected by any na
tion or tribe, it shall be represented in said general assembly by the chief or chiefs and head men of said
tribes, to be taken in the order of their rank as recognized in tribal usage in the number and proportions
above indicated.

3. After the said census shall have been taken and
completed, the superintendent of Indian affairs shall
publish and declare to each tribe the number of members of said council to which they shall be entitled under
the provisions of this article ; and the persons so to
represent the said tribes shall meet at such time and
place as he shall designate, but thereafter the time and
place of the session of the general assembly shall be determined by itself : *Provided*, that no session in any one
year shall exceed the term of thirty days ; and provided
that the special sessions may be called whenever, in the
judgment of the secretary of the interior, the interests of
said tribes shall require it.

4. The general assembly shall have power to legislate upon all subjects and matters pertaining to the
intercourse and relations of the Indian tribes and nations
resident in the said territory, the arrest and extradition
of criminals escaping from one tribe to another, the administration of justice between members of the several
tribes of said territory, and persons other than Indians
and members of said tribes or nations, the construction
of works of internal improvement, and the common defense and safety of the nations of the said territory. All
laws enacted by said council shall take effect at the
times therein provided, unless suspended by the secretary of the interior or the president of the United States.
No law shall be enacted inconsistent with the constitution of the United States or the laws of congress, or
existing treaty stipulations with the United States ; nor

shall said council legislate upon matters pertaining to the legislative, judicial or other organizations, laws or customs of the several tribes or nations, except as herein provided for.

5. Said council shall be presided over by the superintendent of Indian affairs, or, in case of his absence from any cause, the duties of the superintendent enumerated in this article shall be performed by such person as the secretary of the interior shall indicate.

6. The secretary of the interior shall appoint a secretary of said council, whose duty it shall be to keep an accurate record of all the proceedings of said council, and to transmit a true copy thereof, duly certified by the superintendent of Indian affairs, to the secretary of the interior, immediately after the sessions of said council shall terminate. He shall be paid five hundred dollars as an annual salary by the United States.

7. The members of the said council shall be paid by the United States, four dollars per diem, while in actual attendance thereon, and four dollars mileage for every twenty miles going and returning therefrom by the most direct route, to be certified by the secretary of said council and the presiding officer.

8. The Choctaws and Chickasaws also agree that a court or courts may be established in said territory with such jurisdiction and organization as congress may prescribe; *Provided*, that the same shall not interfere with the local judiciary of either of said nations.

9. Whenever congress shall authorize the appointment of a delegate from said territory, it shall be the province of said council to elect one from among the nations represented in said council.

10. And it is further agreed that the superintendent of Indian affairs shall be the executive of the said

territory, with the title of the "Governor of the Territory of Oklahoma," and that there shall be a secretary of the said territory, to be appointed by the said superintendent; that the duty of the said governor in addition to those already imposed on the superintendent of Indian affairs, shall be such as properly belong to an executive officer charged with the execution of the laws, which the said council is authorized to enact under the provisions of this treaty; and that for this purpose he shall have authority to appoint a marshal of said territory and an interpreter, the said marshal to appoint such deputies, to be paid by fees, as may be required to aid him in the execution of his proper functions, and be the marshal of the principal court of said territory that may be established under the provisions of this treaty.

11. And the said marshal and the said secretary shall each be entitled to a salary of five hundred dollars per annum, to be paid by the United States, and such fees in addition thereto as shall be established by said governor, with the approbation of the secretary of the interior, it being understood that the said fee lists may at any time be corrected and altered by the secretary of the interior, as the experience of the system proposed herein to be established shall show to be necessary, and shall in no case exceed the fees paid to marshals of the United States for similar services. The salary of the interpreter shall be five hundred dollars, to be paid in like manner by the United States.

12. And the United States agree that in the appointment of marshals and deputies, preference, qualifications being equal, shall be given to competent members of said nations, the object being to create a laudable ambition to acquire the experience necessary for political offices of importance in the respective nations.

13. And whereas it is desired by the said Choctaw and Chickasaw nations that the said council should consist of an upper and lower house, it is hereby agreed that, whenever a majority of the tribes or nations represented in said council shall desire the same, or the congress of the United States shall so prescribe, there shall be, in addition to the council now provided for, and which shall then constitute the lower house, an upper house, consisting of one member from each tribe entitled to representation in the council now provided for, the relation of the two houses to each other being such as prevail in the states of the United States, each house being authorized to choose its presiding officer and clerk to perform the duties appropriate to such offices; and it being the duty, in addition, of the clerks of each house to make out and transmit to the territorial secretary fair copies of the proceedings of the respective houses immediately after their respective sessions, which copies shall be dealt with by the said secretary as is now provided in the case of copies of the proceedings of the council mentioned in this act, and the said clerks shall each be entitled to the same per diem as members of the respective houses, and the presiding officers to double that sum.

ARTICLE IX.

Such sums of money as have, by virtue of treaties existing in the year eighteen hundred and sixty-one, been invested for the purposes of education, shall remain so invested, and the interest thereof shall be applied for the same purposes, in such manner as shall be designated by the legislative authorities of the Choctaw and Chickasaw nations respectively.

ARTICLE X.

The United States re-affirms all obligations arising out of treaty stipulations or acts of legislation with regard to the Choctaw and Chickasaw nations, entered into prior to the late rebellion, and in force at that time, not inconsistent herewith ; and further agrees to renew the payment of all annuities and other moneys accruing under such treaty stipulations and acts of legislation, from and after the close of the fiscal year ending on the thirtieth day of June, in the year eighteen hundred and sixty-six.

ARTICLE XI.

WHEREAS, The land occupied by the Choctaw and Chickasaw nations, and described in the treaty between the United States and said nations, of June twenty-second, eighteen hundred and fifty-five, is now held by the members of said nations in common, under the provisions of said treaty; and, whereas, it is believed that the holding of said land in severalty will promote the general civilization of said nations, and tend to advance their permanent welfare and the best interests of their individual members, it is hereby agreed that, should the Choctaw and Chickasaw people, through their respective legislative councils, agree to the survey and dividing their land on the system of the United States, the land aforesaid east of the ninety-eighth degree of west longitude shall be, in view of the arrangements hereinafter mentioned, surveyed and laid off in ranges, townships, sections and part of sections; and that for the purpose of facilitating such surveys, and for the settlement and distribution of said land as hereinafter provided, there shall be established at Boggy depot, in the Choctaw territory, a land office; and that in making the said surveys and conducting the business of said office, in-

cluding the appointment of all necessary agents and surveyors, the same system has been pursued which has
heretofore governed in respect to the public lands of the
United States, it being understood that the said surveys
shall be made at the cost of the United States and by
their agents and surveyors, as in the case of their own
public lands, and that the officers and employes shall receive the same compensation as is paid to officers and
employes in the land offices of the United States in
Kansas.

ARTICLE XII.

The maps of said survey shall exhibit, as far
as practicable, the outlines of the actual occupancy of
members of the said nations, respectively; and when
they are completed shall be returned to the said land
office at at Boggy depot for inspection by all parties interested, when notice for ninety days shall be given of
such return, in such manner as the legislative authorities of said nations, respectively, shall prescribe, or, in
the event of said authorities failing to give such notice
in a reasonable time, in such manner as the register of
said land office shall prescribe, calling upon all parties
interested to examine said maps to the end that errors,
if any, in the location of such occupancies, may be corrected.

ARTICLE XIII.

The notice required in the above article shall be
given, not only in the Choctaw and Chickasaw nations,
but by publication in newspapers printed in the States of
Mississippi and Tennessee, Louisiana, Texas, Arkansas
and Alabama, to the end that such Choctaws and Chickasaws as yet remain outside of the Choctaw and Chicka
saw nations, may be informed and have opportunity to

exercise the rights hereby given to resident Choctaws and Chickasaws ; *Provided*, that before any such Choc- taw or Chickasaw shall be permitted to select for him or herself, or others, as hereinafter provided, he or she shall satisfy the register of the land office of his or her intention, or the intention of the party for whom the se- lection is to be made, to become bona fide resident in the said nation within five years from the time of selection, and should the said absentee fail to remove into said na- tion, and occupy and commence an improvement on the land selected within the time aforesaid, the said section shall be cancelled, and the land shall thereafter be dis- charged from all claim on account thereof.

ARTICLE XIV.

At the expiration of the ninety days aforesaid the legislative authorities of the said nations, respectively, shall have the right to select one quarter section of land in each of the counties of said nations, respectively, in trust for the establishment of seats of justice therein, and also as many quarter sections as the said legisla- tive councils may deem proper for the permanent en- dowment of schools, seminaries and colleges in said na- tion, provided such selection shall not embrace or inter- fere with any improvement in the actual occupation of any member of the particular nation without his consent; *and, provided*, the proceeds of sale of the quarter sec- tions selected for seats of justice shall be appropriated for the erection or improvement of public buildings in the county in which it is located.

ARTICLE XV.

At the expiration of the ninety days' notice afore- said, the selection which is to change the tenure of the

land in the Choctaw and Chickasaw nations from a holding in common to a holding in severalty, shall take
place, when every Choctaw and Chickasaw shall have
the right to one quarter section of land, whether male or
female, adult or minor, and if in actual possession or
occupancy of land improved or cultivated by him or her,
shall have a prior right to the quarter section in which
his or her improvement lies; and every infant shall have
selected for him or her a quarter section of land in such
location as the father of such infant, if there be a father
living, and if no father living, then the mother or guardian, and should there be neither father, mother, or
guardian, then as the probate judge of the county, acting
for the best interest of such infant, shall select.

ARTICLE XVI.

Should an actual occupant of land desire, at any
time prior to the commencement of the surveys aforesaid, to abandon his improvement, and select and improve other land, so as to obtain the prior right thereof,
he or she shall be at liberty to do so; in which event the
improvement so abandoned shall be open to selection by
other parties : *Provided*, that nothing herein contained
shall authorize the multiplication of improvements so as
to increase the quantity of land beyond what a party
would be entitled to at the date of this treaty.

ARTICLE XVII.

No selection to be made under this treaty shall be
permitted to deprive or interfere with the continued
occupation by the missionaries established in the respective nations of their several missionary establishments ; it being the wish of the parties hereto to promote
and foster an influence so largely conducive to civilization and refinement. Should any missionary who has

been engaged in missionary labor for five consecutive years before the date of this treaty in the said nations, or either of them, or three consecutive years prior to the late rebellion, and who, if absent from the said nations, may desire to return, wish to select a quarter section of land with a view to a permanent home for himself and family, he shall have the privilege of doing so, provided no selection shall include any public buildings, schools or seminary ; and a quantity of land not exceeding six hundred and forty acres to be selected according to legal subdivisions in one body, and to include their improvements, is hereby granted to every religious society or denomination which has erected, or which, with the consent of the Indians, may hereafter erect buildings within the Choctaw and Chickasaw country for missionary or educational purposes ; but no land thus granted, nor the buildings which have or may be erected thereon, shall ever be sold or otherwise disposed of, except with the consent of the legislatures of said nations respectively and approval of the secretary of the interior ; and whenever such lands or buildings shall be sold or disposed of the proceeds thereof shall be applied, under the direction of the secretary of the interior, to the support and maintenance of other similar establishments for the benefit of the Choctaws and Chickasaws, and such other persons as may hereafter become members of their nations according to their laws, customs and usages.

ARTICLE XVIII.

In making a selection for children the parent shall have a prior right to select land adjacent to his own improvements or selection, provided such selection shall be made within thirty days from the time at which selections under this treaty commence.

ARTICLE XIX.

The manner of selecting as aforesaid shall be by an entry with the register of the land office, and all selections shall be made to conform to the legal subdivisions of the said lands as shown by the surveys aforesaid on the maps aforesaid; it being understood that nothing herein contained is to be construed to confine a party selecting to one section, but he may take contiguous parts of sections by legal subdivisions in different sections, not exceeding together a quarter section.

ARTICLE XX.

Prior to any entries being made under the foregoing provisions, proof of improvements, or actual cultivation, as well as the number of persons for whom a parent or guardian, or probate judge of the county proposes to select, and of their right to select, and of his or her authority to select, for them, shall be made to the register and receiver of the land office, under regulations to be prescribed by the secretary of the interior.

ARTICLE XXI.

In every township the sections of land numbered sixteen and thirty-six shall be reserved for the support of schools in said township; *Provided*, that if the same has been already occupied by a party or parties having the right to select it, or it shall be so sterile as to be unavailable, the legislative authorities of the particular nations shall have the right to select such other unoccupied sections as they may think proper.

ATRTICLE XXII.

The right of selection hereby given shall not authorize the selection of any land required by the United

states as a military post or Indian agency, not exceeding
one mile square, which, when abandoned, shall revert to
the nation in which the land lies.

ARTICLE XXIII.

The register of the land office shall inscribe in a
suitable book or books, in alphabetical order, the name
of every individual for whom a selection shall be made,
his or her age, and a description of the land selected.

ARTICLE XXIV.

Whereas, it may be difficult to give to each occupant of an improvement a quarter section of land, or
even a smaller sub-division, which shall include such
improvement, in consequence of such improvements lying
in towns, villages and hamlets, the legislative authorities of the respective nations shall have power, where, in
their discretion they think it expedient, to lay off into
town lots any section or part of a section so occupied,
to which lots the actual occupants, being citizens of the
respective nations, shall have pre emptive right, and,
upon paying into the treasury of the particular nation
the price of the land, as fixed by the respective legislatures, exclusive of the value of said improvements, shall
receive a conveyance thereof. Such occupant shall not
be prejudiced thereby in his right to his selection else-
where. The town lots which may be unoccupied shall be
disposed of for the benefit of the particular nation, as
the legislative authorities may direct from time to time.
When the number of occupants of the same quarter section shall not be such as to authorize the legislative authorities to lay out the same, or any part thereof into
town lots, they may make such regulations for the dis-

position thereof as they may deem proper, either by sub-division of the same, so as to accommodate the actual occupants, or by giving the right of prior choice to the first occupant in point of time, upon paying the others for their improvements, to be valued in such way as the legislative authorities shall prescribe, or otherwise. All occupants retaining their lots under this section, and desiring, in addition, to make a selection, must pay for the lots so retained, as in the case of town lots. And any Choctaw or Chickasaw who may desire to select a sectional division other than that on which his homestead is, without abandoning the latter, shall have the right to purchase the homestead sectional division at such price as the respective legislatures may prescribe.

ARTICLE XXV.

During ninety days from the expiration of the ninety days' notice aforesaid, the Choctaws and Chickasaws shall have the exclusive right to make selections, as aforesaid, and at the end of that time the several parties shall be entitled to patents for their respective selections, to be issued by the president of the United States, and countersigned by the chief executive officer of the nation in which the land lies, and recorded in the records of the executive officer of the particular nation; and copies of the said patents, under seal, shall be evidence in any court of law or equity.

ARTICLE XXVI.

The right here given to Choctaws and Chickasaws, respectively, shall extend to all persons who have become citizens by adoption or intermarriage of either of said nations, or who may hereafter become such.

ARTICLE XXVII.

In the event of disputes arising in regard to the rights of parties to select particular quarter-sections or other divisions of said land, or in regard to the adjustment of boundaries, so as to make them conform to legal divisions and subdivisions, such disputes shall be settled by the register of the land office and the chief executive officer of the nation in which the land lies, in a summary way, after hearing the parties; and if said register and chief officer cannot agree, the two to call in a third party, who shall constitute a third referee, the decision of any two of whom shall be final, without appeal.

ARTICLE XXVIII.

Nothing contained in any law of either of the said nations shall prevent parties entitled to make selections contiguous to each other; and the Choctaw and Chickasaw nations hereby agree to repeal all laws inconsistent with this provision.

ARTICLE XXIX.

Selections made under this treaty shall, to the extent of one-quarter section, including the homestead or dwelling, be inalienable for the period of twenty-one years from the date of such selection, and upon the death of the party in possession shall descend according to the laws of the nation where the land lies; and in the event of his or her death without heirs, the said quarter-section shall escheat and become the property of the nation.

ARTICLE XXX.

The Choctaw and Chickasaw nation will receive into their respective districts, east of the ninety-eighth degree of west longitude, in the proportion of one fourth in

the Chickasaw and three-fourths in the Choctaw nation,
civilized Indians from the tribes known by the general
name of the Kansas Indians, being Indians to the north
of the Indian territory, not exceeding ten thousand in
number, who shall have in the Choctaw and Chickasaw
nations, respectively, the same rights as the Choctaws
and Chickasaws, of whom they shall be the fellow citizens, governed by the same laws and enjoying the same
privileges, with the exception of the right to participate
in the Choctaw and Chickasaw annuities and other moneys, and in the public domain, should the same, or the
proceeds thereof, be divided per capita among said Choctaws and Chickasaws, and among others the right to
select land as herein provided for Choctaws and Chickasaws, after the expiration of the ninety days during
which the selections of land are to be made, as aforesaid
by said Choctaws and Chickasaws; and the Choctaw and
Chickasaw nations pledge themselves to treat the said
Kansas Indians in all respects with kindness and for-
bearance, aiding them in good faith to establish themselves in their new homes, and to respect all their customs and usages not inconsistent with the constitution
and laws of the Choctaw and Chickasaw nations, respectively. In making selections after the advent of the Indians and the actual occupancy of land in said nation,
such occupancy shall have the same same-effect in their
behalf as the occupancies of Choctaws and Chickasaws;
and after the said Choctaws and Chickasaws have made
their selections as aforesaid, the said persons of African
descent mentioned in the third article of the treaty shall
make their selections as therein provided, in the event
of the making of the laws, rules and regulations aforesaid, after the expiration of ninety days from the date
at which the said Kansas Indians are to make their
selections as therein provided, and the actual occupancy

of such persons of African descent shall have the same effect in their behalf as the occupancies of the Choctaws and Chickasaws.

ARTICLE XXXI.

And whereas some time must necessarily elapse before the surveys, maps and selections herein provided for can be completed so as to permit the said Kansas Indians to make their selections in their order, during which time the United States may desire to remove the said Indians from their present abiding places, it is hereby agreed that the said Indians may at once come into the Choctaw and Chickasaw nations, settling themselves temporarily as citizens of the said nations, respectively, upon such land as suits them and is not already occupied.

ARTICLE XXXII.

At the expiration of two years, or sooner, if the president of the United States shall so direct, from the completion of the surveys and maps aforesaid, the officers of the land-offices aforesaid shall deliver to the executive departments of the Choctaw and Chickasaw nations, respectively, all such documents as may be necessary to elucidate the land-title as settled according to this treaty and forward copies thereof, with the field-notes, records, and other papers pertaining to said titles, to the commissioner of the general land-office, and thereafter grants of land and patents thereof shall be issued in such manner as the legislative authorities of said nations may provide for all the unselected portions of the Choctaw and Chickasaw districts as defined by the treaty of June twenty-second, eighteen hundred and fifty five.

ARTICLE XXXIII.

All lands selected as herein provided shall hereafter be held in severalty by the repective parties, and the unselected land shall be the common property of the Choctaw and Chickasaw nations, in their corporate capacities, subject to the joint control of their legislative authorities.

ARTICLE XXXIV.

Should any Choctaw or Chickasaw be prevented from selecting for him or herself during the ninety days aforesaid, the failure to do so shall not authorize another to select the quarter-section containing his improvement, but he may at any time make his selection thereof, sub-ject to having his boundaries made to conform to legal divisions as aforesaid.

ARTICLE XXXV.

Should the selections aforesaid not be made before the transfer of the land records to the executive authori-ties of said nations, respectively, they shall be made ac-cording to such regulations as the legislative authorities of the two nations, respectively, may prescribe, to the end that full justice and equity may be done to the citi-zens of the respective terrritories.

ARTICLE XXXVI.

Should any land that has been selected under the provisions of this treaty be abandoned and left unculti-vated for the space of seven years by the party select-ing the same, or his heirs, except in the case of infants under the age of twenty-one years, or married women, or persons non compos mentis, the legislative authori-ties of the nation where such land lies may either rent

the same for the benefit of those interested, or dispose
of the same otherwise for' their benefit, and may pass
all laws necessary to give effect to this provision.

_____

ARTICLE XXXVII.

In consideration of the right of selection hereinbefore accorded to certain Indians other than the Choctaws
and Chickasaws, the United States agree to pay to the
Choctaw and Chickasaw nations, out of the funds of Indians removing into said nations respectively, under the
provisions of this treaty, such sum as may be fixed by
the legislatures of said nations, not exceeding one dollar
per acre, to be divided between the said nations in the
proportion of one fourth to the Chickasaw nation and
three-fourths to the Choctaw nation, with the understanding that at the expiration of twelve months the
actual number of said immigrating Indians shall be ascertained, and the amount paid that may be actually
due at the rate aforesaid; and should still further immi-
grations take place from among said Kansas Indians,
still further payments shall be made accordingly from
time to time.

_____

ARTICLE XXXVIII.

Every white person, who, having married a Choctaw
or Chickasaw, resides in the said Choctaw or Chickasaw
nation, or who has been adopted by the legislative authorities, is to be deemed a member of said nation, and
shall be subject to the laws of the Choctaw and Chickasaw nations according to his domicile, and to prosecution
and trial before their tribunals, and to punishment according to their laws in all respects as though he was a
native Choctaw or Chickasaw.

ARTICLE XXXIX.

No person shall expose goods or other articles for sale as a trader without a permit of the legislative authorities of the nation, he may propose to trade in ; but no license shall be required to authorize any member of the Choctaw or Chickasaw nation to trade in the Choctaw or Chickasaw country who is authorized by the proper authority of the nation, nor the authorized Choctaws or Chickasaws to sell flour, meat, fruit and other provisions, stock, wagons, agricultural implements, or tools brought from the United States into the said country.

ARTICLE XL.

All restrictions contained in any treaty heretofore made, or in any regulation of the United States upon the sale or other disposition of personal chattel property by Choctaws or Chickasaws, are hereby removed.

ARTICLE XLI.

All persons who are members of the Choctaw or Chickasaw nations, and are not otherwise disqualified or disabled, shall hereafter be competent witnesses in all civil and criminal suits and proceedings in any courts of the United States, any law to the contrary notwithstanding.

ARTICLE XLII.

The Choctaw and Chickasaw nations shall deliver up persons accused of crimes against the United States who may be found within their respective limits, on the requisition of the governor of any state, for a crime committed against the laws of said state, and upon the requisition of the judge of the district court of the United

States for the district within which the crime was committed.

ARTICLE XLIII.

The United States promise and agree that no white
person except officers, agents and employes of the government, and of any internal improvement company, or
persons traveling through, or temporarily sojourning in,
the said nations, or either of them, shall be permitted to
go into said territory, unless formally incorporated and
naturalized by the joint action of the authorities of both
nations into one of the said nations of Choctaws and
Chickasaws, according to their laws, customs, or usages;
but this article is not to be construed to affect parties
heretofore adopted, or to prevent the employment temporarily of white persons who are teachers, mechanics,
or skilled in agriculture, or to prevent the legislative authorities of the respective nations from authorizing such
works of internal improvement as they may deem essential to the welfare and prosperity of the community, or
be taken to interfere with or invalidate any action which
has heretofore been had in this connection by either of
the said nations.

ARTICLE XLIV.

Post offices shall be established and maintained by
the United States at convenient places in the Choctaw
and Chickasaw nations, to and from which the mail shall
be carried at reasonable intervals, at the rate of postage
prevailing in the United States.

ARTICLE XLV.

All the rights, privileges and immunities heretofore
possessed by said nations or individuals thereof, or to

which they were entitled under the treaties and legislation heretofore made and had in connection with them,
shall be, and are hereby declared to be, in full force, so
far as they are consistent with the provisions of this
treaty.

ARTICLE XLVI.

Of the moneys stipulated to be paid to the Choc
taws and Chickasaws, under this treaty for the cession
of the leased district, and the admission of the Kansas
Indians among them, the sum of one hundred and fifty
thousand dollars shall be advanced and paid to the
Choctaws, and fifty thousand dollars to the Chickasaws
through their respective treasurers, as soon as practicable after the ratification of this treaty, to be paid out of
said moneys or any other moneys of said nations in the
hands of the United States ; the residue, not affected by
any provision of this treaty, to remain in the treasury of
the United States at an annual interest of five per cent.
no part of which shall be paid out as annuity, but shall
be annually paid to the treasurer of said nations, respectively, to be regularly and judiciously applied, under the
direction of their respective legislative councils, to the
support of their government, the purposes of education,
and such other objects as may be best calculated to promote and advance the welfare and happiness of said
nations and their people respectively.

ARTICLE XLVII.

As soon as practicable after the lands shall have
been surveyed and assigned to the Choctaws and Chickasaws in severalty, as herein provided, upon application
of their respective legislative councils, and with the
assent of the president of the United States, all the annuities and funds invested and held in trust by the United

States for the benefit of said nations, respectively, shall be capitalized or converted into money, as the case may be; and the aggregate amounts thereof belonging to each nation shall be equally divided and paid per capita to the individuals thereof respectively, to aid and assist them in improving their homesteads and increasing or acquiring flocks and herds, and thus encourage them to make proper efforts to maintain successfully the new relations which the holding of their lands in severalty will involve: *Provided, nevertheless,* that there shall be retained by the United States such sum as the president shall deem sufficient of the said moneys to be invested, that the interest thereon may be sufficient to defray the expenses of the government of said nations respectively, together with a judicious system of education, until these objects can be provided for by a proper system of taxation; and whenever this shall be done to the satisfaction of the president of the United States, the moneys so retained shall be divided in the manner and for the purpose above mentioned.

ARTICLE XLVIII.

Immediately after the ratification of this treaty there shall be paid, out of the funds of the Choctaws and Chickasaws in the hands of the United States, twenty-five thousand dollars to the Choctaw and twenty-five thousand dollars to the Chickasaw commissioners, to enable them to discharge obligations incurred by them for various incidental and other expenses to which they have been subjected, and for which they are now indebted.

ARTICLE XLIX.

And it is further agreed that a commission, to consist of a person or persons to be appointed by the president of the United States, not exceeding three, shall be appointed immediately on the ratification of this treaty, who shall take into consideration and determine the claim of such Choctaws and Chickasaws as allege that they have been driven during the late rebellion from their homes in the Choctaw [and Chickasaw] nations on account of their adhesion to the United States, for damages, with power to make such award as may be consistent with equity and good conscience, taking into view all circumstances, whose report, when ratified by the secretary of the interior, shall be final, and authorize the payment of the amount from any money of said nations in the hands of the United States as the said commission may award.

ARTICLE L.

Whereas Joseph G. Heald and Reuben Wright, of Massachusetts, were licensed traders in the Choctaw country at the commencement of the rebellion, and claim to have sustained large losses on account of said rebellion, by the use of their property by said nation, and that large sums of money are due them for goods and property taken, or sold to members of the said nation, and money advanced to said nation; and whereas other loyal citizens of the United States may have just claims of the same character: It is hereby agreed and stipulated that the commission provided for in the preceding article shall investigate said claims, and fully examine the same; and such sum or sums of money as shall by the report of said commission, approved by the secretary of the interior, be found due to such persons, not exceeding ninety thousand dollars, shall be paid by the United States to the persons entitled thereto, out of any money belonging to said nation in the possession of the United States: *Provided,* that no claim for goods or property of any kind shall be allowed or paid, in whole or part, which shall have been used by said nation or any member thereof in aid of the rebellion, with the consent of said claimants: *Provided also* that if the aggregate of said claims thus allowed and approved shall exceed said sum of ninety thousand dollars, then that sum shall be applied pro rata in payment of the claims so allowed.

ARTICLE LI.

It is further agreed that all treaties and parts of treaties inconsistent herewith be, and the same are hereby, declared null and void.

Proclaimed July 10, 1866.

In testimony whereof, the said Dennis N. Cooley, Elijah Sells, and E. S. Parker, commissioners in behalf of the United States, and the said commissioners on behalf of the Choctaw and Chickasaw nations, have hereunto set their hands and seals, the day and year first above written:

> D. N. COOLEY, (seal.)
> Comm'r Indian Affairs.
> ELIJAH SELLS, (seal.)
> Sup't Indian Affairs.
> E. S. PARKER, (seal.)
> Special Comm'r.
> Commissioners for United States.

> ALFRED WADE, (seal.)
> ALLEN WRIGHT, (seal.)
> JAMES REILY, (seal.)
> JOHN PAGE, (seal.)
> Choctaw Commissioners.

CAMPBELL LE FLORE, Secretary.

WINCHESTER COLBERT, (seal.)
     Governor Chickasaw Nation.

EDMUND PICKENS,   (seal.)
HOLMES COLBERT,   (seal.)
COLBERT CARTER,   (seal.)
ROBERT H. LOVE,   (seal.)
     Chickasaw Commissioners.

E. S. MITCHELL, Secretary.

Signed, sealed and delivered in the presence of—
                    JOHN H. B. LATROBE,
                    P. P. PITCHLYNN,
                         Principal Chief Choctaw Nation.
                    DOUGLAS H. COOPER,
                    J. HARLAN,
                         U. S. Indian Agent for Cherokees.
                    CHAS. E. MIX,
                         Chief Clerk Indian Bureau.

And whereas, the said treaty having been submitted to the Senate of the United States for its constitutional action thereon, the Senate did, on the twenty-eighth of June, one thousand eight hundred and sixty-six, advise and consent to the ratification of the same, by a resolution, with amendments, in the words and figures following, to-wit:

              IN EXECUTIVE SESSION,   }
          SENATE OF THE UNITED STATES.   }
                              June 28, 1866.

Resolved, (two thirds of the Senators present concurring), That the Senate advise and consent to the ratification of the articles of agreement and convention between the United States and the Choctaw and Chickasaw Nations of Indians, made and concluded at the city of Washington, the twenty-eighth day of April, in the year eighteen hundred sixty-six, by Dennis N. Cooley,

Elijah Sells, and E. S. Parker, Special Commissioners on the part of the United States; and Alfred Wade, Allen Wright, James Riley, and John Page, Commissioners on the part of the Choctaws; and Winchester Colbert, Edmund Pickens, Holmes Colbert, Colbert Carter and Robert H. Love, Commissioners on the part of the Chickasaws, with the following

AMENDMENTS.

1st. At the end of Article 5 add the following:

The people of the Choctaw and Chickasaw nations stipulate and agree to deliver up to any duly authorized agent of the United States all public property in their possession which belong(s) to the late so-called "Confederate States of America," or the United States, without any reservation wha(t)soever, particularly ordnance, ordnance stores, and arms of all kinds.

2d. Article 9, lines 4 and 5, strike out the words "including any errors which may have accrued."

3d. Article 39, lines 1, 2, and 3, strike out the following: "Be licensed to trade with the Choctaws or Chickasaws, except by the agent, with the advice and consent," and insert in lieu thereof: "No person shall expose goods or other articles for sale as a trader without a permit."

4th. Strike out article 42, and insert in lieu thereof the following as a substitute: "The Choctaw and Chickasaw nations shall deliver up persons accused of crime against the United States who may be found within their respective limits on the requisition of the governor of any state, for a crime committed against the laws of said state, and upon the requisition of the judge of the district court of the United States for the district within which the crime was committed."

5th. Article 46, line 13, strike out the words "not less than."

6th. Article 49, line 3, after the words "United States" insert: *"not exceeding three."*

7th. Article [50], line 11, to and including line 15, strike out the following words: "That the President of the United States shall, within three months from the ratification of this treaty, appoint a commission to consist of one or more discreet persons," and insert in lieu thereof : *"that the commission provided for in the preceding article shall."*

Attest: J. W. FORNEY,

Secretary,

And whereas the foregoing amendments having been fully explained and interpreted to the respective commissioners of the Choctaw and Chickasaw nations of Indians hereinbefore named, they did, on the second day of July, one thousand eight hundred and sixty six, give their free and voluntary assent to said amendments, in the words and figures following, to-wit:

Whereas, the Senate of the United States did, on the 28th day of June, A. D. 1866, advise and consent to the ratification of the articles of agreement and convention between the United States and the Choctaw and Chickasaw nations of Indians, made and concluded at the city of Washington the twenty-eighth day of April in the year eighteen hundred and sixty-six, by Dennis N. Cooley, Elijah Sells, and E. S. Parker, special commissioners on the part of the United States; and Alfred Wade, Allen Wright, James Riley and John Page, commissioners on the part of the Choctaws; and Winchester Colbert, Edmund Pickens, Homes Colbert, Colbert Carter, and Robert H. Love, commissioners on the part of the Chickasaws, with the following

6

AMENDMENTS, to-wit:

1st.. At the end of Article 5, add the following:

The people of the Choctaw and Chickasaw nations stipulate and agree to deliver up to any duly authorized agent of the United States, all public property in their possession which belong to the late so-called " Confederate States of America," or the United States, without any reservation whatsoever, particularly ordnance, ordnance stores, and arms of all kinds.

2d. Article 9, lines 4 and 5, strike out the words, " including any arrears which may have accrued."

3d. Article 39, lines 1, 2 and 3, strike out the following:

" Be licensed to trade with the Choctaws or Chickasaws except by the agent, with the advice and consent," and insert in lieu thereof: *No person shall expose goods or other articles for sale as a trader without a permit.*

4th. Strike out Article 42, and insert in lieu thereof the following as a substitute :

The Choctaw and Chickasaw nations shall deliver up persons accused of crime against the United States, who may be found within their respective limits, on the requisition of the governor of any state for a crime committed against the laws of said state, and upon the requisition of the judge of the district court of the United States, for the district within which the crime was committed.

5th. Article 46, line 13, strike out the words, " not less than."

6th. Article 49, line 3, after the word " United States" insert " not exceeding three."

7th. Article 50, lines 11, to and including line 15, strike out the following words : " That the president of the United States, shall, within three months from the ratification of this treaty, appoint a commission, to consist of one or more discreet persons," and insert, in lieu thereof, that the commission provided for in the preceding article shall.

Now, therefore, we, the commissioners on the part of the said Choctaws and Chickasaws, do hereby assent and agree to the said amendments above written, the same having been interpreted to us, and being fully understood by us.

Witness our hands and seals, this 2d day of July, A. D. 1866, at Washington, D. C.

ALFRED WADE,   (seal.)
ALLEN WRIGHT,   (seal.)
JAMES RILEY,   (seal.)
JOHN PAGE,   (seal.)
Choctaw Commissioners.
WINCHESTER COLBERT, (seal.)
his
EDMUND ⋈ PICKENS,   (seal.)
mark.
HOLMES COLBERT,   (seal.)
COLBERT CARTER,   (seal.)
ROBERT H. LOVE,   (seal.)
Chickasaw Commissioners.

In presence of

JOHN H. B. LATROBE,
CHARLES E. MIX,
P. P. PITCHLYNN,
Principal Chief Choctaw Nation.
DOUGLASS H. COOPER,
ALFRED H. JACKSON,
W. R. IRWIN,
LEWIS S. HAYDEN,
E. S. MITCHELL,
Secretary Chickasaw Commission.

Now, therefore, be it known, that I, Andrew Johnson, president of the United States of America, do, in pursuance of the advice and consent of the senate, as expressed in its resolution of the twenty-eight day of June, one thousand eight hundred and sixty-six, accept, ratify and confirm the said treaty, with the amendments as aforesaid.

In testimony whereof, I have signed my name, and have caused the seal of the United States to be hereto affixed.

Done at the City of Washington, this tenth day of July, in the year of our Lord, one thousand eight hundred and sixty-six, and of [SEAL.] the Independence of the United States of America the ninety-first.

ANDREW JOHNSON.

By the President:

WILLIAM H. SEWARD,

Secretary of State.

LAWS

OF THE

CHOCTAW NATION.

EXECUTIVE DEPARTMENT.

SECTION I.

PRINCIPAL CHIEF.

1. Be it enacted by the general council of the Choctaw nation assembled : The principal chief of the Choctaw nation shall have power to remove from office any national, district or county officer, for the causes and under the restrictions following, to-wit : In case the securities, or either of them of any national, district or county officer, who may be required to give bond and security for the faithful performance of his duty, by any law of this nation, shall remove his or their residence out of this nation permanently, or shall become insolvent, or shall be convicted of a violation of any the provisions of an act entitled, " An act to prevent the use of intoxicating liquors in the Choctaw nation," it shall be the duty of the principal chief, on satisfactory information of any such removal or insolvency, to notify such officer to appear before him, at a day and place therein named, within twenty days thereafter, to give a new bond, with other good and sufficient security, in a penalty equal to that of the former bond, with the like con-

dition. And if such officer shall neglect or refuse to do
so, or if, on satisfactory showing of his condition as
aforesaid, the principal chief shall forthwith vacate his
commission, and the vacancy shall be supplied as the
constitution prescribes, and if any national, district or
county officer shall be found by inquest, according to
law, an idiot, lunatic or *non compos mentis*, during the
time for which he is elected or appointed, or shall, during such time, be found, by the verdict of a jury, guilty
of any felony, infamous crime, corruption or peculation
in office, or gambling with public money of the nation,
which may have come into his hand by virtue of his
office, the commission of every such officer shall be
deemed and held to be vacated, and such vacancy shall
be supplied as the constitution provides.

2. The principal chief shall, at stated times, require
information, in writing, from all officers in the executive
department, on any subject relating to their duties, and
embody such parts of the same as are of public concern
in his communication to the general council, to be made
from time to time. He shall have the superintendence
of the officers of national treasurer and national auditor,
during the recess of the general council, and he shall
take care that they respectively perform the duties
required of them by law, without fraud, partiality or
delay: and if it shall satisfactorily appear to him at any
time that the money or other property of the nation in
the treasury has been misapplied, wasted or embezzled,
he shall direct the national attorney, or district attorney, to proceed according to law, against such defaulter
on his or their bonds. He shall have full power and
authority, whenever he may think the public interest
requires it, to make a personal inspection of all the
books, vouchers and other official papers in the offices of
the national auditor and national treasurer, and to count

the moneys in the treasury, and if he shall discover, or have, cause to suspect any embezzlement, peculation, defalcation or frauds to have been committed or perpetrated in either of these departments of the government, he shall forthwith apply to the circuit judge for a warrant, to arrest the officer in whose office such embezzlement, peculation, defalcation or fraud shall have been committed or suspected to have been committed. And it shall be the duty of such judge to grant the said warrant or other process, and to have such officer arrested and brought before him for trial and examination. And if the said judge shall certify that after a full and perfect examination of all the facts in the case there is probably ground to believe that said officer has been guilty of some embezzlement, defalcation, peculation or fraud, then the principal chief shall suspend the said auditor or treasurer, as the case may be, from the further exercise of his official duties, and to make a temporary appointment to fill his place until the court shall determine that said officer was improperly removed or suspended, or that the same was done without a sufficient cause; or if the national treasurer's or national auditor's reports are not accepted by the general council on account of any errors or otherwise, the principal chief is hereby authorized and required to suspend said officer or officers for the time being, or during the term they were elected, and appoint some competent person to fill such vacancy; and the person so appointed and commissioned shall take the oath of office, give bond and report his official doings in every respect as if elected, and in accordance with the law defining the duties of the national treasurer and national auditor, and fixing their salaries; and the person appointed to fill such vacancy shall receive the same pay as is allowed by law to a regularly elected national treasurer or national auditor, and the officer

suspended shall not receive any salary for the time being or for the term he may be suspended.

3. The principal chief shall not appoint any one to
act as delegate, commissioner, agent or attorney, in any
capacity whatever, for this nation, except the appointee
is a legal citizen of the nation, and is and has been a resident of the same for the last three consecutive years
previous to his or their appointment.

4. The principal chief is hereby authorized to appoint some competent person to be his private secretary
with a salary of five hundred dollars per annum, payable quarterly upon the certificate of the principal chief,
whose duty it shall be to do such writing and official
business as the principal chief may require, and whose
term of office shall not be longer than the appointing
principal chief, unless re-appointed.

5. The principal chief of this nation shall receive
for his services the sum of two thousand dollars a year,
payable quarterly, from the date of his installation, out
of the treasury of the nation, upon his written order at
such times, and the national auditor shall issue his warrant therefor, and the national treasurer shall pay the
same; and a sum not exceeding four hundred dollars
shall be annually appropriated for the use of the executive department of the government for the contingent
expenses thereof, to be accounted for by the principal
chief to the general council at each session thereof; and
it shall be the duty of the national auditor, from time to
time, on the written order of the principal chief, stating
the uses of any sum of money for contingent purposes,
to issue his warrant on the treasury of the nation therefor.

SECTION II.   APPROVED COL. 22, 1888.
DISTRICT CHIEFS.

1. Be it enacted by the general council of the Choctaw nation assembled: There shall be elected by the

qualified voters of the Choctaw nation, at the time and in the manner prescribed by the constitution, district chiefs in each district of this nation, who shall be commissioned by the principal chief, and shall continue in the office for the term of two years from the time of having been qualified unless sooner removed, and until their successors be duly qualified; and before they enter upon the discharge of their official duties, they shall take the oath prescribed in the constitution before the principal chief or any judge of the supreme, circuit or county courts of the nation.

2. Each district chief within his district shall be a general conservator of the peace, and shall see that the laws are faithfully executed by the proper officers, especially an act to prevent the introduction and use of intoxicating liquors in the Choctaw nation, and report to the principal chief for the information of the general council, any failures occurring therein ; and shall recommend to him from time to time any matter for the general good, and when the principal chief shall deem it proper and expedient, and shall give them written notice of the time and place of meeting, they shall compose an executive council to furnish any desired information re-respecting their several districts ; but said district chiefs shall in no manner interfere with the proper exercise of the duties prescribed by law of any officers of the nation.

3. Each district chief of the nation shall attend the circuit courts of his own district, and address the people on the importance of obeying and enforcing the law, and maintaining good order throughout the nation, and advocate the practice of temperance, industry and morality ; and their salaries shall be fifty dollars each per annum, payable semi-annually on the certificate of the the circuit judges at the terms of the circuit courts ; but should any district chief fail or neglect to be in atten-

dance at the said courts, to address the people as required of him by law, the circuit judge is hereby required to appoint some suitable person to perform the duties incumbent upon the district chief, and shall give the person performing the duties, a certificate for the sum of ten dollars, to be deducted from the pay of the district chief so failing.

APPROVED OCT. 30, 1888,

SECTION III.

NATIONAL SECRETARY.

1. Be it enacted by the general council of the Choctaw nation assembled: It shall be the duty of the national secretary to take charge of and safely keep in his office the journals, papers, documents and proceedings of both houses of the general council during the recess thereof, and the secretary of the senate and the clerk of the house of representatives shall deliver to him, immediately on the adjournment of the general council every document and paper in anywise appertaining to the same. The national secretary shall also collect together and take charge of all books, papers, documents, journals of both houses of the general council, and shall carefully preserve the official books, public library, papers, records and furniture belonging to the archives of the Choctaw nation. He shall keep a register of all the official acts of the principal chief, and shall, when required, lay the same and all papers, minutes and vouchers, relative thereto, before the general council; and shall perform such other duties as shall from time to time be required of him by law; he shall keep and preserve the returns of all elections held in this nation, and lay the same and all other official documents relating thereto before the general council when required; and he shall receive for his annual salary, in quarterly payments,

after the same shall have been audited according to law, the sum of six hundred dollars.

2. The national secretary shall be required to enter into bond with two or more good and sufficient securities, to be approved of by the principal chief, in the penalty of twenty thousand dollars, payable to the principal chief of the Choctaw nation (by name for the time being) and his successors in office; conditional that, "he shall from time to time, and at all times, produce any document or other property of the nation that is or may be placed in his custody for safe keeping, when thereto required by the general council or principal chief, and shall at the expiration of his term of office deliver over to his successor in office all documents, instruments of writing, papers or books which shall be made, done or committed to him or by him, or by any person or persons by him employed in his office, then this obligation to be void, otherwise to be and remain in full force and virtue;" and if the principal chief approve the bond he shall endorse his approval on the same. The national secretary shall procure a well-bound book and enter therein all documents and instruments of writing in his care, which may be submitted to him by the general council, principal chief or from any other source for safe keeping; the same being necessary to be filed in his office; and each package to be distinctly marked for easy reference.

3. The national secretary shall, upon application of any person or persons, make out a correct copy or copies of any act or acts of the general council, and certify the same to be correct in his official capacity, and shall be entitled to receive for the same six cents for every hundred words thereof; and whenever any person shall desire a certificate under the seal of this nation, of official character, of any judge, or other officer of this

nation, it shall be the duty of the national secretary to furnish the same, under the seal of the nation, signed by the principal chief, and countersigned by himself, and for every such certificate so issued, the national secretary may be entitled to demand and receive from the person desiring the same, fifty cents, out of which he shall defray all expenses attending the same.

4. It shall be the duty of the national secretary, as soon as practicable after each session of the general council, to have enough copies of all the acts, resolutions, treasurer and auditor's report of each session thereof respectively printed and published in substantial pamphlet form, on good paper, in both Choctaw and English, to furnish and send one copy of each language to every officer of the Choctaw government, and reserve for the nation one dozen copies of each besides, to be deposited in the archives of said nation to meet future contingencies, and then if any surplus copies be left, the said national secretary may dispose of the same on his own personal account, and an additional annual compensation of three hundred and fifty dollars is hereby allowed the national secretary to meet and pay for all additional labor herein imposed and all expenses contingent or otherwise of his office; said additional annual compensation to be drawn upon his own certificate, upon which the national auditor shall issue his warrant, and the national treasurer shall pay the same.

5. There is hereby established a permanent annual contingent fund of fifty dollars, for the use and benefit of the national secretary, to enable him to procure the proper amount of stationery for his own, to be paid out of any money in the treasury not otherwise appropriated; and the auditor is hereby directed to issue his warrant in favor of the national secretary for that amount, and the treasurer to pay the same. **APPROVED OCT. 20, 1888.**

ARTICLE IV.

NATIONAL TREASURER.

Be it enacted by the general council of the Choctaw nation assembled.

1. Before the national treasurer shall enter upon the discharge of his official duties, he shall take the oath prescribed in the constitution before some judge of the supreme, circuit or county courts of the Choctaw nation, and enter into bond with two or more good and sufficient securities, to be approved by the principal chief, in the penalty of twenty thousand dollars, payable to the principal chief of the nation by name, for the time being and his successors in office, conditioned as in the following form, to-wit: "The condition of the above obligation is such that whereas the above bound —— was on the —— day of ——, one thousand eight hundred and ——, duly elected as the constitution prescribes, the treasurer of the Choctaw nation for the constitutional term of two years, from the date of this bond and his oath of office, herein written. Now, therefore, if the said —— shall from time to time, and at all times, render a just and true account to the general council of the Choctaw nation, when by them thereto required, of all moneys, securities and other property of the said nation, which shall come into his hands or be committed to his charge, and deliver the moneys, securities and other property of the said nation, in his hands at the expiration of his term of office, together with all documents, instruments of writing, papers or books, which shall be made, done or committed by him, or by any person or persons by him employed in said office, then this obligation to be void, otherwise to be and remain in full force and virtue," which bond shall be submitted to the principal chief and his approbation of the securities therein named shall be endorsed thereon, as also the oath of office written and

certified by the person administering the same, with the proper date, which bond so approved and prepared shall be deposited in the office of the national secretary, there to be recorded and safely kept and preserved, and the said bond shall not be void on the first recovery, but may be put in suit and prosecuted on from time to time, at the cost and charges of any party injured, until the whole amount of the penalty thereof shall have been secured, and an authenticated copy of the said bond shall be received in evidence in any court of law or equity in this nation, and shall be as authentic and valid, as matter of evidence as the original would be if it were produced in court ; and no commission shall issue to the national treasurer elect until bond and security be given, approved of and deposited in the office of the national secretary, as herein before required, and if the same national treasurer elected shall refuse to enter into bond and security as aforesaid, after he shall have been duly elected and informed thereof officially, such election is hereby declared to be absolutely null and void, and the vacancy occasioned thereby shall be immediately filled in such manner as provided in the constitution.

2. It shall be the duty of the national treasurer to receive and keep the moneys of the nation, to disburse the same agreeably to law, and take receipts or vouchers for all moneys which he shall disburse; he shall keep regular, fair and proper accounts of the receipts and expenditures of the public money; he shall open an account in his books in the name of the Choctaw nation, in which account he shall enter the amount of all moneys, securities and other property in the treasury, which may, at any time be received by him, keeping the receipts and disbursements for each fiscal year in separate accounts and closing each with the close of said year: he shall also open an account in the books of the treasury for all

appropriations of money made by law, so that the appropriations of money, and the application thereof, conforme ably thereto, may clearly and distinctly appear on the books of the treasury; and it shall be the duty of the treasurer to pay the salaries of all public officers entitled thereto, quarter-yearly, on the auditor's warrant, unless the time of the payment of the same be otherwise provided for by law; and he shall, at the commencement of every session of the general council, make to them a detailed report of the receipts and expenditures of the fiscal year, and whenever the revenue is likely to prove insufficient for the expenditures of the nation, he shall subjoin to his report such recommendations to the general council as may, in his opinion, be best suited to supply the deficiency.

3. It shall be the duty of the national treasurer to state, in the books of the treasury, separately and distinctly, the amount of money received by him on account of permanent annuities, interest on trust funds, debts, fines, penalties and forfeitures, or on any other account whatsoever, for or in behalf of the nation, and also on account of the same he shall pay out of the same, so that the net amount of the whole revenue, and every branch thereof, and the amount of disbursements in payment of the several demands on the treasury may clearly and distinctly appear; and it shall also be his duty to examine whether any auditor's warrant has been issued agreeable to law, or is signed with the genuine signature of the auditor, before he shall pay the same, and, after making due examination, if he shall find such warrant to have been duly and properly issued, he shall pay the amount called for by the same to the person entitled to receive it, taking his or her receipt thereon, and shall make proper entry in his books of every auditor's warrant, and shall keep the same regularly filed in his office. It

shall be the duty of the national treasurer to furnish to the principal chief, from time to time, when thereto required, a full and complete statement in tabular form, of the situation of public finances, and of the proceedings in his office; the books and accounts of the treasurer shall, at reasonable times, be open to the inspection of the national auditor. The national treasurer shall furnish the national auditor, monthly during each fiscal year, with a list of the receipts at the treasury, numbered as the warrants on which they are founded, and stating in whose name the several receipts have been given, their respective duties, amounts and numbers, and the national treasurer shall not disburse any of the public moneys, except upon the pay warrant of the national auditor, and that when such disbursement is made, he shall make an entry of the date of said warrant in his office, with the word "paid" written in a large, legible hand across the face thereof, and such warrant shall be a full and sufficient voucher for the payment of the same, without the receipt of the person to whom it shall have been paid being given, either upon said warrant or otherwise.

4. That the payee of every warrant issued by the national auditor shall immediately take the same to the national treasurer, whose duty it shall be to countersign and register the same in a well bound book, to be kept in his office for that purpose, in which the treasurer shall note particularly the number of warrants, the amounts, date, and the day on which he countersigned and registered the same, and no warrant which has not been so countersigned and registered shall be transferable or receivable for public duties; and every person or persons paying warrants or grand jury tickets for public duties to the nation, shall endorse his name upon such warrants or grand jury tickets, and no warrant or grand jury

tickets hereafter issued shall be received for any public dues, without the same shall have been so endorsed; and when any person shall desire to make any payments in auditor's warrants into the treasury, it shall be the duty of the national auditor, before issuing his receipt warrant authorizing such payment, carefully to examine all such warrants, and if he shall have any doubts of the genuineness of any warrant he shall compare said warrant with the entries of warrants upon his books and with the entries made in the disbursement book in the treasurer's office; and on the back of all such warrants as he shall judge genuine he shall write the word "genuine," and underneath he shall sign his name officially, and the national treasurer shall not receive any warrant in payment of public dues unless it shall have said endorsement of the auditor upon the same, and it shall be the duty of the national treasurer, before he shall receive in payment or grant his receipt to any person, paying said warrant into the treasury, to have the same compared with the entries on his disbursement book, and if he find that no warrant has been entered in said book, having the same number, bearing date in the same year, or issue to the same person on the same account of expenditure, he shall immediately enter said warrants on said disbursement book, and receive them in payment and receipt for the same, and the treasurer shall not thereafter be liable for the amount of any said warrants, should they prove to be forgeries or suprious, unless proof be made that he received them through carelessness or with fraudulent or felonious intent, or without compliance with the provisions of this act; but if the national auditor shall wilfully, corruptly, or with felonious attempt endorse the word "genuine" and his name upon any such warrant, or with a view to commit a fraud upon the treasury, upon conviction thereof before any court of competent jurisdiction, he shall be fined in a sum equal to double the amount of the warrant so endorsed, and be imprisoned in the nearest jail for not less than six months nor more than eighteen months, at the discretion of the court, and be forever after disqualified from holding any office of profit or honor in this nation.

5. If the national treasurer shall misapply, waste or embezzle any money, securities or other property in the treasury, it shall be the duty of the national attorney, or district attorney, in the absence or inability to act of the national attorney, to proceed against such defaulting treasurer and his securities, for the amount of moneys, securities and other property so misapplied, wasted or embezzled, by motion in the name of the principal chief of the nation for the time being in the circuit court of the county wherein the seat of government is situated, ten days previous notice of such motion being first given to the treasurer and securities; and the court may, on the hearing of such motion, direct a jury to be impaneled *instanter* for the trial of the issue of the defendants, or either of them, to appear and plead, or to inquire of damages of the defendant or defendants, make default, and if on such trial the treasurer be convicted, he and his securities shall be adjudged to pay double damages; and, moreover, such treasurer shall be thereby rendered incapable thereafter of holding any office of profit or honor with and under the authorfty of the nation.

The national treasurer shall be entitled to receive as a compensation for his services, the sum of six hundred dollars a year, payable quarter yearly out of the national treasury upon the auditor's warrant issued in a like manner with warrants for other officers' salaries.

6. The national treasurer shall keep an account with each item of the appropriation bills, and shall class-

ify the items of said bills under eight heads, (see paragraph 3, section 5, of this act), and is hereby required to make his annual report to the principal chief on the first Monday in October of each year, that the principal chief may submit the same to the general council along with his annual message.

SECTION V.   **APPROVED OCT. 30, 1888.**

NATIONAL AUDITOR.

1. The national auditor before he enters upon the duties of his office shall take and subscribe the oath prescribed in the constitution before some one of the judges of the supreme, circuit or county courts of this nation, and enter into bond with two or more good and sufficient securities to be approved by the principal chief, in the penalty of ten thousand dollars, payable to the principal chief of the nation (for the time being), and his successor in office conditioned as in the form following, to-wit: The condition of the above obligation is such that, whereas, the above bound———— was duly elected as specified in the constitution of the Choctaw nation, national auditor of the nation aforesaid, for the term of two years, from the date of the commission, of the qualification, and oath of office herein written: now, therefore, if the said ———— shall faithfully, impartially, and without delay grant and issue his warrant or warrants on the national treasurer for all such sums of money due and payable by law out of any money in the treasury not otherwise appropriated, on the application of any person or persons lawfully entitled to any such warrant or warrants, and shall from time to time, and at all times, render a just and true account of all warrants, in regular order, and all other proceedings in his office to the general council of the nation when thereunto required, and shall carefully keep and preserve the books,

records, papers and other things belonging to his office, and deliver the same without injury or damage to his successor in office; and further, shall well and truly do and perform all other duties required by law of the national auditor during his continuance in office, then this ·obligation to be void, otherwise to be and remain in full force and virtue; which bond shall be submitted to the principal chief, and his approbation of the sureties therein named endorsed thereon, and the same deposited in the office of the national secretary, there to be recorded, and safely kept and preserved therein; and said bond shall not be void on the first recovery, but may be put in suit and prosecuted on from time to time at the cost and charges of the party injured, until the whole amount of the penalty thereof be recovered. Whenever it may become necessary to institute suit on any auditor's bond, an authenticated copy of the same shall be received in evidence in any court in this nation, in the same manner, and it shall be of the same validity, as evidence, as the original would be if it were present in court; and no commission shall issue to the national auditor elect until bond and security be given, approved and deposited in the office of the national secretary as hereinbefore required; the oath of office shall be written upon the bond by the person administering the oath to the auditor, and if the person elected as auditor fail to give bond and security as aforesaid, after he shall have been duly elected and informed thereof officially for the space of ten days, such election is hereby declared absolutely null and void, and the vacancy occasioned thereby shall be filled in such manner as prescribed in the constitution for filling vacancies.

2. It shall be the duty of the national auditor to examine, state, settle and audit all accounts, claims, or demands whatever against the nation, arising under any

act or resolution of the general council, and to grant to
every claimant authorized to receive the same, a warrant
on the national treasury, under his hand and seal of
office, making due entry and register of all his proceedings in a book to be kept for that purpose, and carefully
arranging, filing and preserving in his office all accounts,
receipts, vouchers and papers touching the same ; to examine, settle and audit the accounts for annuities and
interest on trust fund or any other dues of the United
States payable to the national treasurer, and all other
accounts due and payable to the national treasurer from
any other source provided by law; to call upon all such
debtors to render accounts and pay into the treasury all
sums and all balances due, and on failure to do so, if
the debtor be the government of the United States, to use
the best means to ensure the early payment thereof :
and if the debtors be citizens of the nation, to institute
proceedings against them according to law ; to state and
keep the accounts so as to show the amounts of all warrants drawn by him on the treasurer, and for what service or articles of public expenses they were given : and
to lay before the general council and principal chief,
when thereto required, the general accounts, together
with an account of all balances due to and from the nation, with a full and complete statement of the situation
of the public finances and of the proceedings of his
office ; and shall, with the approbation of the principal
chief, purchase all needful supplies of books and sta
tionery and fuel for the general council and national
officers, and issue his warrants on the treasury for the
amount of such purchases in favor of the persons from
whom such purchases shall be made ; *provided*, they
shall not exceed the sum of two hundred dollars in any
one year, and shall file the receipts of the persons for
whom such purchases are made as vouchers in his office;

and make a detailed report of the purchases made by him as aforesaid, and the prices at which they were made.

3. Each fiscal year shall close with the 31st day of July of that year, and no certificate shall be given by any officer who is authorized to make certificates, which will connect one fiscal year with another, or lap one fiscal year onto another, and the auditor is hereby instructed to make no warrants which will so lap or connect the fiscal years into one another; and the auditor is further directed and authorized to return any and all certificates not made in accordance hereto, to the person presenting the same, to have said certificates or certificate made to conform to the requirements of this act, else the auditor shall not issue on the same; and said auditor shall open an account with each item of the appropriation bills, and shall classify the items of said bills under eight heads, viz:

First. Principal chief and his cabinet, national lighthorsemen, clerk of the supreme court, sheriff for attending supreme court, and the contingent funds of the auditor and principal chief.

Second. Supreme and circuit judges, superintendent of public schools, district trustees, district chiefs and district attorneys.

Third. County judges and clerks.

Fourth. Sheriffs and circuit clerks.

Fifth. Election judges and clerks.

Sixth. Jurors and sheriffs for attending circuit courts.

Seventh. School fund.

Eighth. Expenses of the general council.

And all other items shall be classed under the general head of "Miscellaneous;" and the auditor shall number his warrants under each warrant from one (1) up to the maximum, in each fiscal year. All certificates of national indebtedness issued in each quarter of the fiscal year shall be presented to the auditor for his warrant thereon, within one month after the expiration of that quarter. All clerks of courts shall, within three days from the adjournment of their respective court terms, make out certified abstracts of all national certificates, and forward the same immediately by mail or otherwise, to the auditor, in order that the auditor may have the same by which to prove the original certificates as they are presented; and the auditor is hereby required to make his annual report to the principal chief on the first Monday in October of each year, that the principal chief may submit the same to the general council along with his annual message.

4. All warrants drawn by the national auditor upon the national treasury, shall express by references to some one general head of expenditure the cause for which they were drawn, and when the said warrants are drawn for sums chargeable upon the revenue of a different year from out of which they are paid the sum shall be expressed , and all certificates or receipt warrants to the treasury, to receive any money due to the treasury, shall express upon the face thereof the particular head of general revenue on account of which such sum is due, and when the sum is due for the revenue of the past year, that, also, shall be expressed upon the face of such certificate or receipt warrant. All warrants issued by the auditor shall be made payable to order, and shall be negotiable by endorsement and not otherwise.

5. The national auditor shall not issue any warrant upon any allowance made to, or claim in favor of any person, his agent or assignee, who may be a debtor to the nation, against whom the money shall be due or

balance existing in favor of the nation, but he shall allow such debtor a credit on his account for such allowance or claim, and it shall be his duty to furnish the national treasurer monthly with an account of all warrants on the treasury which he shall have issued during the preceding month.

6. The national auditor shall be entitled to receive as a compensation for his services the sum of six hundred dollars a year, payable quarter-yearly, out of the national treasury, from the date of the execution of his bond and its approval by the principal chief. He shall make out his account for each quarter's salary, and receive the approbation of the national secretary thereon in writing, and shall file the same as a voucher for the warrant he shall issue in his own favor, placing his own receipt on said voucher as in other cases.

ARTICLE VI.

APPROVED OCT. 30, 1888.

NATIONAL ATTORNEY.

1. Be it enacted by the general council of the Choctaw nation assembled: Shall, before he enters upon the duties of his office, take and subscribe the oath of office prescribed in the constitution, which oath shall be administered by the principal chief of the nation, any judge of the supreme, circuit or county courts, and certified on his commission; and the national attorney shall be of council for the nation in all cases whatever triable and determinable in the supreme court of the nation, and it shall be his duty to attend the supreme courts at each term thereof, and to appear and prosecute for the nation in all criminal prosecutions, and in all civil cases in which the nation or any county thereof may be interested: *provided*, that if the national attorney fail to attend at any term of the

supreme court, the said supreme court is hereby authorized to employ some attorney to act for the nation in the
place of said national attorney, and the attorney so em,-
ployed shall for his services be paid by the national attorney such sum as shall be allowed by the supreme
court, not in one case to exceed one-fourth part of the
annual salary of said national attorney, and all accounts
of a public nature properly coming before the supreme
court for allowance shall be presented to the national
attorney, and his opinion thereon obtained, in writing if
necessary, and it shall also be his duty to give his opinion in writing in all cases touching the public interest
when thereunto required by the principal chief of the
nation. He shall, also, at the request of the national auditor and national treasurer, or either of them, give his
opinion in writing upon all cases concerning the revenue
or expenses of the nation; and it shall be the duty of
the national attorney, whenever he may be requested, to
give his opinion in writing to any district attorney upon
any cause then pending in which the nation may be interested, and which may be necessary for such district
attorney to prosecute and defend.

2. If the national attorney shall in any manner consult, counsel, advise, or defend a person within this nation charged with any crime or misdemeanor, or breach
of any penal statute, said national attorney so offending
shall, on conviction thereof in any court of competent
jurisdiction, be fined in a sum not exceeding two hundred dollars, and shall, moreover, be removed from
office, and be rendered incapable thereafter of filling any
office of profit or honor in this nation.

3. The national attorney shall be entitled to receive, as a compensation for his services, the sum of four
hundred dollars a year, payable quarter-yearly, out of
the national treasury, upon the issuance of the national

auditor's warrant, in like manner with other officers' salaries.

———

APPROVED OCT. 20, 1888,

SECTION VII.

NATIONAL AGENT.

1. Be it enacted by the general council of the Choctaw nation assembled: There shall be appointed by the principal chief, by and with the advice and consent of the senate, one competent person, a citizen of said nation, to be known as national agent of the Choctaw nation whose duty it shall be to contract for the sale of stone, stone coal and timber of all kinds. Said national agent shall be commissioned, and before he enters upon the duties of his office shall take the oath of office prescribed in the constitution, and enter into bond with good and sufficient securities in the penal sum of ten thousand dollars, payable to the Choctaw nation, conditioned that he will well and truly discharge his duties in accordance with law; which bond shall be filed in the national secretary's office. Said national agent shall hold his office for two years unless sooner removed by the principal chief for malfeasance in office.

2. Said national agent in making contracts with parties for the sale of any of the articles herein mentioned, shall charge royalty, as follows:

On salt, 25 cents per barrel of 240 pounds.
On coal, one-half cent per bushel.
On stone, ten cents per cubic yard.
On walnut timber, $5.00 per thousand feet.
On cypress timber, $3.00 per thousand feet.
On ash timber, $2.00 per thousand feet.
On oak and pine timber, $1.00 per thousand feet.
On cottonwood timber, 75 cents per thousand feet.

TELEGRAPH POLES.

Cedar, 4 to 5 inch deep, 8 to 10 inch bottom, 26 feet long, 40 cents each.

Cedar, 6 inch top, 12 inch bottom, 26 feet long, 50 cents each.

Oak, 6 inch top, 12 inch bottom 26 feet long, 25 cents each.

Oak, 4 to 5 inch top, 8 to 10 inch bottom, 26 feet long, 20 cents rach.

Piling—Cedar, 2 1-2 cents per foot, running measure.

Piling—Oak, 1 cent per foot, running measure.

RAILROAD CROSS TIES—(BRIDGE, HEWN OR SAWED.)

Oak (post, burr, white, red and black), and pine 7 1-2 cents each.

Cedar, bois d'arc, walnut, mulberry, sassafras and red or slippery elm, 25 cents each.

Black locust and coffee bean, 12 1-2 cents each.

RAILROAD SWITCH TIES.

Oak (post, white and burr), 25 cents each; oak (red and black), 15 cents each; pine, 10 cents each.

Tan bark, 75 cents for every tree peeled.

Cord wood, 20 cents per cord.

Shingles—Pine, 25 cents per thousand; cypress 30 cents per thousand.

The above royalty on timber, shingles and tan-bark shall be due and payable on all manufactured in the Choctaw nation; and any other timber not mentioned above the national agent is authorized to make contracts for, on the best terms obtainable, by and with the consent of the principal chief; and all timber contracted by the national agent, to be measured by scale measurement, shall be measured according to Doyle's rule of Scribner's book, and the royalty collected accordingly;

provided, however, that the national agent is hereby instructed to make all contracts for furnishing ties to railroads with Choctaw citizens exclusively. All contracts made hereunder shall expire on the 31st day of December of each year, except contracts for mining coal and quarrying stone, which shall cover a period of six years; and all royalty accruing under the same shall be due and payable monthly.

3. The national agent shall not sell any timber or stone on any citizen's claim except by the consent of such citizen; *provided, however*, that all the royalty arising from the sale of either, whether taken from the claims of individuals or from the public domain, shall be turned into the national treasury.

4. Before contracting with parties who are noncitizens, the national agent shall require them to enter into good bonds of ten thousand dollars to the United States to be approved by the United States commissioner of Indian affairs, and conditioned upon their faithful compliance with their contracts, and all contracts herein provided for shall be executed in accordance with section 2103 United States Revised Statutes; and no noncitizen shall engage in any business contemplated by this act, except a contract be first made with the national agent, and a permit be also obtained according to the laws of the Choctaw nation.

5. No Choctaw citizen shall engage in any business contemplated by this act until they have first made contracts with the national agent in accordance with the law, and shall have made good and sufficient bonds to the Choctaw nation in the penal sum of five thousand dollars, to be approved by the national agent, and sent by said national agent to the national secretary's office for file; said bond to be conditioned upon the faithful compliance of said citizens with said contracts. All violators

of this law shall be fined not less than two hundred and fifty dollars nor more than five hundred dollars in the discretion of the circuit court having jurisdiction, and upon the failure of said offenders to pay their fines in thirty days, they shall each receive thirty-nine lashes on the bare back, and be discharged from further obligations in the particular case; and district attorneys shall prosecute all persons indicted under this act, and if the fines are collected said district attorneys shall receive one-tenth of the same for their services, and the balance shall be placed in the national treasury for public purposes.

6. The national agent shall have general supervision of the offices of inspector, district collectors and coal weighers, and for that purpose he is hereby required to make frequent visits of inspection to the stations of the several coal weighers, and see that their duties are properly performed; and if in his opinion a necessity therefor exists, to require the presence of the inspector and district collector at his office for explanations of their official acts, and the inspector and district collectors shall make quarterly returns of all moneys collected by them to the national treasurer, and quarterly reports of the same to the national agent, with the sworn statement of the persons from whom the royalty was received; and the national agent shall examine the said reports and forward a quarterly abstract thereof to the principal chief for his information; and he shall also prepare an annual abstract of said reports and present the same with the quarterly report, and all vouchers thereto belonging, to the general council for examination and information.

7. In case of any irregularity in the offices of the inspector, district collectors or coal weighers, or of any material error or discrepancy in their reports, the national agent shall report the facts of the case, without

delay, to the principal chief; and the national agent shall also be required to visit the headquarters offices of the railroad and coal companies, and inspect their books and returns, to ascertain if the report made to them correspond with the reports made to the Choctaw nation; and if it be necessary to obtain that power of inspection of said books and returns, he shall insert a provision to that effect in their contracts.

8.   The national agent shall receive for his services eight hundred dollars per annum, payable quarterly, upon the certificates of the principal chief to the auditor, who shall issue his warrants accordingly, and the treasurer shall pay the same; and said national agent shall not be allowed any funds besides his salary for contingent expenses. ————   **APPROVED CCT. 30, 1888.**

SECTION VIII.

INSPECTOR.

1.   Be it enacted by the general council of the Choctaw nation assembled: There shall be appointed by the principal chief, by and with the advice and consent of the senate, one competent person, a citizen of the Choctaw nation, who shall be known and designated as inspector, who shall hold his office two years, and shall be commissioned by the principal chief, and shall take the oath of office prescribed in the constitution, and shall enter into bond, with good and sufficient security, in the penal sum of five thousand dollars, payable to the Choctaw nation, conditioned that he will well and truly count and inspect, in connection with the railway inspector, all railroad ties, both hewn and sawed, and all piling and stone, and whatsover is used by the railroad on which royalty is due, or may be due, and will well and truly measure all lumber and timber, and count all shingles, manufactured along the line of the railroad, which bond

shall be filed in the national secretary's office. It shall
be the duty of the inspector, to count, in connection with
the railroad inspector, all railroad and bridge ties, and
measure all piling, and whatsover else is used by the
railroad, or any railway branch, or railway switch, on
which royalty is due, or may hereafter be due, and shall
make quarterly statement to the principal chief, for his
information, and to the national treasurer for his guidance in the collection of the royalty; and it shall also be
the duty of the inspector to visit all the saw mills along
the line of the railroad, and measure and count all lumber and shingles manufactured by them, and measure all
timber, etc., shipped or used along the railroad, on which
royalty is due or may be due, and collect the royalty on
the same, according to law; and shall make quarterly
statements to the principal chief; and shall, also, make
quarterly statement to the national treasurer, and transmit all moneys collected by him to the treasurer, at the
end of each quarter, and he shall also be required to
make an annual report to the general council for their
guidance.

2. The inspector shall not be allowed to collect any
money, except what may arise from the manufacturing
of lumber and shingles, and timber, that is not used by
the railroad. He shall receive for his services ten per
cent. of all royalties contemplated under this act, to be
paid quarterly; and the principal chief shall issue his
certificate to the national auditor, and the national treasurer shall pay the same.

APPROVED OCT. 30, 1888.

SECTION IX.

DISTRICT COLLECTORS.

1. Be it enacted by the general council of the Choctaw nation assembled : There shall be appointed by the

principal chief, by and with the advice and consent of the senate, a district collector for each district of the nation, whose duty it shall be to collect the tax on licensed traders in their respective districts, and the royalty on lumber and timber of all kinds shipped out of the nation from their respective districts and off the lines of railroads, and keep correct accounts of the same and make quarterly reports of the same to the principal chief for every fiscal quarter; and who shall be entitled to receive for their services each . ten per cent. of the amount of their respective collections, which they are hereby authorized to retain, and shall make quarterly returns to the national treasurer of the remainder. Any appointee under this act shall be a citizen of the nation, and shall make a bond, payable to the Choctaw nation, in the penal sum of five thousand dollars, to be approved by the principal chief, and filed in the national secretary's office; said appointee each to hold his office for the term of two years, unless sooner removed by the principal chief for failure to discharge the duties of his office according to law.

2.   The district collectors of the several districts of this nation, and also the inspector, shall have power to seize and take possession of any timber, lumber, shingles, boards, laths, tan-bark, fire wood or timber in any shape, that he may find prepared or being prepared to be sold or disposed of as merchandise, by any person not authorized by contract with the national agent so to do ; and they are hereby authorized and empowered to sell the same to the best advantage and return to the national treasurer the money so received, deducting the commissions now allowed them by law. *Provided*, that citizens of this nation shall not be deprived of the liberty of making for their own use the articles above specified without first making a contract for that purpose ; and

any person who shall take or cause to be taken and carried off any such material and property as mentioned above and which has been seized by a district collector or by the inspector as by this act authorized, shall be deemed guilty of larceny, and upon indictment and conviction shall be punished accordingly.

APPROVED OCT. 30, 1888.

SECTION XI.

NATIONAL LIGHTHORSEMEN.

1. Be it enacted by the general council of the Choctaw nation assembled: There shall be a corps of nine national lighthorsemen in this nation who shall receive their appoinment by commission from the principal chief, three from each district, and shall take the oath prescribed in the constitution, to be administered by the principal chief or any judges of the nation and subscribed to on the back of their commissions, and who shall serve for the term of two years, unless sooner removed by the principal chief. The principal chief shall commission one of said lighthorsemen so appointed captain thereof, and it shall be the duty of said captain to preserve order and discipline among the rest, and to see that each of them is properly armed, equipped and mounted for immediate service, and to report to the principal chief any improper conduct or failure to discharge the duties required of any or all of them.

2. Said lighthorsemen shall be under the exclusive direction and control of the principal chief of this nation; they shall be messengers of the principal chief upon any matter of national concern ; they shall keep the peace of the nation ; they shall faithfully aid in the execution of the criminal laws of this nation ; they shall suppress, if necessary, with the aid of other citizens, whom they

8

are hereby empowered specially to summon for the purpose, all riots, routs and unlawful assemblies, and report the same, with all other violations of the penal laws, to some judge or other proper officer. The principal chief shall keep the lighthorsemen, or such number as he may deem proper, at the place of holding the general council during the session thereof, and shall specially direct them to keep order and quiet at such time and place ; to see that no intoxicating liquors are brought within two miles in any direction of such place at said time, and, if necessary, the captain or any one of said lighthorsemen shall summon any number of citizens deemed requisite, over eighteen and under sixty years of age, to aid and assist in keeping order, spilling liquor and arresting the offenders. and taking them before a county judge, which judge is hereby empowered and directed to bind such person, or persons, so offending, over to the next circuit court thereafter in a bond not exceeding in penalty two thousand dollars, to appear and answer such charges as may be preferred against him or them ; and any person or persons offending, as hereinbefore stated, shall offer or threaten any forcible resistance with deadly weapons to the captain, or any of the lighthorsemen, or other person or persons summoned, as this act specifies, in the discharge of any of the duties hereinbefore set forth, it shall be the duty of the captain, or any of the light horsemen, and others summoned by them, to shoot down any and all persons so threatening or assisting with deadly weapons. The principal chief is hereby author ized and directed to order the lighthorsemen, or any number of them that may be required, to attend the United States Indian agent for this nation whenever he may call for them, and strictly obey all orders he may give them in the execution of the laws of the United States.

3. The captain of the lighthorsemen shall be entitled to receive, as a compensation for his services, the sum of two hundred dollars a year, and the lighthorsemen shall receive for their services the sum of one hundred and fifty dollars a year each, to be paid quarter-yearly on the principal chief's order to the national auditor, who is directed to issue his warrant on the national treasury for the same. And in addition to the above, the several national lighthorsemen of this nation shall be entitled to and receive the sum of three dollars and fifty cents for each and every day's actual attendance on the general council, and the principal chief shall issue his certificate on the national auditor, and the national auditor shall issue his warrant for the same in favor of each lighthorseman, stating the number of days in attendance and the amount due for the same.

APPROVED OCT. 30, 1888.

LEGISLATIVE DEPARTMENT.

SECTION 1.

GENERAL COUNCIL.

1. Be it enacted by the general council of the Choctaw nation assembled : At the beginning of every regular annual session of the general council, on a quorum of the senate appearing in the senate chamber, they shall call some senator to the chair, who shall call upon some one of the supreme judges to administer the oath prescribed in the constitution to the senators, when they shall proceed to elect a president of the body in such manner as they may, by rule, determine. The senate shall then elect, also, in the manner they may, by rule determine, a recording secretary, journalist and door-keeper, to whom the president shall administer the oaths of office, and also to other senators who may thereafter appear, and all other officers of the senate. At the beginning of each and every regular session of the general council, on a quorum of the members of the house of representatives appearing in the representative chamber, they shall call some member to the chair, which member shall call upon one of the supreme judges to administer the oath required by the constitution, to the members present. The house of representatives shall then proceed to elect a speaker; they shall then elect, in such manner as they may by rule determine, a clerk, journalist and doorkeeper, to whom the speaker shall have power to administer the oath of office, and to other members who may thereafter appear. There shall be elected by both houses of the general council of this nation, in

joint session, during the first week of each and every
regular session thereof, in such manner as may be determined at the time, a sergeant-at-arms, who shall be the
peace officer of the general council, and perform such
other duties as they may prescribe, and to whom the
president of the senate, while in session, shall administer the oath prescribed by the constitution in presence
of that body.

2. The president of the senate and the speaker of
the house of representatives shall each be entitled to receive six dollars per day, and each other member of the
senate and of the house of representatives five dollars
for each and every day's attendance at the general council, and shall, moreover, be allowed, at the commencement and end of every session, at the rate of three dollars for every thirty miles of the estimated distance by
the most direct land route of travel, in coming to and returning from the place where the general council shall
sit; and if any member of either house—the president of
the senate or the speaker of the house—shall be detained
by sickness, in coming to or returning from any session
of the general council, or be unable to attend the house
to which he belongs, he shall be entitled to the same
daily allowance, The recording secretary of the senate,
and clerk of the house of representatives, shall each be
allowed four dollars per day; and the recording secretary of the senate, with the approbation of the president
of the senate, and the clerk of the house of representatives, with the approbation of the speaker of the house
of representatives, shall each appoint as many clerks as
may, from time to time, be necessary to the dispatch of
business in their respective houses, who, when employed,
shall be allowed two dollars per day, and the doorkeeper of each house shall be entitled to four dollars per day;
and the sergeant-at arms shall be entitled to five dollars

per day; the journalist of the senate and the journalist of the house of representatives, shall each receive for their services four dollars per day. The compensation herein allowed to the sergeant-at-arms shall be certified to by the president of the senate, and the compensation which shall be due to the members and officers of the general council shall be certified by the president and speaker, respectively, to the national auditor, who shall issue his warrants on the national treasurer, which shall be paid out of the funds appropriated annually to defray the expenses of the general council.

3. The principal chief of this nation bé and he is hereby authorized to select some competent draughtsman, for both houses of the general council, to prepare bills, or reports of committees, and generally to assist members of each house in all matters of legislation; *that provided*, he shall only appoint a draughtsman whenever requested to do so, by the presiding officers of both houses of the general council, and to dismiss the same when notified by the said officers that said draughtman's services are no longer needed. Said draughtsman shall be allowed five dollars per day, and the auditor shall issue his warrant for the same upon the certificate of the president of the senate for such services.

4. All witnesses that may be legally summonsed, on behalf of this nation, to attend any future session of the general council, in either branch thereof, for the purpose of giving testimony in cases of impeachment, or other matter of investigation, when such testimony may be lawfully required, shall be allowed the sum of two dollars for each and every day he, she, or they, may be so in attendance; and also the further sum of five cents for each and every mile he, she or they may travel in going to and returning from the place where such testimony may be rendered, and the sum or sums due to

such witness or witnesses shall be ascertained by the oath or affirmation of such witness or witnesses, his, her or their agent or attorney, which oath or affirmation the clerk of the house of representatives, or secretary of the senate, as the case may be, is hereby authorized to administer and thereupon to issue a certificate to such witness or witnesses for the full amount of the sum so ascertained, and the national auditor, on the production of such certificate, is hereby authorized and required to issue his warrant on the national treasury for the payment thereof.

5. It shall be the duty of the doorkeepers, when the two houses adjourn, to collect all the remaining stationary and furniture purchased for the use of the general council, and deliver it to the national secretary and take his receipt for the same.

APPROVED OCT. 30, 1888.

JUDICIAL DEPARTMENT.

SECTION I.

THE SUPREME COURT.

1. Be it enacted by the general council of the Choctaw nation assembled: Each judge of the supreme court, before he enters on the duties of his office, shall take and subscribe the oath required in the constitution, endorsed upon the back of his commission, which oath may be administered by the principal chief, or any judge of the nation; and said commission and oath shall be recorded by the clerk of said court, upon the minutes of said court; which judges, or a majority of them, shall have the power to appoint a clerk of said court, to hold his office for the term of four years from the date of his commission.

2. The judges of the supreme court shall choose from among themselves the chief justice, and have the same entered upon the minutes of the court; and in case of his absence or disqualification to sit in any cause, the oldest judge present shall be the presiding judge for the time being, and no judge of said court shall sit in any cause wherein he is connected by blood or marriage with either of the parties, or directly or indirectly interested, or if he shall have been of counsel for either party in such cause; and although one or more of the judges of the supreme court be interested in the event of any suit, matter or thing depending therein, the same shall be finally decided by the other judges, if there by a number not so interested sufficient to constitute a court; and in case a majority of said judges shall be interested in any

cause depending in said court it shall be the duty of the
principal chief to specially appoint and commission one
or more members of the bar learned in the law to supply
the places of the judges so interested, who shall be sworn
to hear and determine that particular cause and no
other ; and whenever the supreme court shall be equally
divided in opinion, on hearing any appeal or writ of
error, the judgment or decree of the court below shall be
affirmed.

3. The supreme court shall have jurisdiction over,
and shall hear and determine all manner of pleas, complaints, motions, causes and controversies, civil and criminal, which may be brought before it from any circuit
court of law or county court of any county in this nation
either by appeal, writ of error, *supersedeas,** or other
legal process, and which shall be cognizable in said court
according to the constitution and laws of this nation;
provided, that no appeal, writ of error, supersedeas or
other process shall be granted in any manner whatsoever until after final judgment or decree in the court below, except in cases especially provided for by law; and
the supreme court or any judge in vacation shall have
power to issue writs and other processes necessary to
their appellate jurisdiction, and may grant writs of error
or supersedeas to the judgments or decrees of the circuit
courts of law, in all cases wherein writs of error or supersedeas may be by law allowed, in the manner, and on
the terms and conditions prescribed by law in such cases,
and also to grant writs of *habeas corpus,*† *certiorari,*‡

*Supersedeas—*is a writ or command to suspend the powers of an
officer in certain cases, or to stay proceedings.

†*Habeas corpus—*is a writ for delivering a person from false imprisonment, or for removing a person from one court to another.

‡*Certiorari—*is a writ issued out of a superior court, to call up the
records of an inferior court, or remove a cause there depending, that
it may be tried in the superior court. This writ is obtained upon complaint of a party, that he has not received justice, or that he cannot
have an impartial trial in the inferior court.

*ne exeat,** and all other remedial writs and process grant-
able by said judges by virtue of their office, agreeably to
the principles and usages of the common law, returnable
as the law directs, either to the supreme court or before any
judge of said court as the nature of the case may require·
Also it shall be the duty of the supreme court to establish rules for the proceeding in said court and also rules
for bringing cases to issue; and the proper conducting of
the business in the several circuit courts of law in this
nation, and to cause a copy thereof to be made for each
circuit court in the nation; and it shall be the duty of
said supreme court whenever they shall alter, amend or
enlarge said rules, as soon thereafter as may be, to cause
a copy to be made as above directed.

4. It shall be the duty of the judges of the supreme
court in every case they may decide or decree, to deliver
their opinions in writing, stating at large the reasons and
principles upon which such decision is made ; which
opinion shall be by the clerk of said court filed among
the records of said court at the time of delivery, and any
judge of said court differing in opinion from a majority
of said court, shall reduce his opinion to writing and
the reasons therefor, and shall likewise be filed among
the records of said court, and any judge of said court
neglecting or refusing to comply with the provisions of
this section shall be deemed guilty of a misdemeanor in
office and shall be liable to removal therefor. It shall be
the duty of the clerk of said court to record in a book, by
him to be kept for that purpose, the written opinions of
said court and the written opinions of any judge thereof;
and the said clerk shall receive ten cents for each hundred words so recorded, payable half-yearly out of the
national treasury upon the certificate of any one of the

Ne exeat—is a writ to prevent a person from going out of the
Nation, without license.

said judges of said court that the services has been performed, and that the account as stated is true and correct. That for preventing errors in entering up the judgments, decrees, orders and decisions of said court, the minutes of the proceedings of each day shall be drawn up at large by the clerk, in a book by him to be kept for that purpose, and read in open court the next day—except those of the last day of each term, which shall be drawn up, read and corrected the same day—and any necessary corrections made therein, when they shall be signed by the presiding judge and preserved among the records; and the supreme court shall annually appoint one of the judges thereof to inspect the clerk's office of said court, and to report the same to the next term of the supreme court, specifying in what condition he finds the records and papers belonging to the office, which report shall be recorded upon the minutes of the court.

5. The supreme court shall have power to punish any person who may be guilty of a contempt of said court, in like manner as a circuit court of the nation. The sheriff of the county in which the supreme court shall be held, shall be an officer of said court and shall attend to the same with a sufficient number of deputies accordingly, and the sheriff and his deputies shall be bound to perform the duties of sheriff and crier.

6. The supreme court shall be held at the seat of government on the first Monday of October and April in each and every year; and may continue until the business therein pending shall be disposed; the judges of said court shall have power to call a special term of said court when deemed necessary, and shall give thirty days' notice of the time for holding the same; and if any judge of the supreme court shall fail to attend any term of said court, it shall be the duty of the clerk of said court to certify the number of days said judge was

absent at each term of his court to the national auditor, who shall deduct the sum of ten dollars for each and every day said judge may fail to attend, if it should appear that the said judge was within the limits of the nation at the time of such failure; *provided, however*, that the said judge shall make oath and file the same at the national auditor's office, that his absence was occasioned by sickness, or that his attendance was prevented by the obstruction of high waters, in which case no deduction shall be made. The supreme court may adjourn from day to day, or for such longer period as they may think necessary to the ends of justice and the determination of the business before them, and there shall be no discontinuance of any suit, process, matter or thing returned to or depending on the supreme court although a sufficient number of judges shall not attend at the commencement or any other day of the term; but if a sufficient number fail to attend at the commencement of any term or at any time during the term, any judge of the said court, or the sheriff attending the same may adjourn the said court from day to day for six days successively.

7. When any cause is finally decided in the supreme court, and the party who is taxed with the cost thereof shall fail to pay the same, the clerk may issue execution therefor returnable to the next term of said court, and direct to the sheriff of the county where the party resides; and the first Monday of October and April shall be the return days in the supreme court in each and every year, to which all executions issuing from said court shall be made returnable; and all officers failing to return said executions at the proper time, or to pay over the money collected thereon, shall, on motion, be made liable therefor, as in cases of sheriffs failing to return executions to or pay over moneys on executions returnable to the circuit courts of this nation.

8. The judges of the supreme court of this nation shall be entitled to and receive as a compensation for their services the sum of four hundred dollars a year, each to be paid quarter-yearly out of the national treasury when the account for the same shall be presented, audited, and the auditor's warrant on the treasury issued therefor.

APPROVED OCT. 30, 1888.

SECTION II.

THE CLERK OF THE SUPREME COURT.

1. Be it enacted by the general council of the Choctaw nation : The supreme court shall appoint a clerk in the following manner : In term time the appointment shall be made by any order entered upon record in the proceedings of said court, and the person so appointed, before he shall enter on the duties of his office, shall take the oath prescribed in the constitution in open court, and shall enter into bond with two securities to be approved by the court, payable to the principal chief of the nation for the time being and his successors in office, in the penalty of two thousand dollars, conditioned for the faithful performance of the duties of his office, and that he, in due time, records the judgments, decrees, orders and decisions of said court, and deliver over to his successor in office all records, minute books, papers, presses, seal and whatever belongs to his said office of clerk, which bond shall be recorded in the clerk's office of said court, and immediately thereafter be deposited in the office of the national secretary, and shall not be void on the first recovery, but may be put in suit and prosecuted at the cost and charges of any party injured until the whole amount of the penalty thereof be recovered. In vacation the appointment shall be made by commission under the hands and seals of a majority of the judges of said court, and the person so appointed shall

execute bond with security as above prescribed, and produce the same to any one of said judges for his approbation, and if he approve it he shall endorse his approbation thereon and administer the proper oath of office, and endorse his certificate thereof also on said bond, and said judge shall cause the bond with the endorsement thereon to be recorded, and shall deposit the same in the office of the national secretary as aforesaid, which bond may be put in suit and prosecuted in like manner as before directed in the case of bonds taken in open court. A certified copy of such bond shall be received in evidence in any court of law in this nation, in the same manner as the original would be if it was present in court. Said clerk may be removed for neglect of duty or misdemeanor in office by the supreme court, on motion of which, the clerk against whom complaint is made, shall have ten days' previous notice, specifying the particular negligence or misdemeanor in office with which he stands charged; and in every such case the court shall determine both the law and the fact.

2. The clerk of the supreme court shall have power to appoint a deputy with the approbation of the court, and he shall take the oath of office prescribed in the constitution, and thereupon said deputy shall have power and authority to do and perform all the several acts and duties enjoined upon his principal; and the clerk of the court aforesaid shall keep his office at the place in which said court shall be holden. During a vacancy in the office of clerk of the supreme court, and during the unavoidable absence of the principal clerk and his deputy, if he have one, the court, in term time, or a majority of the judges in vacation, may appoint a clerk *pro tempore*,* who, after taking the oath of office, shall be authorized to perform the duties of a clerk, and during his

Pro tempore—for the time being.

continuance in office shall be entitled to all the fees thereof. Whenever the office of the clerk of the supreme court shall become vacant from any cause whatsoever, the records, papers, books, stationery, and everything belonging to, or pertaining to said office, shall be delivered over to his successor in office by the person or persons having the same, whenever demanded; and it is hereby declared to be the duty of such successor to demand, receive, and take the same into his care and safe keeping, and in case of a refusal or detention of any such records, papers, books, stationery, or other things appertaining to said office, of which he is appointed successor, after demand as aforesaid, he shall, moreover, give information thereof to the national or district attorney, who shall prosecute each person or persons by action of debt, and have recovery of the same by execution and sale of the personal property of said defendants, by the proper officer of the court, on information, in the name of the nation, in any court of competent jurisdiction, and on conviction thereof by the verdict of a jury, the person or persons so refusing or detaining as aforesaid, shall be fined in the sum of five thousand dollars, to the nation, for the use of the library fund.

3. If the clerk of the supreme court shall knowingly or willfully make any false entry, or erase a letter, or change any records in his office or keeping, said clerk, so offending, shall, on conviction thereof, be fined and imprisoned at the discretion of the court, and shall also be liable to the action of the party aggrieved.

4. The supreme court shall make allowances to the clerk for all needful sums for supplying the office with necessary books and presses for the records, and for the safe keeping of the books and papers belonging to the office, and shall make allowance to sheriff, as officer of said court, for all necessary fuel furnished in term time,

which allowances, being certified to the national auditor, he shall give a warrant therefor on the treasury of the nation.

5.   It shall be the duty of the clerk of the supreme court to make out and keep a distinct docket of all cases pending in the supreme court—for each one of the dis tricts electing judges to the supreme court—and to place on the docket, for each district, all cases, criminal or civil, emanating from counties in the same; *provided* that all civil cases in which the nation may be a party. shall be placed on the docket of that district in which the seat of government is situated, and all criminal cases shall be placed first on the docket to which they respectively belong; and it shall be lawful for the clerks of the supreme court to demand, receive and take for the several services by him performed, the fees hereafter annexed to said services, viz: For filing records and writs of error or appeal, twenty-five cents; entering appearance of each party, twenty-five cents each; every continuance, twenty-five cents; each oath, twenty-five cents; for docketing cause, twenty-five cents, to be charged but once; for entering each final judgment, one dollar; for copy of the same, for court below, fifty cents; for taxing costs and entering the same on fee book, twenty-five cents, and, for each execution, fifty cents; and in addition to the fees above allowed, the clerks shall receive, out of the national treasury, the sum of one hundred dollars, to be paid quarter-yearly, upon the presentation of his account, endorsed as correct by the chief justice of the court, when the national auditor shall issue his warrant for the same upon the national treasurer.

6.   It shall be the duty of the clerk of the supreme court, at the close of each term of said court, to make out and transmit to the court, or the clerk thereof, from which the cause was brought, a copy duly certified, with

the seal of the court affixed,of each and every final judgment and decree of said supreme court, unless the same
shall be sooner demanded by the person or his attorney
entitled to the same, when he shall deliver said copy
upon the payment of all cost due in said court, in the
cause in which the copy of the judgment or decree is demanded; otherwise he shall retain said copy, and transmit the same as hereinbefore directed,and,as in all cases
where the costs have not been paid, send out an execution for the same; and it shall also be the duty of the
clerk of the supreme court to furnish any person, on application, with a copy of the opinion of said court, and a
copy of any record, paper or judgment, or anything on
file in his office, and the clerk shall be entitled to receive ten cents for every hundred words contained in
each copy so furnished, and twenty-five cents for a certificate, with seal of the court attached, when required.

SECTION III.   APPROVED CCT. CO, 1888.

CIRCUIT COURT.

1. Be it enacted by the general council of the Choctaw, nation assembled: The Choctaw nation shall be
divided into three judicial districts, viz: Mosholatubbee
district shall be called the First judicial district; Apuckshunubbee district shall be called the Second judicial
district, and Pushmataha district shall be called the
Third judicial district; and a circuit court shall be held
in each, twice in each year, to commence and continue,
viz:

AN ACT repealing an act passed and approved June 29,
1893, locating the circuit court ground of the Mosholetubbee District in Gaines county.

Be it enacted by the general council of the Choctaw
nation assembled: That an act passed June 29, 1893, be

9

and the same is hereby repealed and the following is hereby substituted: The circuit court ground of Mosholetubbee district in Gaines county is hereby removed to one mile southwest of the said James Brown's, and shall be called and known as Hochubbee court ground. The district court of Mosholetubbee district shall hold its first session at Hochubbee court ground on the second Monday of November, 1893 and all courts special and regular, shall henceforth be held there, and all acts or parts of acts coming in conflict with provision of this act are hereby repealed, and this act shall take effect and be in force from and after its passage.

Approved Oct. 19, 1893.

W. N. JONES, P. C. C. N.

In the Second judicial district, on the first Mondays of December and July, at the Sulphur Springs, near the residence of Simon P. Willis, in Nashoba county, and shall be known and called Apuckshunubbee circuit court ground.

In the Third judicial district, at the Monday of Februrary and second Monday of August, at a point where Hon. L. S. W. Folsom caused a court house to be built for said district, near the meeting house known as "Tiakhali," in Jackson county, and the same shall be called and known as Pushmataha circuit court ground. And each may continue in session thirty judicial days, if business requires it, but no longer.

2. The judges of the circuit courts shall be elected by the qualified voters of their districts, in the same manner as provided for electing district and county officers; and the person having the highest number of legal votes, shall be declared duly elected, and shall be promptly commissioned by the principal chief and shall continue in office for the term prescribed by

the constitution, unless sooner removed; and shall take
the oath of office prescribed in the constitution, before
the principal chief, or any judge of a court of record;
a certificate of which shall be filed in the clerk's office
of the district where they shall first sit; without which
oath and certificate, if they shall be deemed guilty of a
high misdemeanor, and may be removed from office
therefor.

3. The circuit courts in the several districts of this
nation shall have power to hear and determine all prosecutions of criminal cases, by information or by indictment, in the name of the Choctaw nation, for treason,
murder, and all other felonies, crimes and misdemeanors
committed in their respective jurisdictions, except such
as properly belong to the United States court: and shall
exercise all the powers incident to, or belonging to, a
court of oyer and terminer, and general jail delivery,
and to do and perform all other acts properly pertaining
to circuit courts of law; and the judges of said courts
shall each have power, either in vacation or term time,
to grant writs of *habeas corpus,** *ne exeat injunction,*† to
stay waste, to enjoin execution of a judgment, or to stay
proceedings at law, and all other remedial writs returnable to a court of law; said courts shall have power to
fine and imprison any person who may be guilty of contempt of court, while sitting, either in the presence or
hearing of the court; *provided,* such fine shall not exceed one hundred dollars, and imprisonment shall not be
for a longer time than the term of the court at which the
contempt was committed. The circuit courts shall have
original jurisdiction of all suits and actions for the recovery of money, founded on any bonds or contracts,

---

Habeas corpus—is a writ for delivering a person from false imprisonment, or for removing a person from one court to another.

†*Ne exeat*—is a writ to prevent a person from going out of the
Nation, without license.

when the principal of the sum in controversy exceeds fifty dollars, and all causes, matters and things arising under the constitution and laws of this nation, which are not expressly cognizable in some other court, as well as all cases of divorce, alimony and foreclosure of mortgages; and shall also have power to hear and determine all motions, on reasonable notice to adverse party, against sheriffs or other officers, for money received under execution, or other process or order of the court, which shall not be paid to the party entitled to the same, his agent or attorney, on demand, and all motions against attorneys and counsellors at law for failing or refusing to pay money received for their clients, and to give judgment according to the statutes in such cases made and provided, and award execution therefor; *provided, however,* that the circuit courts of said nation shall not have power to issue writs of injunction or other process to stop the operation of any public works or public enterprise under contract with the proper authorities of the Choctaw nation, whereby said nation is receiving or to receive a royalty. The mining of coal or other mineral substances, the manufacture of lumber, and otherwise converting any of the natural appurtenances of the soil into merchantable goods, shall be held to be public works and shall not exist in the Choctaw nation, (except under contract with the proper legal authorities of the Choctaw nation) to pay a stipulated royalty, and said contracts to have a fixed limited time to run; *provided, however,* that the limitation of the jurisdiction of said circuit courts imposed by this act shall not be so construed as to exclude said circuit courts from exercising complete jurisdiction in all matters hereinbefore provided for, except wherein said nation is being excluded, or attempts are made to exclude said nation by any person or persons whomsoever from rights which are secured to said nation under this act.

4. The judges of the circuit courts may alternate and exchange temporarily their districts, with each other, whenever, in their opinion, the public interests may require it; and whenever they may be absent, from any cause, from any term of their courts, the sheriff of the county wherein the court is held, shall adjourn same from day to day for two consecutive days, and after that time the adjournment shall be to the next succeeding term. If from any cause a circuit court shall not be held at any term thereof, or shall not continue to sit the whole term, or before the end of the term, shall not have heard and determined all matters ready for its disposition, then all processes, pleadings and proceedings of whatever nature, remaining in said court, pending and undecided, shall stand continued, of course, until the next succeeding term ; and if from any cause a court shall not sit on any day in a term, after it shall have commenced, there shall be no discontinuance, but the court may proceed to business on any subsequent day, until the end of the term, if business before said court shall not be sooner disposed of.

5. Clerks of circuit courts, in making out their issue dockets for each term, shall set as many suits for each day, beginning on the first day, and proceeding as far in the term as the number of suits may make it necessary, or the judges may direct, or, in their opinion, may best suit the business of the courts ; and no cause shall be taken up for trial or hearing on a day previous to that for which it may have been set; and the clerks shall issue subpœnas for witnesses to attend on the days on which their respective cases have been set. Clerk's shall draw up the minutes of each day previous to the next day's sitting of the courts, when the same shall be read in open court, and after such corrections as are necessary being made, if any, therein, the same shall be

signed by their respective presiding judges, and carefully preserved by the clerks, in well bound books kept for the purpose; and on the last day of each term the clerks shall draw up the minutes of that day in the same way as before, which shall be read and corrected and signed by the judges on that day. Clerks of circuit courts shall make out, for each term of their respective courts, separate dockets, in one of which shall be placed all civil causes, and in the other all criminal causes; and it is hereby expressly declared to be the duty of the judges of the courts aforesaid, to give preference to and take up said criminal docket for trial, on motion of the district attorney, unless good cause is shown to the contrary.

6. Whenever the regular term of any circuit court shall have failed, and in the opinion of the judge presiding therein, the business of the court requires it, the said judge is hereby authorized and directed to order a special term of said circurt court to be holden: which order shall be entered upon the minutes of the special term, and on receiving notice of said order, the clerk and sheriff of the county in which said court may be located, to make out and draw a panel for said special term, upon which panel, so drawn, a *venire facias** shall issue, all to be summoned accordingly; and at any such special term the said court shall have power to hear and determine all business remaining in the said court unfinished and not specially continued at the preceeding regular term, and shall also have and exercise full jurisdiction of all jail delivery in all cases which have not been so continued; which said special terms, whenever so ordered, shall continue until all the

Venire facias—a writ directed to the sheriff, requiring him to summon twelve men, to try an issue between parties. It is also a writ in the nature of the summons to cause the party indicted on a penal statute to appear.

business therein pending shall be finished; *provided*, that
no special term shall be ordered to be holden on shorter
notice than thirty days from the date of the order, written notices of which shall be put up by said clerk, in at
least five public places in the district, giving twenty
days' notice of the time and place of holding the same.

7. Clerks of the circuit courts are authorized to
procure seals for the use of their courts, at the expense
of the nation with the styles of their respective courts
around the margins, and an eagle in the center of each.

8. Until provision is made by the county courts of
the different counties in the nation, for the erection of
jails within their limits, the jail situated within each
judicial district shall, in all cases, be used as the jail
of the circuit court for that district; and the sheriffs of
the counties wherein such jails are situated, shall be the
jailors for the circuit courts of their respective districts,
and shall take into custody all persons committed by
process from said courts; and all persons committed, by
whatever lawful authority for trial in such courts, the
sheriff of the counties in which any circuit court shall
sit, shall execute all judgments and sentences rendered
by such courts in any criminal case; *provided*, such
judgments are by law to be executed in the said counties in which the circuit courts shall be holden, and shall
in all respects act as sheriffs of said courts; and it shall
be the duty of the sheriffs of the counties in which the
circuit courts are located, to deputize three suitable persons, citizens of said counties, to act as deputies during
the terms of said courts, in addition to the number now
allowed to sheriffs under the law; said deputies shall be
sworn and qualified as other deputies are qualified and
shall receive like fees as other deputies; and the execution of any judgment rendered in the circuit courts, to
be made in any manner in any county of the judicial

district, other than in the counties in which the circuit court shall be holden, shall be by the clerks issued and directed to the sheriff of the county in which the cause of action shall accrue, to be by said sheriff executed, and returned to said clerks in like manner as executed by the sheriffs of the counties in which the circuit courts are held.

9.   Whenever any judge of any circuit court shall be disqualified, from any cause whatsoever, for sitting on any case in his court, he is hereby authorized to appoint any legal voter present, who may be qualified to try such case, and no other; and if any judge shall try any case in which he may be interested, or otherwise disqualified without the consent of the parties to the case, he shall be deemed guilty of a high misdemeanor in office, and shall be liable to impeachment therefor.

10.   If at any time when a special term of any circuit court ought to be holden, it should happen that the presiding judge of that district should be sick, absent or prevented by any other cause besides being interested, from holding said special term, then it shall be the duty of the presiding judge of the adjoining or other distrtct, on being notified of such incapability or inability, by the judge of the district in which such special term ought to be holden, to make the order for holding such special term to the clerk of the proper district, when he, the said clerk, and sheriff, shall proceed as in paragraph six of this section; and said judge so ordering said special term shall attend and hold it.

11.   The judges of the circuit courts shall each be entitled to receive five hundred dollars per annum, to be paid quarterly out of the national treasury, upon presentation of their accounts therefor to the auditor.

APPROVED OCT. 30, 1888.

SECTION IV.

CLERKS OF THE CIRCUIT COURTS.

1. Be it enacted by the general council of the Choctaw nation assembled: The clerks of the several circuit courts of this nation shall be appointed by the circuit judges and shall hold their office for the term of two years, unless sooner removed; and before they enter upon the duties of their offices the clerks of the circuit court of each district shall enter into bond, with good security, to be approved by the court of which he is clerk, payable to the principal chief, for the time being, or his successor in office, in the penal sum of two thousand dollars conditioned for the faithful performance of his duties of office, and that he in due time record the judgments, decrees and orders of the court, and deliver over to his successor in office all records, minutes, books, papers, presses and whatever belong to said office of clerk; which bond shall be recorded in the clerk's office of said court, and immediately thereafter deposited in the office of the national secretary, by the judge approving the same, and shall not be void on the first recovery, but may be put in suit and prosecuted at the costs and charges of any party injured, and levied of the goods and chattles of said clerk and sureties, until the whole amount of the penalty thereof be recovered, and a certified copy of any such bond shall be received in evidence in any court of law of this nation, in the same manner as the original would be if it were present in court.

2. The clerks of said circuit courts shall have power to appoint deputies, with the approbation of their several courts, who shall take the oath of office; and thereupon such deputies shall have full power and authority to do and perform all the several acts and duties enjoined upon their principals; and the said clerks of the said courts shall have power to appoint deputies in vacation,

with the approbation of the judge of the district in which said appointment may be made, and which approval shall be given in writing, and carefully filed away by said clerk in his office, and shall be entered upon the minutes of the regular term of the circuit court. The clerks of said circuit courts shall keep their offices at the place of holding the circuit court of the district in which they are 'clerks; but in all cases where offices have not been provided for the clerks of said courts, such clerks may keep the records and papers of the said courts at such places as the judge thereof may direct, and enter of record.

3. In case a vacancy shall occur in the office of clerk of the circuit court, in any district in this nation, by death, resignation, or other cause, it shall be the duty of the circuit judge of such district, or the judge presiding, to appoint a clerk *pro tempore*,* to fill such vacancy until a clerk is duly appointed and qualified according to law, which appointment shall be entered upon the minutes of the court; and such clerk appointed shall enter into bond, and take the oath of office as in other cases; and when so qualified, his acts shall be as valid, and he shall have all the powers and emoluments for the time, that regular clerks have by law; and whenever the office of clerk to any court shall become vacant, from any cause whatever, the records, papers, books, presses and stationery, and everthing belonging or appertaining to said office, shall be delivered over to the successor in office by the person, or persons, having the same, whenever demanded; and it is hereby declared to be the duty of such successor, to demand the same, and take in his care and safe keeping all such records, books, papers, presses, stationery, and whatsoever belongs to the said office; and in case of refusal or detention of the

Pro tempore—for the time being.

same, or any part thereof, after demand aforesaid, he shall give information to the district attorney, who shall prosecute such person, or persons, by action of damages or information; in the name of the nation, in any court of competent jurisdiction, and on conviction thereof by the verdict of a jury, the person, or persons, so refusing or detaining, as aforesaid, shall be fined in the sum of two thousand dollars, to be levied of their goods and chattels, and delivered over to the national treasurer, to be used for schools.

4. If any clerk of the circuit courts of this nation shall knowingly make any false entry, or erase a letter, or change any record in his keeping, belonging to his office, every such clerk so offending shall, on conviction thereof, be fined and removed from office by court, and shall be liable to be prosecuted by the party aggrieved.

5. The several circuit courts shall make an allowance to the clerks thereof, of all needful sums of money for supplying their offices with all necessary books, stationery and presses, for the records and safe keeping of the books and papers belonging to their offices respectively; on which allowance being, in equal proportion, certified to the county treasurers of the several counties of their respective district, they shall pay the same out of any money in their treasuries not otherwise appropriated.

6. The several clerks of the circuit courts of this nation, and their deputies, shall be, and they are hereby empowered, to administer oaths in all cases wherein an affidavit is necessary, as the foundations of any official act to be performed by such clerks, which affidavit shall be filed, and in every respect be as effectual as if the oath had been administered by any judge or a court of record; and any person sworn by any such clerk, or his deputy, by virtue of this act, shall give evidence under such circumstances, as would have constituted the same

to be perjury if done in the presence of a court of record, the same shall be deemed perjury to all intents and purposes.

7. The clerks of the several circuit courts of this nation shall, in addition to the fees allowed them by law, be entitled to the sum of three hundred dollars a year, to be paid quarterly, upon the certificate of the circuit judge, to the national auditor, who shall issue his warrant and the national treasurer shall pay the same.

8. It shall be the duty of circuit clerks of the several judicial districts within this nation, to make out and certify to the national auditor, or county treasurers of the several counties of their respective districts, as the case may require, within one month after the adjournment of each term of the circuit court of their respective judicial district, a fair abstract of all fines and penalties, which shall be assessed, had or recovered in his court at the term thereof, specifying therein the names of the person, or persons, the amounts of the fines and penalties, and the offenses for which the same are assessed; and in case such clerk shall wilfully neglect to transmit such abstract as above specified, he shall forfeit and pay into the national treasury the sum of twenty-five dollars, to be assessed by the circuit judge, and collected by the sheriff, as other fines are collected and paid over.

9. The circuit clerks of each judicial district in this nation are hereby required to cause to be removed all cases properly belonging to the courts of which they are clerks now pending untried, and place such cases on docket for trial at the first term of the circuit court for the judicial district hereafter to be holden; and the circuit clerk of each district shall tax, with his own bill of costs upon the decision of any and all suits or causes, civil and criminal, so removed, the costs due thereon, to

the clerks of the courts from whence they were removed;
and all the costs so taxed shall be collected by execution and sale on failure of the party who may be adjudged to pay the same to do so, and the circuit clerks
aforesaid are hereby required and directed to take
charge of all books, papers, and record of cases, civil
and criminal, that have been disposed of in any of the
circuit courts aforesaid, and which the judge of the circuit courts of the particular judicial districts shall say
belong to the court of which he is judge, and shall file
away and preserve the same in his office in the order in
which they were decided. **APPROVED OCT. 30, 1886.**

SECTION V.

DISTRICT ATTORNEYS.

1. Be it enacted by the general council of the Choctaw nation assembled: District attorneys shall continue
in office during the term of two years; and said district
attorneys shall before they enter upon the duties of their
office severally take and subscribe the oath prescribed
in the constitution, which oath shall be administered by
the principal chief, or any of the several judges, and
certified on their commissions, and shall reside within
their respective districts; and it shall be the duty of said
district attorneys to appear and prosecute for the nation
in all cases in their respective circuits in all criminal
prosecutions and in all civil cases where the nation or
any county in their respective circuits may be a party
interested; and all accounts of a public nature before
they are allowed by any of the circuit courts shall be
presented to the district attorney of the proper circuit
for his approval in writing; and it shall be the duty of
the district attorney to give his opinion in writing to the
county treasurer in all cases concerning the revenue and
expenses in any county of their respective circuits when-

ever required, and shall when thereunto required by any treasurer of any county in his circuit institute and pros-ecute to effect before the proper court, all persons in-debted to the nation, or any county within the same, in the manner that may be prescribed by law.

2. *Be it further enacted*, That if any district at-torney through neglect fail to attend any term of the circuit court of their respective circuits, the circuit court in which such failure is made is hereby authorized and required to employ some attorney to act for the nation in the place of such district attorney so failing to attend, and the attorney so employed shall for his services be paid by the district attorney so failing to attend, such sum as shall be allowed by the said circuit court, not in any one case, and for one failure to exceed twenty-five dollars ; *provided*, said district attorney so failing shall have been prevented to attend by sickness or high water, which are satisfactory to the circuit court, then such at-torney *pro tempore* * be allowed twenty-five dollars out of the national treasury, upon the certificate of such cir-cuit judge to the national auditor, who is hereby re-quired to issue his warrant therefor.

3. *Be it further enacted*, That in all cases of con-viction of felonies, the district attorney shall be allowed a fee of ten dollars, and in all cases of conviction for mis-demeanors a tax fee of five dollars shall be allowed said district attorney, which shall be taxed in the bill of costs collected, and paid over to the district attorney entitled to the same.

4. *Be it further enacted*, That if any district attor-ney in this nation shall in any manner consult, counsel, advise or defend a person within this nation charged with any crime, misdemeanor, or breach of any penal

* *Pro tempore*—for the time being.

statute, the district attorney so offending shall, on con-viction thereof in any court of competent jurisdiction, be fined in a sum not exceeding two hundred dollars, and shall be removed from office, and be rendered incapable thereafter of filling any office of profit or honor in this nation.

5. *Be it further enacted*, That in addition to the fees allowed the district attorneys by this act, they shall each be entitled to receive, as a compensation for their services, out of the national treasury, viz: District attorneys of Mosholatubbee and Pushamataha districts each receive the sum of three hundred dollars, and the district attorney of Apuckshunnubbee district the sum of three hundred and fifty dollars, to be paid quarter-yearly upon presentation of the account therefor, when the national auditor shall issue his warrant for the same upon the national treasury.

APPROVED OCT. 30, 1888.

SECTION VI.

COUNTY COURTS AND COURTS OF PROBATE.

1. Be it enacted by the general council of the Choc-taw nation assembled: The county court and court of probate established in each county of the Choctaw na-tion, shall be styled the county court of —— —— county, (as the case may be) and the judges elected therefor, be-fore entering upon the duties of their office, shall take and prescribe the oath prescribed in the constitution be-fore any judge of a court of records, which oath thus taken and subscribed, shall be recorded on the minutes of the county court, and on failure of such judge-elect to qualify, as prescribed by law, for the space of twenty days after said election, shall be deemed disqualified to hold the office, and the vacancy shall be filled in the same manner as other vacancies in said office.

2. The county court in each county shall have a a seal of said court, with the style of the court around the margin, and an eagle in the center, which shall be kept by the clerk and affixed to all letters of administration, testamentary and guardianship; to all certificates of the court or of the clerk, and to every writ and process of every kind issued from said court; the cost of which shall be paid out of the county funds upon the certificate of the county judge.

3. The county court shall have jurisdiction in all cases relative to probate of last wills and testaments, the granting of letters testamentary, and of administration, and repealing the same; in the appointment and displacing of guardians of orphans, minors, and persons of unsound mind or idiotic; in the settlement and allowance of accounts of executors, administrators and guardians; to hear and determine all controversies respecting last wills and testaments, the right of executorship, administration or guardianship, or respecting the duties or accounts of executors, administrators and guardians; to award process, and cause to come before such court all persons whom they may deem it necessary to examine, whether parties or witnesses, or who as executors, guardians or administrators or otherwise, shall be interested or in anywise accountable for any lands, tenements, goods, chattels, moneys or effects, belonging to any minor, orphan or persons of unsound mind, or idiotic, or the estate of any deceased person. Said county courts shall have exclusive original jurisdiction in all matters of contract or controversy, where the sum in controversy is not over fifty dollars. The several county courts of this nation shall have power to punish any person who may be guilty of a contempt of such courts in like manner as a circuit court of law.

4. Any person who has been, is, or may hereafter be, elected to the office of county judge of any county in this nation, and who shall at the time of his election be executor, administrator or guardian in such court, and not having settled his final account thereof, shall be disqualified from acting as county judge in such case, but it shall be his duty to apply to the county judge of an adjoining county, who shall have full authority to proceed therein, and shall cause his proceedings thereon to be recorded in the clerk's office of the county court of the county from which the same shall have been so removed. When any judge of a county court shall be related by affinity or consanguinity to either party, or having any interest in the cause pending in said court, such judge shall be incompetent to try said cause, and it shall be his duty to appoint any discreet person qualified to try that case for which he is disqualified; *provided*, that the incompetency of such judge may be waived by the interested parties, and entered of record, and his competency to try the cause be restored. The election of an attorney-at-law, to the office of county judge shall not deprive such attorney of the right to practice in his profession, in any court of law, except the court of which he is judge; *provided*, that he shall not prosecute, or defend, or advise either party in any matter or cause which he may have decided, and on which an appeal or other proceedings are had in any other court in this nation; and if any judge of a county court shall aid, abet, or counsel, or advise in any such matter, cause or controversy, he shall be deemed guilty of a high misdemeanor, and may, for the same, be removed from office.

5. It shall be the duty of the county judge of each county in this nation, to hold a court at the place fixed by law for holding county court in his county on the first Monday in every month, which may continue for

10

four days, if business so long requires, and no longer, and the sheriff of the county shall attend said courts and shall serve all summons or process to him directed, from the county court of his or any other county within the nation, and shall make returns thereof, according to the tenor of the same ; and on failure, he shall be liable to be proceeded against in the same manner as for the like failure in other cases. Each county judge may hold a special term of his court by giving ten days' notice, in three public places, and specifying the causes to be tried at such special term, and no other business shall be disposed of at that term.

6. It shall be the duty of the judges of the county courts to keep respectively in their courts a docket-book of all causes pending in their courts, on which docket shall be entered, in the order in which they are made, all applications for letters testamentary, of administration and guardianship, and all other suits and causes, in said courts, whether commenced by bill, petition, or motion, and whether the same be *ex parte*,* or between one or more persons or parties litigant in said courts ; and at each term of said courts, it shall be the duty of the judges thereof to take up and dispose of the business pending between them in the order in which the same is entered upon their docket.

7. In all cases in which any county court shall make and enter a judgment and decree against any party litigant therein, or against any executor, administrator or guardian, for payment of a sum of money by said party litigant, executor, administrator or guardian, to any other party entitled to the same, by the terms of said judgment or decree, said court shall have power to enforce a compliance with the terms of such judgment or decree

---

Ex parte—"on one part;" as, *ex parte* evidence, that which is brought forward by one side only.

by process of *fieri facias*,* issued by said court, returnable to a term of said court, not less than thirty, nor more than ninety days from the date of the process, which process shall be executed by the sheriff of the proper county upon the tenements, goods and chattels of the party against whom the same shall be issued, or by process of attachment against the person of the party against whom the judgment or decree shall have been rendered ; *pro.vided*, that no such attachment shall issue until the party against whom the same is prayed shall have been cited to appear at some regular term of the court to show cause why it should not be issued ; and if upon the service of the citation, the party shall fail to appear, and show cause aginst the issuing of the attachment, the court shall issue a peremptory attachment commanding the sheriff to imprison the person or the party, until they comply with the judgment of the court. The county courts shall have power, and are hereby required to entertain bills of review, for the correction of any interlocutory order, or final decree of said courts in proceedings for the final settlement of any executor, administrator or guardian ; any person interested by bill of review may open and cause to be examined by the courts, any annual or partial settlement made by such executor, administrator or guardian, and surcharge and falsify the accounts rendered upon such settlement, and any person interested may, at any time within two years after final settlement, by bill of review, open the account of any executor, administrator or guardian, and surcharge and falsify the same, and not after, saving to minors and married women, the same time after the removal of their disability. No order or decree affecting the rights or interests of any minor, shall be valid and binding upon

*Fieri facias—a writ for one who has recovered a debt, damages or costs, commanding the sheriff to levy the same on the goods of him against whom the recovery was had.

said minor, or his or her interest in any estate administered in any county court in this nation, unless his or her
guardian, if a resident of the county in which the proceedings are had, shall be first personally served with
five days' notice to appear and defend the rights of said
minor, or if the guardian of such minor be not a resident
of said county, and do not apper, or if the guardian,
whether resident or not of the county, be a party personally interested to give validity and effect to any such
order or decree, the court shall appoint a guardian *ad
litem,** to protect the interest of such minor.

8. Any person or persons who may wish to adopt
any illegitimate or orphan child or children, shall file a
petition to that effect with the county clerk of the county
they may reside in, which shall remain on file for thirty
days, and if no legal or just cause is shown why the petition shall not be granted, then the county judge shall
grant the petition, and cause the same to be recorded in
the county clerk's office, after which the adoption shall
be as binding as if done by special act of the general
council.

9. The following procedure shall be established in
the probate courts of this nation, viz.: When any person
shall die intestate, being a citizen of this nation, the probate court of the county in which the party died, or the
greatest portion of his effects were at the time of his
death, shall have the right to entertain petition for letters
of administration upon the estate of said decedent, and
the nearest of kin by blood or marriage shall have the
preference to administer; *provided*, they file their petition within thirty days from the death of the party. But
if no petition is filed by the kin aforesaid, then any person interested in the administration of said estate shall
have the right to administer. All petitions filed in courts.

Ad litem—Guardian to defend a minor sued.

for letters of administration shall set forth the time and place of the death of the party, and the probable amount of the estate, and the heirs interested in said estate: the petition so filed shall be received in court for thirty days before acted upon, in which time all persons interested in said estate shall file in writing if they wish objections, to the granting of the petition on file at least five days before the hearing term thereof; if no objections are filed the court shall proceed to action upon the petition on file. If the petition is granted the petitioner shall execute bond ;with approved securities, payable to the county judge and his successor in office, in a sum equal to the value of the estate to be administered, which bond, if deemed sufficient, shall be approved by the judge and filed in the clerk's office to be sued upon by any person injured by the illegal administration of the estate upon the part of the administration; the court shall, after the approval of the bond, cause the clerk to issue letters of administration to the party, which letters shall authorlze the administrator to collect the estate by suit or otherwise, and true inventory return into court, under oath. The personal estate of the deceased, if any, shall be appraised by three disinterested persons commission ed and sworn by the clerk to receive and appraise the personal effects of the said deceased, and return an appraisement of the same in to court, and the amount of appraisement shall be charged against the administrator to be accounted for in the final settlement of his administration. The administrator shall settle and collect all claims and accounts for and against the estate, as decreed by the court; *provided*, if on the return of the inventory of any intestate estate, it shall appear that the value of the whole estate does not exceed the sum of one hundred and fifty dollars, the probate court may, by a decree for that purpose, assign for the use and support of the widow and children of such intestate, or for the support of the children under seven years of age, if there be no widow, the whole of such estate, after the payment of the funeral charges and expenses of administration. But in case the personal estate shall amount to more than the allowances mentioned herein, fifty per cent or one-half of the value of the whole estate shall be applied to the payment of ihe debts of the deceased, with charges of his funeral and of settling his estate.

10. That all proceedings in court shall be in writing and filed in court five days before hearing term thereof and the court shall consider and adjudge the same. That it shall be the duty of the administrator to settle up the estate as soon as the interest of the estate will allow. The final settlement of an administrator shall remain on file for inspection thirty thirty days, and objections thereto shall be filed in writing, if any; and the court shall consider and dispose of them according to law. If the final account of an administrator is allowed by the court he shall transfer the residue of the estate in his hands to the county clerk and take his receipt therefor, and the said administrator's bond shall then be cancelled. The appraisers of an estate shall each receive one dollar and a half per day during the time they are engaged in making the appraisement, and to be paid by the administrator and charged to the estate. And the administrator shall be allowed a compensation not less than five per centum nor more than seven per centum upon the whole value of the estate administered which shall be allowed by the court in the final settlement of the estate.

11. The law in reference to administrators shall be also applicable to executors and guardians, and all written wills shall be attested by two or more witnesses and be exhibited for probate within six months after the

death of the party ; and wills not written shall be pro-
bated within three months after the death of the party,
and be attested by at least two witnesses not interested
in the estate conveyed in the will; and no guardian shall
be allowed to sell the effects of any minors in his hand
except for the support and education of the "ward;" but
it shall be lawful for any person who may be appointed
guardian of minor children to get an order from court
to sell any of their real estate or personal property for
the benefit of such minors, either in or out of this nation,
and such sales shall be good and binding on such minors
when they become of age ; also, when any person is
proved to be in a state of derangement of mind, or an
idiot, and possessed of property, there shall be a guardian appointed, with the same power and instructions as
specified in the law in reference to minors ; and all judgments and decrees of the probate courts shall be enforced by law for and against the estates of deceased
persons.

12. The property of all persons who die intestate,
or without a will, shall descend to his legal wife, or husband, and their children; and in case such deceased
person has neither wife, nor husband, nor children, his
or her grandchildren (if any) shall inherit the estate;
and in case there is no grandchild the father or mother
of such deceased person, or either of them shall heir the
estate; and in case such deceased person has neither
wife, nor husband, children, or grandchildren, or father
or mother, his or her estate shall go to his or her brothers and sisters, and if none, to ther lawful children.
Should there be none of the above mentioned relatives
to the intestate deceased person, the estate shall descend
to the half brothers and sisters of the deceased person
and to their legal issue.

13. The judge of the county court, without the consent of either party to a suit, may, if necessary adjourn the cause, not exceeding thirty days. The judge of the county court, on the application of either party, on good cause shown, may adjourn a cause not exceeding thirty days for any one adjournment, and may adjourn for a longer period with the consent of both parties. No adjournment shall be allowed upon the application of a party, unless such party satisfy the judge by his own affidavit, or the affidavit of some other person, that he cannot safely proceed to trial for want of some material testimony or witness; that he has used due diligence to obtain the same, and that if an adjournment be allowed he will be able to procure such testimony or witness in time to be used on the trial.

14. A subpœna by a county judge shall be valid to compel the attendance of a witness before such judge in the same county where the cause is to be tried, or being in an adjoining county. Whenever it shall appear to the satisfaction of a judge by proof made before him that any person duly supœnaed to appear before him in a suit, shall have failed, without just cause, to attend as a witness in conformity to such subpœna, and the party in whose behalf subpœna was issued, or his agent, shall make oath that the testimony of such witness is material, the judge shall have power to issue a writ of attachment to compel the attendanoe of such witness. Every person duly subpœnaed as a witness who shall not appear shall forfeit and pay a fine for the use of the county in which he is subpœnaed to appear, unless some reasonable excuse shall be shown on the oath of such witness or the oath of some other person—such fine not exceeding ten dollars, as the judge shall think reasonable to impose; and the judge shall make an entry in his docket of the conviction and of the cause thereof.

15. Either party to a civil suit depending before a county judge upon notice to the other party, may cause the deposition of every witness therein to be taken by any judge of this nation. No such deposition shall be taken unless notice in writing of the time and place of taking the same, shall have been previously served on the other party at least three days before the taking thereof.

16. Any person aggrieved by the judgment rendered by a county judge, and accept a judgment of non-suit, may, in person or by his agent, make his appeal therefrom to the district circuit court of the same district where the judgment was rendered. No appeal shall be allowed, unless the following requisites be complied with: First, the applicant, or some person for him, shall make and file with the judge an affidavit within ten days after the judgment was rendered, setting forth that the appeal is not taken for the purpose of delay, but that justice may be done him; second, the affidavit must also set forth specially, what part of the judgment or decree of the court he may take exceptions to, when all of which is complied with, the judge may grant such applicant an appeal, which shall be delivered to the clerk of the circuit court at least ten days before the first day of the term of the circuit court, and enter on the docket for trial before the circuit court.

17. When a man and woman intermarry with each other, each one shall retain the right of the property that he or she may bring into the marriage union at the time they are joined together in the bonds of matrimony, and neither party shall have the right to dispose of the other's property without the consent of the other; and if the property of the wife or husband is disposed of by either party without the consent of the other, a suit may be instituted in the courts of this nation, and the

property so disposed of, restored to its proper owner, or the value thereof recovered. But property that may be accumulated by the joint exertions of a man and his wife after they are married, shall be held in common, and subject to the disposal of the husband for the mutual support and benefit of the family. No will that is made by the husband or wife, conveying such property without the consent of the other, shall be valid.

18. It shall be lawful for the clerks of the county courts to issue execution for the cost of any suit or proceeding which may originate in said court, and the sheriff shall collect and return the same in the same manner as if issued by the clerk of the circuit court.

19. All books for minutes, records, and other matters deemed necessary for the use of the clerks of the several counties in this nation, shall be procured by the clerks thereof, and the accounts therefor certified to by the judges of said courts, and paid out of the county treasury of their respective counties.

20. The county judges of this nation shall receive as a compensation for their services, the sum of one hundred and fifty dollars each per annum, to be paid quarter-yearly; when they present their accounts to the national auditor he shall issue his warrant for the same out of the national treasury. But whenever the county revenue in any county exceeds the sum of five hundred dollars per annum, the county judge thereof shall be allowed an additional salary of fifty dollars, and the same sum for every additional five hundred dollars of revenue until the revenue reaches the sum of fifteen hundred dollars, beyond which no additional sum per annum shall be allowed said county judges; *provided*, the increase of compensation allowed by this act shall be payable out of the county treasury.

21.   Judges of the county courts of this nation shall
have the power to direct the clerks thereof to issue summons for jury of seven disinterested persons of the county to try such cases as properly belong to the jurisdiction of said court, if they deem necessary ; and such
writs of summons shall be executed by the sheriff in
their proper county ; and the party or party losing such
suits shall pay said jurymen one dollar each per day,
for every day's attendance on court, and five cents per
mile traveled, going to and returning therefrom, and the
cost of summoning witnesses and other expenses, etc.
shall be paid, as provided for by law, in the circuit
court.   APPROVED OCT. 30, 1888.

SECTION VII.

CLERKS OF COUNTY COURTS.

1.   Be it enacted by the general council of the Choctaw nation assembled :   The clerks of the county courts
shall hold their offices for the term of two years, unless
sooner removed for misdemeanor, or other disqualifying
cause, from office, and before entering upon the duties
of their offices shall take the oath of office prescribed in
the constitution, which oath, when taken and subscribed
shall be entered on the records of said court; and any
judge of a court of record shall be qualified to administer such oath to the clerks aforesaid; any clerk failing
or refusing to take the oath of office for fifteen days after
his appointment, shall be incompetent to hold the office,
and the vacancy shall be filled in the same manner as
other vacancies in said office are filled. Also, they shall,
before they enter upon the duties of their office, enter
into bond with good security, payable to the principal
chief of the nation and his successors in office, in the
same manner, and in the same penalty, and with the

same conditions as is required of the several circuit clerks of this nation, which bond shall be recorded and filed, as is prescribed for the said circuit clerks' bond.

2. It shall be the duty of the clerks of the county courts to keep and preserve all records, files, books, papers, and the proceedings of said court, to record all last wills and testaments, duly proved and approved, all accounts finally allowed, all inventories and appraisements duly made and sworn to, to issue all citations, subpœnas and other process, as issue of course, and all such as are directed by the court in 'term time, or the judge in vacation, and to do and perform all those things that appertain to the office of a clerk of the county court; and the clerk's office in term time shall be under the direction of the court, and in vacation under the direction of the judge of said court.

3. The clerks of the county courts in this nation shall keep their offices at the places designated by law for holding said courts; but in all cases where offices have not been provided for the clerks of the courts, such clerks may keep all the books, records and papers belonging to their offices, at such places as the county judges may direct and so enter of record. Said clerks may appoint deputies in the same manner as is provided by law for the appointment of deputy clerks of the circuit courts, and such deputies shall have power to act in the name of their principals; and the said clerk, or his deputy, may, either in term time or vacation, administer oaths in relation to the probate of accounts, and as to all matters connected with the proceedings of the county court, and also to administer oaths in all cases wherein an affidavit is necessary, as to the foundation of any official act to be performed by any such clerk. And whenever the office of county clerk shall become vacant from any cause whatsoever, the records, books, papers,

stationery and everything in anywise belonging to, or
appertaining to said office, shall be demanded, delivered over and secured in the manner; and in case of refusal or detention, under the penalties prescribed in the
law defining the duties of the clerks of the circuit courts
in this nation. In case the clerk of the county court in
any county shall be at any time unable to attend said
courts, from any cause whatever, it shall be lawful for
the judges of the county courts, in case there is no deputy clerk of said court present, to appoint a person to
act as clerk *pro tempore*,* who shall take the oath of
office faithfully to discharge the duties of the same, and
for his services as clerk he shall be entitled to the fees
allowed by law to the clerk of said court.

4. The county court in each county shall make
allowances of all sums necessary for furnishing the
clerk's office with tables, chairs, and presses to preserve
papers, to be paid out of the county treasury of the
proper county, under direction of the county judge.

5. It shall be the duty of each clerk of the county
courts to record in the books provided for his office all
deeds, mortgages, conveyances, deeds of trust, bonds,
covenants, or other instruments of writing, or of concerning any tenements, or goods and chattels, which
shall be proved or acknowledged according to law, and
all marriage contracts and marriage certificates, and all
commissions and official bonds, required to be recorded
in his office. And shall record immediately upon recep-
tion all and every character of instruments of writing
filed in said office, if in conformity with the requisitions
of the law, by entering them word for word, and letter
for letter, and noting at the foot of the record the day of
the month and year the same was deposited in his office
for record. And when any deed, mortgage, deed of

*Pro tempore—for the time being.

trust, bond, conveyance, or other instrument of writing, authorized by law to be recorded, shall be deposited in the office of the county clerk of any county for record, the clerk shall enter in a book, to be provided for the purpose, in alphabetical order, the names of the persons, and date, and nature thereof, the time of delivery for record, and shall, if required, give the person delivering the same a receipt specifying the particulars thereof; and it shall be considered as recorded from the day it was delivered for record, and the clerk shall certify and attach to every such deed, mortgage, conveyance or deed of trust, bond, and other instrument of writing so recorded, the day of the month and year when he received it, and the book and pages in which it was recorded, and deliver the same to the party entitled thereto or his order.

6. Each county clerk shall provide and keep in his office a well bound book, and make and enter therein an index in alphabetical order to all books of records, wherein deeds, mortgages, or other instruments in writing are recorded, distinguishing the books and papers in which every such deed of writing is recorded. Said index shall contain the names of the several grantors and grantees, in alphabetical order; and in case the deed be made by a sheriff, the name of the sheriff and the name of the defendant in execution; and if by executor or administrator, their names and the names of their testator or intestate; and if by attorney, his name, and that of his constituents; and if by a commissioner, his name, and that of the person whose estate is conveyed. That each clerk shall, in like manner, make, keep and preserve a full and perfect alphabetical index to all books and records in his office, wherein all deeds and instruments of writing in relation to personal property, marriage contracts, certificates of marriage, and all other pa-

pers and records, and a like index of all the books of records wherein commissions and official bonds are recorded; the names of the officers appointed or elected, and of the obligors in any bond recorded, and a refer ence to the book and page where the same are recorded; and that each clerk shall make a reference in the several indexes of all deeds and conveyances which may be hereafter recorded, so as to afford at all times an easy reference to such records.

7. Any county clerk to whom any deed or other writing proved or acknowledged according to law shall be delivered for record, shall neglect or refuse to make an entry thereof, or give receipt therefor as required by law, or shall neglect or refuse to record such deeds or other writing within a reasonable time after receiving the same, or shall record any deeds or instruments of writing before another first deposited in his office, and entered to be recorded, or shall record any deed or other writing incorrectly, or shall neglect or refuse to provide and keep in his office such indexes as required by law, he shall forfeit and pay the sum of one hundred dollars, to be recovered by action of damages, one-half to use of the county and the other half to the use of the person who shall sue for the same, and also be liable to any person injured for all damages he may have sustained thereby, to be recovered by action of damages on the official bonds of such clerk or by special action the case. And if any clerk shall wilfully neglect to perform any of the duties required of him by law, or shall perform them in any other manner than is required by law, he shall be deemed guilty of a misdemeanor in office and shall be removed therefrom; *provided*, that no clerk shall be bound to record any deed or other instrument of writing for which a fee may be allowed by law, until such fee shall have been paid or tendered to him by the party

requring the record to be made. And if any clerk shall
knowingly make any false entry, or erase a letter, or
change any records in his keeping, belonging to his
office, every such clerk so offending shall, on conviction
thereof, be fined and imprisoned at the discretion of the
court, and shall, moreover, be liable to the action of the
party aggrieved.

8.   The county clerks of the several counties in this
nation shall be entitled to receive as a compensation for
their services, the sum of fifty dollars a year, each to be
paid quarter-yearly on the county judge's order to the
national auditor, who is directed to issue his warrant on
the national treasurer for the same.

9.   The clerk of the county court in each county
within this nation shall be county treasurer, who shall
hold his office for the term of two years, unless sooner
removed; shall be commissioned by the principal chief,
and before he enters on the duties of his office, he shall
take and subscribe the oath prescribed in the constitution before the county judge of the county for which he
is appointed, which shall be certified by the county
judge administering the same on the back of his commission, and shall also give bond with two or more good
and sufficient securities to be approved by the judge of
the county court, in such penalty as said judge may direct, payable to said judge of said court of —— county
for the time being, and his successor in office with the
like condition, after making the necessary changes as is
directed by law to be given in the bond of the national
treasurer, which bond, with the approbation of the securities therein named endorsed thereon, shall, together
with the endorsement be recorded in the office of the
clerk of the county court of the county for which said
treasurer is appointed, and the bond filed in the same
office, there to be safely kept and preserved, and may be

sued on in the like manner, and with like effect, in all respects as the bond given by the national treasurer. And if any county treasurer shall neglect or refuse to give bond and security, and take the oath of office as aforesaid, for the space of ten days after he shall have been appointed, such appointment is hereby declared absolutely null and void, and the judge of the county court shall immediately appoint another in his place, with the like conditions aforesaid in this paragraph.

10. It shall be the duty of each county treasurer to receive and keep the moneys of the county, to disburse the same agreeable to law, and take receipts for all moneys he shall so disburse; and he shall keep regular accounts of the receipts and expenditures of the funds of the county, and of all debts due to or from the county of which he is treasurer, and direct prosecutions according to law, for all debts that are or shall be due to the county for which he is appointed. It shall be the further duty of the several county treasurers to make a detailed report, quarter-yearly, of his county, of all moneys received by them, and the disbursement thereof; that all debts due to and from the county, may clear and distinctly appear; and if any county treasurer shall neglect or refuse to make such report, he shall forfeit and pay the sum of one hundred dollars for every such neglect or refusal, to be recovered by action of debt, or information in the name of the judge of the county court of such county in any court of competent jurisdiction, and applied to the use of the county; *provided*, that if the county treasurer fail to make the reports on account of sickness, or any other lawful excuse, then he shall not be prosecuted for the same. The county treasuer of each county is hereby empowered and required to examine the accounts, dockets and records of the sheriff and ranger of his county, for the purpose of ascertaining

11

whether any moneys, of right, belonging to such county, may be in their hands.

11.   When any allowance shall be made by any court to any person payable out of the county treasury, the clerk of such court shall make out a fair copy of the account so allowed, and certify such allowance under his hand and seal of office, and recite therein under what statute it was made; and if the county treasurer shall have any doubt of the propriety of any such allowance made as aforesaid, he shall not pay the same, but shall make report thereon to the next succeeding meeting of the county court, for its consideration; and no court shall be authorized to make any allowance payable out of the county treasury, unless the same be provided for by some act or resolution of the general council; and no money shall be paid out of the county treasury to any person or persons unless the same shall have been previously allowed by the county court of the proper county, or some other court or officer lawfully authorized to make allowance, and duly certified.

12.   If any county treasurer shall misapply, waste or embezzle any money in the treasury of the county, it shall be the duty of the national attorney, or district attorney of the proper district, to proceed against such defaulting treasurer and his sureties, for the amount of the money so misapplied, wasted or embezzled, by motion, in the name of the judge of the county court, for the time being, in the circuit court for the county wherein such default was made, ten days' previous notice of such motion being first given to such county treasury and his sureties; and the court may, on such motion, direct a jury to be impanneled instantly for the trial of the issue, if the defendants appear and plead, or to inquire of damages, if the defendants make default; and if, on such trial, the treasurer shall be convicted, he and

his sureties shall be adjudged to pay double damages; and, moreover, such county treasurer shall be thereby rendered incapable thereafter of holding any office of honor or profit under this nation.

13. It shall be the duty of the clerks of the circuit courts in this nation, within ten days after the adjournment of their courts respectively, to return to the county treasurer of the proper county, a list containing a statement of all fines, penalties and forfeitures imposed by said courts respectively, which may be payable, in whole or in part, into the county treasury of such county, not contained in any previous return, together with the name of the sheriff, clerk, or other officer, who has received any such fines, penalties, forfeitures, or become liable to pay the same by law, in order to enable the said county treasurer to collect the same according to law; and every clerk failing to perform the aforesaid duty shall forfeit and pay the sum of one hundred dollars, to be recovered by the county treasurer of the proper county, by action of debt or information in any court of competent jurisdiction, and paid into the county treasury for county purposes.

14. When any sheriff, clerk, or other officer who has received, or become liable by law, for the payment of any fine, penalty, or forfeiture, and shall not within twenty days after his having received the same, or become so liable, account with the county treasurer of the proper county, and pay the same into the treasury thereof, then, and in every such case, it shall and may be lawful for the said treasurer, upon motion made in the circuit court for said county, to demand judgment against such sheriff, clerk or other officer, and their sureties, for the amount of such fines, penalties, forfeitures, as afore-said, and such court is hereby required to give judgment accordingly, and award execution thereon; *provided,*

that such sheriffs or other officer have ten days' previous notice, in writing, of every such motion. And it shall be the duty of the national attorney and district attorneys, in their respective pistricts, to attend to the prosecution of all suits against any defaulting officers named in this act.

15. If the county treasurer of any county within this nation shall be convicted of having violated any of the duties enjoined on him by law, the judge of the county court shall vacate the commission of such county treasurer, and the vacancy occasioned thereby shall be supplied by the judge of the county court, to be commissioned by the principal chief; oath, bond and securities to be given, as is required in the ninth paragraph of this section.

16. The judge of the county court of each and every county in this nation is hereby required to allow the county treasurer of each and every county a recompense of five per cent on all moneys paid into the county treasury for county purposes.

—————

APPROVED OCT. 30, 1888.

SECTION VIII.

SHERIFFS.

1. Be it enacted by the general council of the Choctaw nation assembled: Every sheriff in the Choctaw nation shall be commissioned by the principal chief, and before he enters on the duties of his office, he shall take the oath of office prescribed in the constitution before the county judge, and enter into bond with good and sufficient securities, to be approved by the county judge of such county, in the penalty hereinafter specified, payable to the principal chief of the nation for the time being and his successors in office; the condition of such bond shall be in the form or to the effect following, to-wit: The con-

dition of the above obligation is such, that, whereas, the
above bond ———— was duly elected by the qualified
electors of the county of ———— sheriff of said county,
at an election held on the — day of ————, for the
term of two years; now, therefore if the said —,————
shall well and truly collect all fines and forfeitures accruing to or becoming due to the nation, or any county
within the same, which may lawfully come into his
hands for collection against any person or persons residing or being found within the county of which he is
sheriff, and shall punctually pay all such fines and forfeitures so collected to the person or persons entitled by
law to receive the same, and shall also well and truly
execute and make due return of all process and precepts
to him lawfully directed, and pay and satisfy
all sums of money by him received by virtue of any civil process or precepts to the person or persons to whom the same are due, his agent or
attorney, lawfully authorized to receive the same, his or
her executors, administrators, or assignees, and in all
things shall well and truly execute and faithfully perform the said duties of the office of sheriff during the
term of his continuance therein, then the above obligation shall be void, otherwise to be and remain in full
force and virtue. The county judge shall endorse on
said bond his approbation of the sureties therein named,
and a certificate that he has administered to the sheriff
the oath of office, and shall cause the bond, together with
the endorsement thereon, to be recorded in the office of
the clerk of the county court, and immediately thereafter
deposit the same in the office of the national secretary,
there to be safely kept and preserved ; and shall not be
void on the first recovery, but may be put in suit and
prosecuted from time to time at the cost and charges of
any party injured, until the whole amount of the penal-

ty thereof be recovered. An authenticated copy of any such bond shall be received in evidence in any court of law in this nation in the same manner as the original would be if it were present in court. The sheriffs of the several counties in this nation shall respectfully execute bonds, with security as aforesaid in the following penalties, to-wit: The sheriffs of Sans Bois, Gaines, Tobucksy, Wade, Nashoba, Jack's Fork and Atoka counties each in the sum of five hundred dollars; those of Skullyville, Towson and Kiamichi counties each in the sum of fifteen hundred dollars; and those of Sugar Loaf, Eagle, Boktuklo, Red River, Cedar and Blue counties each in the sum of one thousand dollars.

2. If the candidate having the greatest number of votes as sheriff of any county in this nation, shall fail or refuse to take the oath of office, and give bond, as by law directed, for the space of ten days after he shall have been duly elected, and notified thereof officially, such election is hereby declared void, and it shall be the duty of the county judge to certify the fact to the principal chief, who shall thereupon fill such vacancy by appointment, as the constitution directs. And in case the securities, or either of them, of any sheriff, shall remove his or their residence out of this nation permanently, or shall become insolvent, it shall be the duty of the county judge, on satisfactory proof of such removal or insolvency, to notify such sheriff to appear before him at a day and place therein named, within ten days thereafter, to give a new bond with other good and sufficient security, in a penalty equal to that of the former bond, with the like conditions; and if such sheriff shall fail so to do, the said county judge shall certify the fact to the principal chief, who shall forthwith vacate the commission of the sheriff so refusing or neglecting, and he shall fill such vacancy by appointment; and if any sheriff shall

be found, by inquest according to law, an idiot, lunatic, or *non compos mentis*,* during the period for which he is elected, or appointed, the principal chief shall fill such vacancy by appointment. And if any sheriff elect shall presume to execute the duties of sheriff before he shall have given bond and taken the oath of office, agreeable to the directions of law, all such of his acts and proceedings done under color of office, shall be absolutely void, and he shall for such offense be liable to be indicted for a misdemeanor, and on conviction thereof, before any court of competent jurisdiction, fined in any sum not exceeding five hundred dollars.

3. The sheriffs of the several counties in this nation shall have power to appoint one or more deputies, who shall have full power to do and perform all the several acts and duties enjoined upon the principals, and every such appointment shall be in writing under the hand and seal of the sheriff, and every deputy sheriff, before he enters upon the duties of his office, shall take and subscribe before any judge of a court of records, an oath faithfully to execute the office of deputy sheriff, according to the best skill and judgment, which appointment, with the certificate of the oath thereupon, endorsed and attested by the said judge, shall be by said deputy sheriff carefully filed, in the office of the clerk of the county court in and for the same county ; *provided*, that nothing in this section shall be construed to prevent the sheriff from removing his deputy or deputies at pleasure; and if any person shall proceed to execute the office of deputy sheriff, before he shall have received an appointment as aforesaid, and taken the oath of office, and filed the said appointment and certificate of such, oath in the clerk's office as aforesaid, then all such of his acts and proceedings done under color of office shall

Non compos mentis—"not sound of mind."

be absolutely void; provided, no person who may be
deputized by any sheriff to do a particular act only
shall be required to take the oath directed by this act to
be taken by the deputy sheriff.

4. Every sheriff by himself or deputy shall, from
time to time, execute all writs and other process to him
legally issued and directed in his county, and shall make
due return thereof to the proper court on the day to which
the same is returnable; and if any sheriff shall fail herein,
or shall make a false return on any such writs or other
process issued and directed to him as aforesaid, such
sheriff shall, for every such offense, be fined by the courts
into which such writs or other process is returnable, in
any sum not exceeding one hundred dollars, on motion,
reasonable notice being first given to the sheriff of such
motion, one moiety thereof to the party agrieved, and the
other moiety to the nation for the benefit and use of the
library fund, and such sheriff shall, moreover, be liable
to the action of the party injured by such default, for all
damages which he, she, or they may have sustained
thereby, and also such other fines, penalties and forfeitures as may be provided by law against sheriffs for failing to return writs and other process directed to them,
or for making a false return thereon.

5. The sheriff of any county shall have the same
remedy and judgment against his deputy failing to pay
the money by him received on any execution or other
process to the sheriff or the party to whom the same is
payable, his agent or attorney, or suffering any person
in his custody to escape, as the party for whose benefit
such process was issued may have against the sheriff or
his deputy, or the securities of such sheriff. In order to
prevent disputes between sheriffs and their several deputies, which of them may have acted in serving executions or other process, that when any deputy sheriff hath

served any writs, executions, attachments or other process whatever, he shall indorse on such writs or other
process the day of the month and year he or they shall
have served the same, and subscribe his name as well
as that of his principals to the return of such writs or
other process; and every deputy sheriff failing herein
shall be liable to the same penalty as is by this act inflicted on the sheriff for a false return, and to be recovered and appropriated in the same manner. When any
fine, penalty, or judgment which may be assessed or
rendered against any sheriff, his heirs, executors or administrators, for or on account of any default or miscon-
duct of any deputy of such sheriff, it shall and may be
lawful for the court in which such fine, penalty or judgment may be assessed or rendered, upon motion to them
made by such sheriff, his heirs, executors or administrators, to give judgment against such deputy and his securities, their heirs, executors or administrators, jointly
and severally, for the full amount of all such fines, penalties or judgments, and to award execution for the
same; *provided*, such deputy and his securities and their
legal representatives have ten days' notice of such motion.

6. Every sheriff who shall have levied any writ of
execution or process on goods and chattels which shall
remain in his hands and possession, unsold at the expira
tion of his term of service, shall be and is hereby required
to deliver over such goods and chattels so levied upon
and remaining unsold to his successor in office, taking
his receipt for the same ; and it shall be the duty of the
sheriff to whom such goods and chattels are delivered as
aforesaid, to proceed to sell the same, after giving thirty
days' notice at three public places, one of which shall
be at the court house or ground, in like manner as his
predecessor ought to have done had he continued in

office ; and to account for and pay the proceeds of such
sale to the party or parties entitled thereto by law ; and
if any sheriff shall fail or refuse to deliver over to his
successor in office any goods and chattels so levied on
and remaining in his hands as aforesaid, on demand
thereof made, it shall be lawful for the party for whose
benefits such writs of execution or other process issued,
to move the court from which the writs or process issued
against the sheriff so failing or refusing, and his securities and their legal representatives upon which motion
judgment shall be entered up for the amount of the execution or other process which came to the hand of such
defaulting sheriff, with interest at the rate of fifteen per
centum from the return day of such execution; *provided*,
that such sheriff shall have ten days' notice of such
motion.

7.   Every sheriff shall, at the expiration of his office
deliver all writs in his possession unexecuted to his successor in office, who shall give a receipt for the same,
and shall execute and return all such writs; and shall
also deliver to his successor a certified list of the names
of all persons confined in the jail of his county, when
there shall be one jail, in each county, otherwise in the
jail of the judicial district in which his county is situated, and the cause of commitment, a copy of which list
shall be filed in the clerk's office of the county court by
the sheriff receiving the same; *provided, however*, until
jails are erected in each county of this nation, it shall be
lawful for any sheriff of this nation to receive into their
custody all persons committed to their care as aforesaid.

8.   It shall be the duty of every sheriff to keep the
peace within his county, by causing all offenders against
the law to enter into bond with securities for keeping the
peace and appearing at the next term of the circuit court
to answer to the charge alleged against them: it shall be

his duty to suppress all unlawful assemblies, for which
end he is hereby empowered to call to his aid the power
of the county; he shall pursue, take and commit to jail
all persons charged with treason, felony and all other
crimes; and he is authorized to take good bond from the
parties arrested for their appearance at the next term of
the circuit court, except in cases of murder which shall
only be bailable by the judge of the county court or
circuit court; he shall duly attend upon all the
courts of records at their respective terms in his county,
and for such services shall receive, in addition to the
fees of office, the sum of twenty-five dollars, to be paid
out of the county treasury of his county, upon the certi
ficate of the circuit clerk, and one hundred and fifty
dollars out of the national treasury; upon the certificate
of the circuit judge, the national auditor shall issue his
warrant on the national treasurer for the same, payable
quarterly. It shall also be the duty of the sheriffs of
the several counties of this nation to execute all orders
or requisitions of the principal chief or United States
agent for this nation, whether verbal or written, for the
arrest and safe keeping of any and all persons and property charged with a violation of laws of the United
States, and the safe guarding and transmission of such
person or persons or property either beyond the limits
of the nation, or taking him, her, or them, before said
agent, at such time and place as may be by said agent
or the principal chief of the nation directed as aforesaid.
And it shall be the duty of every sheriff, without warrant, to seize, spill and search for all kinds of vinous or
intoxicating liquors, and to destroy all barrels, kegs,
jugs and whatever character of vessels may contain such
liquors, and to arrest and take before some judge all
persons introducing, buying, selling, bartering, or giving
away the same, to be dealt with as the law directs. And

when any sheriff or deputy finds that resistance is going to be made to the execution of any writ or process directed to him, or any duty that he is officially authorized to perform, he shall take the power of the county with him and execute the same, and report the person or persons resisting to the next term of the circuit court to which the resistance is made, to be proceeded against as the law directs.

9.   In case the sheriff of any county shall be amenable to the law, and it shall be necessary to issue a writ or summon for his arrest or appearance in court, the process or writ shall issue as in other cases, and shall be by the officer issuing such writ or process directed to any deputy sheriff of his county, who shall, to all intents and purposes of law, be principal sheriff in such cases and execute writs, take bonds and execute the judgments of the court in such cases.

10.   All warrants, mittimusses, writs, process, or precepts of any and all kinds, by which any person is arrested or committed to jail, shall be filed away and safely kept by the sheriff, and shall be turned over to his successor in office as other papers are directed to be turned over. And the sheriffs are by virtue of their office, jailors of their several counties, and shall receive all persons legally committed to their care, and keep them safely until discharged by due course of law; *provided*, that this section shall apply alone to those sheriffs in each judicial district in whose counties there is a jail until there be one erected in each of the other counties. When any prisoner in jail shall not be able to support himself, the jailor shall be allowed fifty cents per day for the maintenance of every such prisoner, to be paid out of the county funds upon affidavit of the sheriff; and in case any prisoner in jail shall be sick, and the jailor shall be of the opinion that medical attendance is necessary, he

shall call some physician to attend such prisoner and in case he be unable to pay the physician so called, the district attorney shall examine and allow the account to be paid out of the national treasury; *provided*, the prisoner be held in jail to answer the nation in a charge against him, otherwise the account shall be paid out of the county funds. And any person convicted of any crime or misdemeanor whatever in this nation, who may take an appeal or writ of error to the supreme court, shall remain in the jail of the county or circuit, as the case may be, wherein he was convicted, and shall not be removed to the place where the supreme court may be in session.

11. The sheriffs of the several counties in this nation shall keep their offices at the place of holding the courts of their respective counties; but in case where no office has been provided, they may keep their offices at such places as the county judges shall direct.

12. The sheriffs shall receive two dollars per day for their attendance on the circuit courts upon the certificates of the judges, which certificates shall be recorded and placed in the hands of the national auditor, who shall thereupon issue warrants upon the national treasurer for the amounts.

13. In addition to the fees already allowed deputy sheriffs by law, each regularly appointed deputy sheriff in this nation, shall receive fifty dollars a year, to be paid out of the national treasury on the certificates of the several principal sheriffs; said certificate to be made out at the end of each quarter of the fiscal year, and for twelve dollars and fifty cents each. *Provided, however,* said sheriffs shall appoint five deputies in Blue and Kiamitia counties, and not more than four in other counties.

14. The sheriffs of the counties in which the several circuit courts of this nation are held, shall be vested with

the authority to appoint special deputy sheriffs to serve
under their direction during the terms of the several circuit courts, in the following manner, to-wit: In the first
judicial district one from each county, except the county
of Gaines; in the second judicial district, one from each
county except the county of Nashoba, and in the third
judicial district two from each county except the county
of Atoka; and the sum of two dollars per day shall be
allowed said special deputy sheriffs for every day's actual attendance upon the circuit courts, payable out of
the national treasury upon the certificates of the circuit
judges of their respective districts, and the national auditor is hereby required to issue his warrant upon the national treasury for the amounts; and said auditor shall
not issue any warrants on certificates unless made in accordance herewith, and all persons purchasing illegally
issued certificates will do so on their own responsibility.

SECTION IX.   **APPROVED OCT. 23, 1888.**

JURIES.

1.   Be it enacted by the general council of the Choctaw nation assembled :   The county court of this nation
shall, at the term next preceding the terms of the circuit
courts of their districts, draw and make out a list of
jurors, duly qualified according to law, to serve as grand
and petit jurors of said circuit court, in the counties of
the First judicial district, viz :   Eight jurors each. In
the counties of the Second judicial district—in Towson,
five ; in Boktuklo, five ; in Red River, seven ; in Eagle,
seven ; in Wade, six ; in Cedar, five ; in Nashoba, five.
In the counties of the Third judicial district, ten each.
Which said list shall be furnished the sheriff by the
county clerk, and the sheriff shall, within ten days after
receiving such list, either in person or by deputy, sum-

mon said jurors to be and personally appear at the circuit court of the district to serve as jurors. The list of jurors summoned as aforesaid, with the return of the sheriff thereon, shall be returned to the circuit clerk of the district from which said list of jurors had been summoned from the several counties. The clerk of the circuit court, with the sheriff of the court, shall draw, alternately, by lots, twelve jurors, who shall constitute the grand jury to serve during the term for which they are summoned, who shall be sworn by the clerk and charged by the judge to enquire of all treasons, murders, crimes, felonies or misdemeanors against the laws of this nation within their respective districts, and the same present to the district attorney. That, from the whole number of grand jurors, the court shall appoint a foreman, and a concurrence of nine out of twelve shall, in every case, be necessary for the indictment of any person for violating the laws of this nation. The grand jurors, when sitting for that purpose, shall have power to summon any person or persons as witnesses in case of offenses against the laws of this nation, and the sheriff, or his deputy, shall be subject to their orders to cause the attendance of such witnesses. The remaining jurors, after the grand jury has been selected, as required in this act, shall constitute the petit jury, and any twelve of whom shall contitute a petit jury to try any case that may come before the circuit court at the term for which they were summoned to attend under the following rules, viz: The names of the petit jurors shall be written down and presented by the clerk to the district attorney, who shall be entitled to four peremptory challenges. The list shall then be presented to the defendant, and if charged with a felony shall be entitled to eight peremptory challenges, and the court shall, if necessary, order the sheriff or his deputy to summon from the bystanders other persons qualified to serve as jurors, subject to rejection by either party, the nation having the first right to object; *provided*, sufficient cause be shown the court for such rejection, and the court shall continue to cause suitable persons to be summoned as jurors until twelve shall be empanneled. No person shall serve as a petit juror who is related to either party to a suit, within the fourth degree of consanguinity or affinity, unless by the consent of both parties, and no exception to any juror on account of his age, non-residence, citizenship or other disability shall be allowed after the jury is sworn. The following oath shall be administered to all petit jurors: "You, and each of you, do swear that you will well and truly try the issue of the case now before you, and a true verdict give, according to law and evidence, unless dismissed by the court, or withdrawn by either of the parties." That the service of jurors shall be equalized as nearly as practicable among the citizens liable to be summoned as jurors and that all jurymen summoned according to the provisions of this act shall be entitled to receive five cents per mile going to and returning from court, and two dollars per day, to be paid out of the national treasury, excepting those jurors who shall serve on civil cases, whose per diem shall be the same, to be paid by the party losing the suit; and the same shall be attached to the bill of costs. The grand and petit jurors for the circuit courts, shall be drawn and certified to the clerk of the circuit court by the county clerks and sheriffs of the county, at least twenty days before the time said circuit court is to be holden, in case the county court shall from any cause, fail to draw the jury as provided herein. And no term of a circuit court, regular or special, shall be held without empaneling a grand and petit jury, as herein provided.

2. Every juror shall be a citizen of the Choctaw nation, over the age of twenty-one years, resident of the

county, and otherwise qualified according to law; and every juror shall be summoned by the sheriff, or other officer, either personally or by a written notice, left at the residence of the juror. Any person having been duly summoned as a juror accordingly, and failing to attend the term of the circuit court for which he was summoned shall pay a fine not less than five nor exceeding ten dollars, unless a good and sufficient cause of such failure shall be shown to the circuit judge thereof on or before the next term of said court; and such court shall order the sheriff or his deputy forthwith to summon a sufficient number of persons qualified to serve as jurors, to supply the deficiency.

3. Any grand juror may be indicted by the grand jury of which he is a member; but, where any complaint shall be lodged against any grand juror, the foreman shall inform the district attorney, and if, on examination, there are any grounds for proceedings against such juror, he shall inform the court thereof, and the court shall discharge such juror, and cause another to be summoned, if necessary.

4. That from and after the passage of this act, if any person is summoned or sworn as a juror in any case shall take anything to give his verdict for or against any party in any case or proceeding, civil or criminal, or shall receive any paper, evidence, or information from any one, in relation to any matter or cases for trial, for which he shall be summoned, he shall be deemed guilty of a misdemeanor, and on conviction shall be fined in any sum not exceeding fifty dollars, and such fine, one-half shall go to the district fund, and the other half shall be equally divided between the district attorney and the light-horse, who shall be at the trouble of collecting such fine. That every judge or other persons, whose duty it shall be to select or summon any jurors in any court or

before any officers who shall be guilty of any unlawful, partial, or improper conduct in selecting or summoning any jurors, shall be deemed guilty of a misdemeanor, and be fined in any sum not exceeding fifty dollars, and such fine shall be collected by the light-horse men, and one half go to the district funds, and the other half shall be divided between the district attorney and the light-horse, who shall be at the trouble of collecting such fine.

SECTION X.   APPROVED OCT. 23, 1888.

FEES OF OFFICERS OF COURTS.

1. Be it enacted by the general council of the Choctaw nation assembled: *To Clerks of the Circuit Courts in Civil Cases*—For each writ other than those hereinafter mentioned, seventy-five cents; docketing each case (to be charged but once), twelve and a half cents; filing all papers in each case, twenty-five cents; entering its appearance, twelve and a half cents; entering each motion, rule of order, twelve and a half cents; declaration in ejectment, one dollar; entering non-suit, discontinuance or *noll prosequi*,* twelve and a half cents; swearing each witness, six and a fourth cents; entering each continuance, twelve and a half cents; *venire facias*,† in every case tried by a jury, twelve and a half cents; *scire facias*,‡ (except against jurors where excused), one dollar; swearing and empaneling every jury, twelve and a half cents; receiving and entering verdict, twelve and a half cents; entering each judgment in court, twenty-five cents; each subpœna, for one witness, twenty-five cents;

Nolle prosequi—these words denote that a plaintiff or attorney for the public withdraws a suit.

† *Venire Facias*—a writ directed to the sheriff, requiring him to summon twelve men, to try an issue between parties. It is also a writ in the nature of the summons to cause the party indicted on a penal statute to appear.

‡*Scire Facias*—a judicial writ summoning a person to show cause to the court why something should not be done.

and for every other name inserted, six and a fourth cents; entering surrender of principal by bail, twenty-five cents; commission to take deposition, fifty cents; copies thereof, for every hundred words, ten cents; taking a recognizance, fifty cents; each execution, fifty cents; for certificate to witness, each to be taxed on the bill of costs, twelve and a half cents; each separate certificate (except to jurors) twenty-five cents.

In criminal cases—For entering pending indictments, or filing information, twenty-five cents; each writ, other than hereinafter named, fifty cents; arraigning prisoner and entering plea, fifty cents; taking recognizance, fifty cents; swearing and empaneling every jury, twenty-five cents; entering judgment or verdict, each twenty-five cents; swearing every witness, six and a fourth cents; each suboepna with one name, twenty five cents; and for every other name inserted, six and a fourth cents; each motion or order, twelve and a half cents; *venire facias*,† in each cause tried, fifty cents; all copies, each one hundred words, ten cents; each certificate, twen-five cents For all public services, not herein particularly provided for, the clerks shall, at each term, exhibit a detailed fee bill, to be examined by the district attor ney, previous to allowance by the court, and the court is hereby authorized to allow the same, not exceeding ten dollars, to be paid out of the county treasury.

2. *To the clerks of the county courts*--For like services by them performed, the same fees as are by law allowed to the clerks of the circuit courts: For recording each deed, bill of sale or other conveyance, for each one hundred words, ten cents; certifying the official acts of a county judge, or other official certificate with seal, fifty cents; registering the probate of any will or testament, and for letters testamentary thereon, one dollar; recording a will, testament, or codicil, for every hun-

dred words, ten cents: administering oath to executors, administrators, collectors, or guardians, taking bond and recording the same, one dollar; letters of administrtion, collection or guardianship and order granting the same, one dollar; order, appointing appraisers of an estate and copy, fifty cents; ordering an inventory appraisment for executors, administrators, collectors or guardians' account, for every hundred words, ten cents; recording certificate of marriage, fifty cents, recording and filing officers' bonds, one dollar.

3. *To the Sheriffs* — For executing the process, judgment or decree of a circuit court and for similar services in other courts : For copying execution, one dollar ; entering each writ in his office, twenty-five cents; returning execution, twenty-five cents ; each bail bond or recognizance, fifty cents ; summoning each witness, fifty cents ; for making deed to purchaser, two dollars ; each day's attendance on county court, two dollars ; attending prisoner on habeas corpus, each day, in vacation, two dollars ; each commitment or release, one dollar; feeding a prisoner, each day, forty cents ; serving a declaration in ejectment and copy thereof, one dollar ; taking bonds of every kind, each fifty cents ; executing death warrant, to be paid out of the national treasury, five dollars ; removing a prisoner, every mile going and returning, ten cents ; impanneling a jury in each cause where a jury is sworn, twenty-five cents ; collecting moneys by virtue of an execution, for the first one hundred dollars, three per cent, for all sums above one hundred dollars and not exceeding two hundred dollars, two per cent, and for every one hundred dollars over in said execution, one and one-half per cent; whipping person by order of court, two dollars ; serving attachment for contempt and returning the same, one dollar ; summoning a special jury, two dollars ; for impanneling grand juries,

advertising and attending elections, serving all public orders of courts in his county, and for all other public services not otherwise provided for, a sum not exceeding twenty dollars for each year, to be allowed by the circuit court, and paid out of the county treasury ; *provided*, that no fees shall be allowed for service of *scire facias** against a defaulting juror, if not fined by the court ; for executing all process, orders, and citations of county court, the same fees as are allowed for similar services in a circuit court of law.

In the Supreme Court.—For an arrest, one dollar; docketing process and return thereof, twenty-five cents; serving *scire facias** or summons, fifty cents. For all other services required by the sheriff in the supreme court, the fees shall be the same as are allowed for similar services in the circuit courts.

APPROVED OCT. 30, 1888.

SECTION X.

RANGERS.

1. Be it enacted by the general council of the Choctaw nation assembled: The ranger of each county shall be commissioned by the principal chief, and before he enters upon the duties of his office he shall take and subscribe the oath required by the constitution, before any judge of a court of record, which shall be certified on the back of his commission by the judge administering the oath, and shall give bond with good security to be approved by the county judge in the penalty of five hundred dollars payable to said county judge and his successors in office, conditioned for the faithful performance of the duties of his office, which bond, with the approbation therein named, endorsed thereon, shall together with the endorsement, be recorded in the office of the clerk of the

Scire Facias—a judicial writ summoning a person to show cause to the court why something should not be done.

county court of the county for which said ranger is elected, and shall not be void on the first recovery, but may
be put in suit and prosecuted by any party injured until
the whole penalty thereof be recovered. The ranger of
every county shall keep a book in which he shall register all the certificates of strays delivered to him by the
taker-up of strays, or transmitted to him by any county
judge of the county, and shall file the same in regular
order; it shall be his duty to cause a copy of the certificate of every appointment to be posted in the public
places in his county; he shall also make out a fair and
and correct list of all strays, and post the same at the
place of holding the county court of his county, on the
first day of each meeting of said court, omitting such
strays as are proven away, sold, or escaped, or dead,
under a penalty of ten dollars for every such neglect or
omission. And it shall be the ranger's duty to record
all marks and brands of his county.

2. When any stray shall be proven away, the
owner thereof shall pay to the taker-up and the ranger
one dollar and fifty cents each for every horse, mule or
pony ; fifty cents for every cow, oxen, or other head of
cattle ; and twelve and a half cents for every sheep, hog
and goat. When any stray shall have been found dead,
or shall have escaped, the taker up shall, without delay,
report thereof to the ranger, on oath, who shall make a
memorandum of the same, on the margin of his book,
where the certificate of such stray was registered.

3. After the expiration of twelve months from the
date of the certificate of strays, as aforesaid, and if no
owner appear and prove his or her property, the stray
or strays so taken up and appraised, as aforesaid, shall
be exposed to public sale for cash or county paper, by
the ranger, who shall give public notice of such sale, at
least twenty days previous thereto, by advertisement

thereof, in writing at the place where the courts are usually held, and at two other public places in the county, and
he shall describe the stray or strays, intended to be sold,
in the advertisement, and from the proceeds of such sale,
the ranger is hereby directed to pay to the taker-up one
half the sum thereof, and the other half to the county
treasurer for county purposes; *provided*, that such taker-
up shall pay the ranger one dollar and fifty cents, and
all other expenses that may be prescribed by law. It
shall be the duty of the ranger, as soon as money shall
be made by the sale of the stray or strays, to pay the
net proceeds thereof to the county treasurer to be appropriated to county purposes, deducting five per centum
commission for his services; and in case of default of
the ranger, his bond shall be put in suit by the county
judge, for the time being, for such delinquency ; and it
shall be lawful for any person claiming the proceeds of
the sale of such stray or strays, within twelve months
thereafter, to make claim to the same before the county
judge of the county, and an order shall issue for the net
proceeds thereof, on the county treasurer, on proof of
title of same.

4. All strays, horses, mares, mules, jacks, jennets,
ponies, and colts and cattle, shall be brought to the place
where the county court sits in each county, where said
strays have been taken up, on the day of sale, and there
publicly exposed from ten till three o'clock of said day.
The sale days of the rangers shall be quarter-annually
in each county on the first day of each regular term of
the county court, and they shall report to the judges of
the county courts of their respective counties, quarter-
yearly, the amount of moneys received by them, on account of the sale of strays.

5. The ranger of each county shall receive, as fees
of office, for every horse or mule sold, one dollar and

fifty cents; for every cow, oxen, or other head of cattle
sold, fifty cents; for every sheep, hog, or goat sold,
twelve and a half cents; for every certificate posted up,
fifty cents, to be paid out of the proceeds of sale.

SECTION XII.   APPROVED CCT. CO, 18C

WITNESSES.

1. Be it enacted by the general council of the Choctaw nation assembled : All witnesses who are subpœnaed by the proper authority of the several courts in
this nation, shall make their appearance according to
the subpœnas served on them, and forthwith go to the
clerks of their respective courts and register their names
and mileage, and also what cases they are witnesses in,
and whether for or against the nation; and all witnesses
summoned to attend court, shall be allowed five cents
per mile each way, going to and returning from court,
and one dollar and fifty cents per day while attending
court until discharged, to be paid in county scrip in their
respective counties where their services are rendered.
It shall be the duty of their respective circuit and county
judges, in all cases continued in their courts, to have the
witness called up and paid off, and notified when to appear again, and that they will not be summoned any
more; and if they fail to appear at the time and place
they have been notified to, shall be fined. All parties
losing their cases in civil suits, shall pay the witness
fees in bill of cost, and the witness fees be retained to
reimburse the county by the county treasurer.

2. When two or more witnesses shall appear before
any court of justice to testify to any case pending before
the court, it shall be the duty of the judge to order the
sheriff to keep such witnesses separate from each other
at court until their whole testimony is taken separately,

that the trial may be fair and impartial. In every case when the testimony of a witness, with answers to the cross questions thereon, are given before any of the courts of this nation, the clerk thereof shall read the testimony so given to such witness and inform the witness that it is his or her privilege to correct any mistakes, by omission or otherwise, found therein, before signing the same. When corrected, such witness shall sign it, and when so corrected and signed such testimony shall be endorsed by the judge presiding and attested by the clerk.

APPROVED OCT. 29, 1888.

SECTION XIII.

ATTORNEY-AT-LAW.

1. Be it enacted by the general council of the Choctaw nation assembled: Any person who may hereafter apply for admission to practice as an attorney at-law, may undergo an examination before any one of the judges of the supreme court, in or out of term time; and if such persons applying, be found to possess a competent share of law knowledge, and be of good character, such judge shall grant him a license under his hand and seal, to practice as an attorney-at-law in all the courts of law in this nation. The attorney-at-law who shall be permitted to practice law in this nation, will pay for the license granted ten dollars, and that the funds shall be applied for county purposes in which he shall reside.

2. Any attorney who may have been paid to prosecute or defend any suit in any of the courts of the Choctaw nation, and who after receiving such pay shall accept or receive any compensation or pay from the opposing parties, for services rendered them in the same suit, shall, after the fact has been established to the satisfaction of the court wherein such suit may be tried or pending, be thenceforward prohibited from practicing in said

courts, or others in the Choctaw nation. An order prohibiting such attorney so offending from practicing
therein shall be entered upon the records of said court,
and a copy of such order shall be furnished by the clerk
to the clerk of the supreme 'court.

APPROVED CCT, 30, 1888

SECTION XIV.

SENTENCES AND EXECUTIONS.

1. Be it enacted by the general council of the Choctaw nation assembled: When any defendant shall be
sentenced to the punishment of death, the court shall
make out, sign and deliver to the sheriff of the county a
warrant stating the conviction of such defendant, and
the sentence of court, and appointing a day for the execution of such sentence, not less than two nor more than
four weeks from the date of such sentence, unless the
court shall suspend sentence and execution on account
of some matter of law arising on the trial, or some other
legal cause. And any person in custody after conviction of a criminal offense, who may desire his, her or
their case revised by the supreme court, upon writ of
error, may prosecute such writ without being present in
person before said court. But if the defendant be not
removed on writ of error, by order of court, he, she or
they shall be detained according to the judgment of the
circuit court in which he, she or they was convicted, until the supreme court shall have decided his, her or their
case, and the judgment thereof shall have been certified
to the circuit court, and the same fully executed.

2. The punishment of death shall be inflicted by
shooting the convict until he, she or they be dead, and
shall be inflicted at the circuit court ground, in each district of this nation, where he, she or they were convicted,
and that ministers of the gospel, physicians and deputy

sheriffs of the county in which the convict is confined, may, on notification of the sheriff, attend such execution, and the sheriff shall make due return of the warrant of execution, of the execution thereof, which shall be attested by two of the deputy sheriffs present, and said warrant of execution shall be returned by the sheriff to the clerk of the court from which said warrant was issued, to be filed by the clerk among the proceedings in said case as a part thereof.

3. Whenever, from any cause, any convict, under sentence of death, shall not have been executed according to the order and judgment of the court, and the same shall stand in force and unrevised in the court where such sentence was pronounced, the judge of said court shall in term time or vacation, upon the application of the district attorney, stating such facts of the non-execution of convicts, according to the sentence of court, which said application shall be filed by the clerk among the proceedings in said case thereof, the judge of said court shall issue a writ of habeas corpus, to bring such convict before such judge, or if he, she, or they be at large, shall issue a writ for his, her or their apprehension, and, upon such convict being brought before such judge by virtue of said writ, the judge shall, if no legal reason exist against the execution of such sentence, immediately thereafter issue a warrant to the sheriff of the proper county, reciting the facts and commanding the sheriff, on a day to be specified in said warrant, to execute said sentence according to law.

SECTION XV. APPROVED OCT. 20, 1888

DEPOSITIONS.

1. Be it enacted by the general council of the Choctaw nation assembled : It shall be lawful for parties litigant in any of the courts of this nation to take the

depositions of any and all parties absent from the limits of this nation, or beyond the limits of the county or district in which the cause may be on trial, or in the following cases, to-wit : If the witness be sick or of old age, so that it would be impossible for them to attend without danger to their health, and when the witness is absent or about to be absent from the nation at the term of the court to which the cause is triable ; *provided*, that any person wishing to take deposition shall give the opposite party or their attorney ten days' notice of the time and place of taking such depositions, which depositions shall be taken before the county judge of the county where the witness resides ; the said judge shall first administer an oath to the party giving depositions, etc., and the depositions so taken, shall be read in evidence in any court or courts of this nation, and shall have the same force and effect as if the person was personally present.

APPROVED OCT. 20, 1888.

SECTION XVI.

ARBITRATION.

1. Be it enacted by the general council of the Choctaw nation assembled : When an arbitrator or arbitrators are chosen by two or more persons to decide and settle any matters in controversy, it will be necessary for each person in controversy to furnish their arbitrator or arbitrators, all proofs, facts, and statements, or any evidence they may possess in finding the case, and upon impartial trial of the same by the arbitrators, as well as his or their opinion and judgment rendered on the matter in controversy, shall be as final and binding on all the persons concerned in choosing an arbitration as if it were done in any court of justice. But in case the arbitrators cannot agree in forming a decision on any case before them, they shall have the right of choosing an

umpire whose decision shall be final and conclusive. When a decision is rendered by an arbitrator or arbitrators on any matter in controversy, such decision shall be recorded in the nearest county court.

SECTION XVII.

APPROVED OCT. 29, 1883.

FINES AND BONDS.

1. Be it enacted by the general council of the Choctaw nation assembled: The circuit courts of the Choctaw nation shall have jurisdiction in all matters of fines and bonds to be collected, and that all suits to be instituted against delinquent parties resting under fines, and against the principal and securities to all bonds forfeited to said nation, the district attorney shall commence by information to the circuit court in the district wherein the prime delinquent may reside. To begin action on fines and the forfeitures of bonds, the evidence in such cases must be records of courts, or such as required by law, and the rules of the several circuit courts in criminal cases, except as to cases which come within the personal knowledge of the circuit courts themselves, when an action will lie. In all cases of imposition and conviction of fines and the forfeitures of bonds, the circuit courts shall direct their clerks to enter up judgments thereon upon the records of said courts, in the necessary amounts, and to issue writs of execution thereon directed to the sheriff of the county of the delinquents, commanding said sheriff to levy upon and sell any property of said delinquents, not exempt under existing laws (act approved Nov. 14, 1854.)

2. Said sheriff, before selling any property under the requirements of this act, shall give at least thirty days' notice by putting up notices in at least three public places in the county, such sale to be to the highest

bidder, and at the court grounds for that county, and between the hours of nine a. m. and five p. m. on the first Monday of some month.

3. All recoveries under this act shall first be pevoted to the payments of costs, the balance to go to the Choctaw nation, and the first recovery, either upon fines or forfeitures of bonds, shall be final in that county; but the circuit courts may have certified copies of writs of execution forwarded to such other counties as defendants or sureties may have property in, there to be executed as a similar process from the circuit court would be, if first directed to the sheriff in that county.

4. In all cases coming up under this act, the circuit court shall direct its clerk to make an entry on his docket as in criminal cases; for instance: The Choctaw nation vs. A. B., or E. F., as the case may be.

5. In making up bonds, the securities shall be required to make oath before some officer competent to administer oaths, as to what the cash valuation of their property is, over and above what is exempt from execution.

APPROVED OCT. 00, 1888.

SECTION XVIII.

EXEMPTIONS.

1. Be it enacted by the general council of the Choctaw nation assembled: When any fine is imposed upon offenders against the laws of the Choctaw nation, and when the sheriffs are ordered by the judges as directed by law to levy upon property, and sell the same to pay the fine or fines imposed, there shall be reserved unto the offenders the house furniture and farming utensils from being taken and sold.

APPROVED OCT. 00, 1888.

ELECTIONS.

SECTION I.

1. Be it enacted by the general council of the Choctaw nation assembled : The several county judges of the nation shall, at the term of their respective courts, one month immediately preceding each general election, appoint three discreet persons for each precinct in their respective counties having the qualifications of electors, to act as judges of election in their respective beats; and the judges so appointed shall select two persons having the like qualifications to act as clerks thereof; but if the court shall fail to appoint election judges, or those appointed shall fail to act, it shall be the duty of the voters, when assembled, to appoint suitable persons to fill such vacancies. And it shall be the duty of the judges of the county courts, at least twenty days previous to any election, to make or cause to be made out four blank poll books, two for district and county officers, and two for principal chief, or national officers, and to provide for each precinct ink, pens, paper and wafers, sufficient for the purposes thereof, the same to be paid out of the county treasury upon the certificate of the judge so providing the same, etc., and shall deliver the said books so made out to the sheriff or his deputy, to be used at their respective precincts, etc.

2. It shall be the duty of the several sheriffs of the counties of this nation, at least one month before each election, to make public proclamation throughout their respective counties of the time and places of holding the election, and the officers to be elected at that time; and post up notices of the same at each precinct, or at two or more public places in their respective counties.

3. The judges and clerks of election shall severally take and subscribe before some judge of a court of record the following oath to-wit: "I do solemnly swear that I will perform the duties of judge of the present election, according to law and the best of my abilities, and that I will studiously endeavor to prevent fraud and deceit in conducting the same." And the clerks of election shall take the following oath, viz: "I do solemnly swear that I will faithfully record the names of all voters voting at the present election, and carry out in lines and columns all the votes polled, etc." But in case there be no person present at the opening of any election, authorized by law to administer the oath of office, it shall be lawful for the judges of the election appointed to administer the oath to each other, and then to the clerks, and such judges shall be vested with full power to administer all oaths that may be necessary in conducting any election.

4. The judges of each election shall open the polls in the morning at eight o'clock, and shall close the same at sunset on the same day, and the judges of election shall order the sheriff or his deputy to take and confine any person for misbehavior or contempt of such judges holding any election, and may impose a fine upon such offender not to exceed ten dollars.

5. The election judges of each election precinct shall have power and are hereby authorized to appoint two clerks whose duty it shall be to write election tickets for voters; said clerks to be sworn by the election judges and shall receive two dollars each for such service, to be paid from the county treasury; and any such clerk who shall falsely write or insert other names in the election ticket than those desired and mentioned by the voter, shall be deemed guilty of a felony, and upon indictment and conviction be punished with thirty lashes on the bare back; and then every voter takes a ticket

and presents the same to the judges of election, who being satisfied with the qualification of such voter, shall number the ticket which shall correspond with the number of such voter named on the margin of the poll box, and the judges shall deposit the ticket in the ballot box. The clerks of the election shall write the name of each and every voter voting on the poll book, numbering the same on the margin from one to the whole number of votes polled at such election, thus:

No.	Names of Voters.

6. Whenever any person offers to vote, and the judges have any doubts as to his qualifications, they are hereby authorized to examine the party under oath to satisfy themselves as to his qualifications, and may call upon any other parties to answer questions as regards such person's qualifications. Any person or persons, not being qualified voters according to the constitution and laws of this nation, and shall wilfully and knowingly vote in any election, shall forfeit and pay in the sum of twenty-five dollars, to be recovered before any circuit judge, one-half for the use of the county, and the other half for the use of the person suing for the same, and any person or persons voting more than once in any one election held in this nation, shall forfeit and pay the sum of fifty dollars, to be recovered before any circuit judge, one-half for the use of the county, and the other half for the use of the person suing for the same. If any judge or clerk of any election, or any other officer concerned in conducting an election shall neglect, improperly delay, or refuse to perform any of the duties required by law, having undertaken to do so, or shall knowingly permit any person to vote not qualified according to the constitution and laws, or shall not seal their poll book,

or shall unduly attempt to influence the election, or shall knowingly do any other improper act, during his term of office, in any manner interfering in the election shall forfeit the sum of fifty dollars, to be recovered before the circuit judge, one-half for the use of the county, the other half for the use of the person suing for the same.

7. At the close of every election the judges of the election shall certify under their hands and seals the number of votes given to each person, and the office for which such votes were given, and it shall also be attested by the clerks of the election, and after closing the polls and making the certificates required by law, the judges of the election shall fold up one of the poll books for district and county offices, enclosing the certificate required by law, and shall seal and endorse the same, and direct to the supreme judge of the district; and the package so endorsed and directed shall be carried by the sheriff or his deputy to the supreme judge of the district within five days after the closing of the polls, and the other poll book for district and county offices shall be returned by the election judges to the clerk of the county court for the inspection of all persons interested. "*Provided*, that in case there should be no sheriff nor deputy sheriff present at the election, the judges of the election shall have power to appoint some discreet person, who shall be sworn by the election judges, to take charge of said poll books and safely carry them to the sheriff of the county; and that the person so appointed shall be allowed two dollars for the services so rendered to be paid from the county treasury upon the certificate of the election judges. It shall be the duty of the judges of the election to certify to their poll books in the following form, to-wit:

"We do certify that the votes given in this poll book

are true and correct, this the —— day of —— A. D. 18——.
Signed and Sealed   [SEAL.]
                                                     [SEAL.]
                                                     [SEAL.]

8. On the tenth day after the close of such election,
or sooner, if all the returns have been received, the supreme judge shall call to his assistance three or more
county judges of his district, or other competent persons,
and shall proceed to open poll books for district and
county officers, and compare the several election returns
which may have been forwarded to such supreme judge,
and make abstracts of the votes given for the several
candidates for such office on separate sheets of paper,
but he shall not open the election returns for the prin·
cipal chief or national officers, but forward them as the
constitution directs, in reference to principal chief. Such
abstract of votes made by said supreme judge according to law, shall be signed by him and forwarded to the
national secretary. The candidates receiving the highest number of legal votes for district and county offices
shall be by such supreme judge declared elected, and he
shall issue certificates to the persons elected, district
and county offices. But in the election of district and
county officers, if there should be a tie vote, or if two or
more candidates shall be equal, or highest in votes, the
supreme judge shall forthwith report the fact to the principal chief, giving the names of the two or more candidates so tied; and the principal chief shall forthwith ap
point one of the candidates to the position mentioned
in the report of the supreme judge. And in the election
of national officers, the poll books shall be delivered by
the national secretary to the speaker of the house of
representatives, who shall proceed to examine and count
all of the legal votes in the presence of both branches
of the general council. And in the event of a tie vote,

or if two or more candidates shall be equal or highest in votes then the speaker shall notify the two houses, and the members thereof shall proceed to vote, as directed in section three, article five, executive department of the constitution, for the officers, after the manner of electing the principal chief.

9. It shall not be lawful for the supreme judges of the several districts of this nation to receive and include the votes in any of the poll books returned to him, without the same shall be in strict conformity to law. But he shall re-seal and forward the same, with his endorsement thereon, considered illegal, to the national secretary, to be by him laid before the general council at its next regular session, for the consideration of that body. If any supreme judge or other person concerned in comparing the returns of any election, shall neglect, improperly delay, or refuse to perform any of the duties required by law, having undertaken to do so, or shall refuse to take any poll book or books or shall refuse to count any of the legal votes, or any one legal vote of a citizen entitled to vote according to the constitution and laws of this nation, shall each forfeit and pay the sum of five hundred dollars, to be collected in the circuit court of his district, one half for county purposes wherein he was convicted, and the other half for the use of the person suing the same. Any person or persons who shall order or direct, or who may be engaged as judge, clerk, sheriff, or returning officer, or in any other capacity, at an election in the nation, held by direction of any person other than an officer duly elected, qualified, and so empowered under the Choctaw government, or under any law not legally passed by the proper and regularly constituted law-making power of this nation, or at such times and places as may be prescribed therein, shall, upon conviction by indictment, before the circuit court,

be deemed guilty of a misdemeanor, and shall be fined in a sum not less than one hundred dollars nor more than five hundred dollars, and also, be imprisoned in the county jail of any county the court may direct, for a term not less than six months nor more than twelve months, at the discretion of the court; and all fines thus collected shall be paid, one-half to the informer and the other half to the proper county for county purposes.

10. The judges and clerks of election shall each receive for their services the sum of two dollars, to be paid out of the national treasury. APPROVED OCT. 30, 1888.

AN ACT making the killing a person for a witch a capital offense.

SEC 3. Be it enacted by the general council of the Choctaw nation assembled: That any person or persons who shall kill another for a witch or wizard, shall suffer death.

And any person who shall publicly state that he himself or she herself is a witch or wizard, or shall say that such a person or persons are witches or wizards, and he or she knows it to be so, shall receive sixty lashes on the bare back.

Approved November 6, 1834.

AN ACT respecting Wills.

SEC. 4. Be it enacted by the general council of the Choctaw nation assembled: That all wills made either verbally or in writing, in the presence of two or more witnesses, shall be valid to all intents and purposes.

Approved November 7, 1834.

An Act forbidding compensation for damages, and making the person destroying the stock of another, when the fence is not lawful, liable to make restitution.

SEC. 6. Be it enacted by the general council of the Choctaw nation assembled : That no person or persons shall be allowed any compensation for any damage that he may sustain from stock breaking into his farm, unless his or her fence be made of good rails and ten rails high.

And be it further enacted, That if any one not having a lawful fence should destroy or injure the stock of another for breaking into his or her farm, he or she shall be liable to pay the value of the stock so injured or destroyed.

Approved November 8, 1834.

An Act making the owners of hogs responsible for all damages where the fence is lawful.

SEC. 1. Be it enacted by the general council of the Choctaw nation assembled: That a fence of four inch cracks between each rail, for two and a half feet from the ground, shall be considered a lawful fence; and hogs breaking into a field having such fence, the owner or owners of such hogs shall be responsible for all the damages sustained, and the courts of the several districts shall have cognizance of such cases.

Approved October 4, 1836.

An Act declaring the punishment for selling of the country.

SEC. 2. Be it enacted by the general council of the Choctaw nation assembled: That any chief, captain or citizen of this nation who shall sign any instrument of writing in any way conveying or making sale of any portion or the whole of the Choctaw nation, shall be deemed a traitor and an enemy to his country, and shall suffer death.

Approved October 9, 1839.

AN ACT entitled an act repealing certain laws, acts and resolutions of the Choctaw general council, passed between the 1st February, 1861, and 1st September, A. D. 1865.

SECTION 1. Be it enacted by the general council of the Choctaw nation assembled: That all laws, acts, and resolutions, or parts thereof, in any way abridging or impairing any rights and privileges previously existing; and all laws, acts, and resolutions, or parts thereof, in any way conflicting with the constitution and laws of the United States, and which may have been passed at any session of the general council of the Choctaw nation, between the first day of February, A. D. 1861, and and the first day of September, A. D. 1865, be and the same are hereby repealed.

SEC. 2. Be it further enacted: That this law take effect and be in force from and after its passage.

Approved October 13, 1865.

CRIMINAL OFFENSES.

SECTION I.

TREASON.

1. Be it enacted by the general council of the Choctaw nation assembled : Levying war against this nation or adhering to its enemies, giving them aid and comfort, shall be deemed and adjudged treason against this nation, and shall be punished with death upon conviction thereof. But no person shall be convicted of treason against this nation unless upon the testimony of two witnesses to the same overt act or on his own confession in open court.

APPROVED OCT. 30, 1888.

SECTION II.

MURDER.

1. Be it enacted by the general council of the Choctaw nation assembled: The killing of a human being without the authority of law, by any means, or in any manner, shall be murder in the following cases: When done with deliberate design to effect the death of the person killed or of any human being. When done in the commission of an act eminently dangerous to others, and evincing a depraved heart, regardless of human life, although without any premeditated design to effect the death of any particular individual. When done without any design to effect death, by any person engaged in the commission of the crime of rape, burglary, arson or robbery, or in an attempt to commit such felonies. And every person who shall be convicted of murder, shall suffer death.

2. The killing of a human being, by the act, procurement or admission of another, shall be justifiable in the following cases : When committed by public officers or those acting by their command, in their aid or assistance, in obedience to any judge of a competent court ; or, when necessarily committed in overcoming actual resistance to the execution of some legal process, or to the discharge of any other legal duty ; or, when neces sarily committed in retaking any felon who has been rescued or has escaped ; or, when necessarily committed in arresting any felon fleeing from justice. Such homicide or murder shall also be justifiable when committed by any person : In resisting any attempt unlawfully to kill such person or to commit any felony upon him, or upon, or in any dwelling house in which such person shall be ; or when committed in the lawful defense of such person or any other human being, where there shall be reasonable ground to apprehend a design to commit a felony, or to do some great personal injury, and there shall be imminent danger of such being accomplished ; or when necessarily committed in attempting by lawful ways and means, to apprehend any person for any felony committed, or in lawfully suppressing any riot, or in lawfully keeping and preserving the peace.

3. The killing of a human being by the act, procurement, or admission of another, shall be excusable when committed by accident and misfortune, in lawfully correcting a child or servant, or in doing any other lawful act by lawful means, with usual ordinary caution, and without any unlawful intent ; or, by accident and misfortune, in the heat of passion, upon any sudden and sufficient provocation, or upon any sudden combat, without any undue advantage being taken and without any dangerous weapons being used, and not done in a cruel or unlawful manner.

APPROVED OCT. 23, 1888.

SECTION III.

MANSLAUGHTER.

1. Be it enacted by the general council of the Choctaw nation assembled : The killing of a human being without malice, by the act, procurement, or culpable negligence of another, while such other is engaged in the perpetration of any felony, except rape, burglary, arson or robbery; or while such other is attempting to commit any felony, besides such as are above enumerated and excepted, shall be deemed manslaughter ; or the killing of a human being, without malice, by the act, procurement or culpable negligence of another, while such other is engaged in the perparation of any crime, or misdemeanor not amounting to felony ; or, in the attempt to perpetrate any crime or misdemeanor, in case when such killing would be murder under former laws, shall be deemed manslaughter. Every person deliberately assisting another in the commission of self-murder, shall be deemed guilty of manslaughter. The wilful killing of an unborn quick child, by any injury to the mother of such child, which would be murder if it resulted in the death of the mother, shall be deemed manslaughter. Every person who shall administer to any woman pregnant with a quick child, any medicine, drug or substance whatever, or shall use or employ any instrument or other means, with intent thereby to destroy such child, unless the same shall have been necessary to preserve the life of such mother, or shall have been advised by a physician to be necessary for such purpose, shall be deemed guilty of manslaughter. The killing of a human being, without malice, in the heat of passion, but in a cruel or unusual manner, without authorty of law and not in necessary self-defense,shall be deemed manslaughter. Every person who shall unnecessarily kill another, either while

resisting an attempt by such other person to commit any felony, or to do any other unlawful act, or after such attempt shall have have failed, shall be deemed guilty of manslaughter. The killing of another, in the heat of passion, without malice, by the use of a dangerous weapon, without authority of law, and not in necessary self-defense shall be deemed manslaughter. The involuntary killing of a human being, by the act, procurement, or culpable negligence of another, while such other person is engaged in the commission of a trespass, or other injury to private rights or property, or engaged in an attempt to commit such injury, shall be deemed manslaughter. Any person navigating any boat or vessel for gain, who shall wilfully or negligently receive so many passengers, or such quantity of other loading. that by means thereof such boat or vessel shall sink or overset, and thereby any human being shall be drowned, or otherwise killed, shall be deemed guilty of manslaughter. If any physician or other person, while in a state of intoxication, shall, without a design to effect death, administer, or cause to be administered, any poison, drug, or other medicine, or shall perform any surgical operation on another which shall cause the death of such other, he shall be deemed guilty of manslaughter. And every other killing of a human being, by the act, procurement, or culpable negligence of another, and without authority of law, not provided for in this section shall be deemed manslaughter. Any person convicted of the crime of manslaughter, under this section, shall receive one hundred lashes on the bare back.

ARTICLE IV.   **APPROVED OCT. 20, 1888.**

ASSAULT WITH INTENT TO KILL

1. Be it enacted by the general council of the Choctaw nation assembled: Any person who shoots at or

wounds any person, or persons, with a fire-arm of any
kind ; or who cuts, or attempts to cut, any person or
persons, with a knife or any other kind of pointed or
edged tool or instrument, thereby endangering the life
of any person or persons, shall be deemed guilty of
assault with intent to kill ; and any person or persons
so assaulting another, shall be indicted by the grand
jury, and shall be tried in the circuit court the same as
other crimes against the laws of the Choctaw nation are
tried, and upon conviction thereof shall be fined not less
than twenty-five dollars, nor more than five hundred
dollars, and costs of the suit, to be levied on his goods
and chattels ; one-half the fine for the benefit of the
person or persons assaulted, the other half for the use of
the county.

APPROVED OCT. 30, 1888

ASSAULT AND BATTERY.

2. Be it enacted by the general council of the Choctaw nation assembled : If any person or persons should
strike or otherwise injure another person without provocation, through malice, so that such injured person
should lose any time from his business, the person so
offending shall be liable to be sued in the courts of this
nation, and shall be subject to fine and be compelled to
pay such fine as the jury may determine, which fine,
when collected, shall be paid over to the person so
maimed or injured.

APPROVED OCT. 30, 1888.

SECTION V.

RAPE.

1. Be it enacted by the general council of the Choctaw nation assembled: Any person convicted of the
crime of committing rape, or forcibly ravishing a woman
or girl, shall receive one hundred lashes laid on his bare
back, and for the second offence of the same nature, the

offender shall suffer death. But in case of an attempt only, to ravish a woman or girl, the court shall determine the penalty; *provided*, the guilty person shall not receive more than thirty lashes on the bare back, for an attempt.

SECTION VI.

APPROVED OCT. 20, 1888,

POLYGAMY AND ADULTERY.

1. Be it enacted by the general council of the Choctaw nation assembled: Any person or persons who shall be convicted of polygamy, or living with each other in adultery, shall be liable to indictment before any court in this nation, and fined not exceeding twenty-five dollars, nor less than ten dollars for each of such offenses. Any person or persons who may be living together out of wedlock, shall be compelled to be lawfully joined together, or the party refusing so to do, shall be indicted and fined not less than ten dollars, nor exceeding twenty-five dollars for every such offense; and the informant in all such offenses as above specified, shall be entitled to, and receive one-third of the fines that may be so collected, and after deducting the fees of the district attorney, the remainder shall become county funds.

SECTION VII. APPROVED OCT. 20, 1888,

INCEST.

1. Be it enacted by the general council of the Choctaw nation assembled: The son shall not marry his mother; the son shall not marry his step-mother; the brother shall not marry his sister nor his sister's daughter; the father shall not marry his daughter; the father shall not marry his daughter's daughter begotten of his step mother, nor his aunt, being his father's or mother's sister; the father shall not marry his son's widow; a man

shall not marry his wife's daughter, or his wife's daughter's daughter, or his wife's son's daughter, and the like
prohibition shall extend to females within the same de-
gress, and all marriages of this nature are hereby declared incestuous and void. If any person shall marry
within the degrees prohibited by law, on conviction thereof, they shall be fined two hundred dollars, or each receive one hundred lashes well laid on their bare backs,
and such marriage is declared incestuous and void. If
any persons who have been divorced for incest, shall,
after such divorce, cohabit or live together as man and
wife, such persons so offending shall be deemed guilty
of incest, and fined on conviction, two hundred dollars,
or receive two hundred lashes, during two days, well
laid on the bare back, or both at the discretion of the
court.   APPROVED

SECTION VIII.

INTER-MARRIAGE BETWEEN CHOCTAWS AND NEGROES,

1. Be it enacted by the general council of the Choctaw nation assembled: It shall not be lawful for a
Choctaw and a negro to marry; and if a Choctaw man
or Choctaw woman should marry a negro man or negro
woman he or she shall be deemed guilty of a felony, and
shall be proceeded against in the circuit court of the
Choctaw nation having jurisdiction the same as all other
felonies are proceeded against; and if proven guilty
shall receive fifty lashes on the bare back.

APPROVED OCT 20 1888

SECTION IX.

UNNATURAL INTERCOURSE.

1. Be it enacted by the general council of the Choctaw nation assembled ; Every person who shall be convicted of the detestable and abominable crime against

nature, committed with mankind, shall, upon conviction, suffer death by being hung by the neck until dead. Any person convicted of having intercourse with any beast shall receive on his, her, or their bare backs thirty-nine lashes well laid on.

SECTION X.

POISONING.

APPROVED OCT. 30, 1888.

1. Be it enacted by the general council of the Choctaw nation assembled : Every person who shall be convicted of having administered, or having caused, or procured to be administered, any poison to any human being with intent to kill such being, and which shall have been actually taken by such being, whereof death shall not ensue, shall be punished by imprisonment not less than three months in the county or district jail and receive one hundred lashes well laid on the bare back. Every person who shall mingle any poison with any food, drink, or medicine with intent to kill or injure any human being, or who shall wilfully poison any spring, well, or reservoir of water shall, upon conviction, be punished by imprisonment in the county or district jail not exceeding three months, and receive one hundred lashes well laid on their bare back, or by such imprisonment and a fine not exceeding two hundred dollars, or all, at the discretion of the court. Every person who shall wilfully and unlawfully administer any poison to any horse, mare, colt, mule, jack, jennet, cattle, dog, or sheep, or shall maliciously expose any poisonous substance, with the intent that the same should be taken or swallowed by any horse, mare, colt, mule, jack, jennet, cattle or sheep, shall upon conviction, be punished by imprisonment in the county jail not exceeding one month, by a fine of not exceeding fifty dollars and receive thirty-nine lashes well laid on the bare back.

APPROVED OCT. 30, 1888.

SECTION IX.

MAYHEM.

1.   Be it enacted by the general council of the Choctaw nation assembled: Every person who, from premeditated design, or with intent to kill, or commit any felony, shall mutilate, disfigure, disable or destroy the tongue, eye, lip, nose, or any other limb or member, of any person, shall be guilty of mayhem, and on conviction thereof shall receive one hundred lashes well laid on the back.

APPROVED OCT. 30, 1888

SECTION XII.

KIDNAPING.

1.   Be it enacted by the general council of the Choctaw nation assembled : Every person who shall without lawful authority, forcily seize and confine any other, or shall inveigle or kidnap any other, with intent either to cause such other person to be secretly confined or imprisoned in this nation, against his will ; or to cause such other person to be sent out of the nation against his or her will ; or to cause such other person to be sold as a slave, or to be deprived of his liberty, or in any way held to service against his or her will, shall upon conviction, be punished by being branded with the letter "T" on the forehead and receive one hundred lashes well laid on the bare back; and every offense prohibited herein may be tried in the district where the same may have been committed, or in any district into or through which any person so kidnaped or confined shall have been taken while under such confinement; and upon the trial of any such offense, the consent of the person so kidnaped or confined, shall not be defense unless it appear satisfactorily to the jury that such consent was not by threats or duress.

APPROVED OCT. 30, 1888

SECTION XIII.

ROBBERY.

1. Be it enacted by the general council of the Choctaw nation nation assembled: If any person or persons shall assault another, and shall feloniously rob, steal and take from his or her possession, any money or other property which may be the subject of larceny, such robber being armed with a dangerous weapon, with intent, if resisted, to kill or maim the person robbed, or if being so armed, he, she or they shall shall wound or strike the person robbed, he, she or they shall be punished by death. If any person or persons shall by force and violence, or by assault, or putting in fear, feloniously rob, steal and take from the person or premises of another, any money or other property which may be the subject of larceny, such robber, not being armed with a dangerous weapon, he, she or they shalle be punished with one hundred lashes well laid on his, her, or their bare backs, and further pay damages to the party from whom such arrest shall have been made, to be assessed by the petit jury of the circuit court, etc.

SECTION XIV.

APPROVED OCT. 20, 1888.

CRUELTY TO STOCK.

1. Be it enacted by the general council of the Choctaw nation assembled: Every person who shall maliciously, either out of a spirit of revenge, or wanton cruelty, or who shall mischievously kill, maim, or wound any horse, mare, gelding, mule, sheep, cattle, hog, poultry, or other live stock, or cause any person to do the same, shall be fined in any sum not less than fifty dollars and receive thirty-nine lashes well laid on the bare back.

SECTION XV.

MALICIOUS MISCHIEF.

1. Be it enacted by the general council of the Choc-taw nation assembled: Every person who shall ma-liciously destroy disfigure, or injure, or caused to be de-stroyed or injured, any property of another, either per-sonal or tenements, shall be deemed guilty of malicious mischief, and upon conviction thereof shall be fined in a sum two-fold the value of the property destroyed or the damage done, and receive thirty-nine lashes well laid on the bare back.

SECTION XVI.

APPROVED OCT. 30, 1888.

BURGLARY.

1. Be it enacted by the general council of the Choc-taw nation assembled: Any person or persons, with or without arms, who shall break into or otherwise enter unlawfully and without permission, any dwelling house, store, house, or out building of any kind, with felonious intent, the same being lawfully occupied by any person, shall be held guilty of the crime of burglary, and shall be fined upon conviction thereof by the court having jurisdiction, twice the amount or value of property so taken or destroyed, and shall be compelled to return all property so taken found in his, her, or their possession, and shall receive not less than ten nor more than one hundred lashes well laid on his, her, or their bare backs, at the discretion of the court having jurisdiction of the same.

APPROVED OCT. 30, 1888.

SECTION XVII.

LARCENY.

1. Be it enacted by the general council of the Choc-taw nation assembled: Every person who shall be con-

victed of taking and carrying away, feloniously, the personal property of another, of the value of twenty-five dollars, or more, shall be guilty of grand larceny, and shall return such property or pay the value thereof and shall receive one hundred lashes well laid on the bare back, and on conviction of a second offense of horse-stealing, shall suffer death by hanging.

2. If any person shall feloniously take, steal, and carry away, any personal property of another, under the value of twenty-five dollars, he shall be deemed guilty of petit larceny, and shall return or pay for the property so stolen, and shall receive not more than one hundred lashes, at the discretion of the court.

3. The stealing and carrying away, or fraudulently withdrawing, concealing, or destroying, or taking away, by any person, any record, paper, or proceeding of a court of justice, or any paper or proceeding filed or deposited with any officer, or in any public office, shall be deemed larceny, without reference to the value of the record, paper, or proceeding, so stolen, taken away or destroyed, and shall receive thirty-nine lashes well laid on the bare back.

4. If any person shall be guilty of stealing or selling any stray animal, knowing the said animal stolen sold, to be a stray, and shall thereof be convicted, shall be deemed guilty of larceny, without reference to the value of such animal, and shall receive one hundred lashes well laid on the bare back. Any and all persons who shall kill or destroy cows, oxen, steers, heifers, bulls or calves, or sows, boars, barrows, or shoats, or sheep or lambs, or goats, either for the subsistence of himself, herself or themselves, or for purposes of sale, exchange, barter, and bargain, and shall cut off and secrete the ears and head, or the heads and ears and hides or skins,

or in any manner destroy the same so that such property cannot be properly identified as to true ownership thereof, shall be deemed and held as guilty of larceny, without reference to the ownership or value thereof, and upon conviction thereof, shall receive not less than twenty lashes nor more than one hundred lashes well laid on the bare back, at the discretion of the court having jurisdiction thereof.

5. Any person buying or receiving, in any manner, or on any consideration, any personal property of any value, feloniously taken away from another, knowing the same to have been so taken, shall receive one hundred lashes well laid on the bare back.

APPROVED OCT. 30, 1888

SECTION XVIII.

ARSON.

1. Be it enacted by the general council of the Choctaw nation assembled: Any person or persons who shall be convicted of the crime of burning another person's house or houses, or in any manner destroying the property belonging to a citizen of this nation, shall be subject to a fine equal to the value of the property so destroyed, and in addition thereto, shall receive such corporeal punishment as the court may determine; but such punishment shall not exceed thirty-nine lashes on the bare back, unless such person shall be unable to pay the fine, in which case he, she or they shall receive one hundred lashes.

APPROVED OCT. 30, 18

SECTION XII.

PERJURY,

1. Be it enacted by the general council of the Choctaw nation assembled: If any person or persons shall be convicted of false swearing, or making false state-.

ments in a court of justice, such offenders shall be fined not less than ten dollars nor exceeding one hundred dollars, and shall receive not less than five nor exceeding thirty-nine lashes on the bare back.

SECTION XX. APPROVED OCT. 30, 1888.

FORGERY.

1. Be it enacted by the general council of the Choctaw nation assembled: Every person who shall be convicted of having forged, counterfeited, or falsely altered any deed of gift, note or order, or any other instrument in which any valuable consideration may be in question, shall be guilty of forgery, and shall be punished with not less than thirty-nine lashes, and fined not less than twenty-five, nor exceeding five hundred dollars.

SECTION XXI. APPROVED OCT. 30, 1888.

ALTERATION OR DESTRUCTION OF WILLS.

1. Be it enacted by the general council of the Choctaw nation assembled: If any person shall wilfully alter or destroy any will or codicil, without the consent of the party making the same, or shall wilfully secrete the same for six months after the death of the testator shall be known to him, the person so offending, on conviction thereof, shall be fined or imprisoned in the county or district jail, or both, at the discretion of court.

SECTION XXII. APPROVED OCT. 30, 1888.

CHANGING RECORDS.

1. Be it enacted by the general council of the Choctaw nation assembled. If any clerk of any court, or public officer, or any other person, shall wittingly make any false entry, or erase any word or letter, or change any record belonging to any court or public office what-

ever, in his keeping or not, he shall, on conviction thereof, be imprisoned in the county or district jail for a term
not exceeding six months, pay a fine in a sum not exceeding one hundred dollars, and be liable to the action
of the party aggrieved.

APPROVED Oct. 30, 1888

SECTION XXIII.

LIBEL AND SLANDER.

1. Be it enacted by the general council of the Choctaw nation assembled: All words which from their
usual construction and common acceptation, are considered as insuits and lead to violence and breaches of
the peace shall, hereafter, be actionable, and no plea,
exception or demurrer, shall be sustained, in any court
within this nation to preclude a jury from passing thereon. who are hereby declared to be the sole judges of the
damages sustained.

2. Every person who shall be convicted of writing
or publishing any libel, or speaking words made actionable by the preceding paragraph, shall be fined in such
sum and receive such a number of lashes on the bare
back, as the court, in its discretion, may adjudge, having
regard to the nature and enormity of the offense ; but in
every criminal prosecution for libel or actionable words,
it shall be lawful for the defendant upon the trial, to
give in evidence in his defense the truth of the matter
written, spoken, or published.

APPROVED Oct. 30, 18

SECTION XXIV.

EMBEZZLEMENT OF PUBLIC MONEY.

1. Be it enacted by the general council of the Choctaw nation assembled : Any holder or receiver of public
money who shall waste, squander or embezzle the same
shall be guilty of a felony and, in addition to the for-

feiture of his official bond, shall be subject to indictment and trial before the circuit court of the district having jurisdiction, and upon conviction shall receive one hundred lashes on the bare back.

SECTION XXV.

APPROVED OCT. 30, 188?

INTRODUCTION OF WHISKY.

1. Be it enacted by the general council of the Choctaw nation assembled: It shall not be lawful for any person or persons to introduce, or cause to be introduced, for their own use, or to sell, give or barter, any vinous, spirituous, or intoxicating liquors, to any person or persons within the limits of this nation in any quantity whatever, (except wines, which may be introduced by a member of any church for sacramental uses), and such offense shall be subject to prosecution, by indictment and punishment upon conviction, according to the following provisions : Such person or persons so offending violating the provisions of this act, upon conviction thereof before the circuit court, having jurisdiction of the same, shall forfeit and pay a sum of not less than ten dollars, nor more than one hundred dollars for each and every offense; and, in default of payment of any such fine, he, she, or they, shall be imprisoned for a term of not less than one month, nor more than three months, at the discretion of the court; and any person or persons within the limits of this nation, found with any liquors, specified above, in their possession, shall be deemed guilty, upon full proof of such possession, in like manner, as if they had introduced the same, and shall be punished according to the preceding provisions of this act, unless his or her innocence of such charge be satisfactorily proven to the court.

2. It shall be the duty of the circuit judges of this nation to give this act in charge to the grand jury, each

of his own district, who shall make diligent inquiry con-concerning any and all violations of this act; and it shall be their duty, when they have reason to suspect or be-lieve that a violation of this act has taken place, to have a subpœna issued for such person or persons as they be-lieve can give information upon the subject, and such witnesses when summoned and appear, shall give evi-dence of every offense against the provisions of this act that may have come to his or her knowledge, without any special inquiry directed thereto; and in case any witness so summoned shall fail, or refuse to appear and testify, such witness shall suffer a penalty of ten dollars for each offense, to be collected by execution, unless by a *scire facias*, such witness shall be able to give suffi-cient excuse for such non appearance, or such refusal to testify.

3.   The sheriff, lighthorsemen and deputy sheriffs of each and every county of this nation, are hereby author-ized, upon suspicion, without warrant for the purpose, forcibly to enter all places, search for and seize, break and destroy all bottles, barrels, jugs, or any and every vessel of any description whatever, containing any liquors specified by this act, and shall arrest and convey before the nearest county judge the person or persons in whose possession such liquors may be found, which county judge shall bind such person or persons after proper and satisfactory showing to appear at the next term of the circuit court of his district, when he shall re-port the same to the court and grand jury; and for the hearing of each one of such cases, the county judge shall be entitled to receive one dollar, and the sheriff, light-horsemen or the deputy sheriffs two dollars, to be recov-ered upon conviction of the offender, and upon his fail-ure to pay the same, it shall be recovered by execution with the costs of prosecution; and if any person or per-

sons refuse to have his or her whisky or other intoxicating liquors destroyed by taking up arms, and should any one of the sheriffs, lighthorsemen, or deputies, in self-defense, kill or destroy the life of the person or persons having whisky, or any intoxicating liquors, he shall be protected by the laws of this nation. But should any offender kill or destroy the life of any person or persons authorized by this act, to destroy all whisky, or other intoxicating liquors, such person shall suffer death. But should the offender only destroy or injure the property or limbs of any of the above mentioned officers, he or she shall be liable to a fine or punishment, to be determined by the circuit court of the district wherein such offense may be committed.

4. If any person or persons shall give or barter any vinous, spirituous or intoxicating liquors, to any person or persons within the limits of this nation, and any person thereby be maimed or injured, such person who sold, gave or bartered the same, shall be liable to an action in court, and on conviction, shall be made to pay a fine of not less than five nor exceeding one hundred dollars, to the person so maimed or injured, and upon failure to pay the said sum, execution shall issue therefor, with the cost of prosecution.

5. For every conviction under this section, the district attorney shall be entitled to a fee of five dollars, to be paid by the person convicted, and on failure to pay said sum, execution shall issue therefor, with the cost of prosecution.

6. All fines collected from conviction had under the first and third paragraphs of this section shall be paid into the treasury of the county wherein the offense was committed, to be expended for such purposes as the county court thereof may direct.

APPROVED OCT. 30, 1888.

SECTION XXVI.

CARRYING PISTOLS.

1. Be it enacted by the general council of the Choctaw nation assembled : It shall not be lawful for any person to carry a pistol of any kind within the limits of the Choctaw nation, except the sheriffs and their deputies and the lighthorsemen and militia on duty and officers connected with the reserve service of this nation; and the grand jury shall indict all violators of this act, and all citizens that are convicted for violating this act shall be fined in any sum not exceeding fifty dollars and not less than five dollars, at the discretion of the circuit court having jurisdiction.

2. It shall be the duty of the sheriff and his deputies and lighthorsemen, to arrest all violators of this section without written process, upon their own sight or upon the information of any citizen of said nation, and require them or him to give bond to appear at the circuit court from day to day while said court is in session until discharged by due course of law; to dispossess all citizens and non-citizens residing in the Choctaw nation under a permit, and freedmen that formerly belonged to the Choctaws or Chickasaws, of any and all pistols they may be carrying in violation of this section and hold the same until the fines and costs of the court are paid; but if the said offenders are unable to pay said fine and costs then the circuit court shall issue execution against the pistols of said offender or offenders, which pistols shall be sold by the sheriff of the county wherein the arrest was made at auction, to pay costs first, and the remainder to be devoted to the payment of the fines; *provided*, *however*, that the circuit court shall have power to issue execution against any property of the offender, or offenders, liable to execution, to pay the penalties imposed by this section. Sheriffs, their deputies and lighthorse-

men, who refuse or neglect to discharge their duties under this section shall, on information before the circuit court having jurisdiction, be fined one hundred dollars for each offense; and all fines collected of sheriffs, their deputies or lighthorsemen, shall be turned into the county treasury of the county wherein the offense was committed, for county purposes.

3. If the information herein provided for shall be given by a private citizen of the nation, one-half of the fine shall be paid to the said informant, and the other half paid into the county treasury of the county wherein the offense was committed. No person or persons shall carry a gun of any kind to a religious meeting, school or gathering of any kind, except sheriffs, their deputies and lighthorsemen, and militia on duty; any persons violating this paragraph shall be fined in any sum not exceeding fifty dollars, nor less than five dollars; and it shall be the duty of the circuit judges of this nation to charge the grand jury to make inquiry for all violations of the provisions of this section.

APPROVED OCT. 30, 1888.

SECTION XXVII.

DISTURBANCE OF SCHOOLS, RELIGIOUS DEVOTION OR FAMILIES, ETC.

1. Be it enacted by the general council of the Choctaw nation assembled : Any person or persons who shall, under the influence of intoxicating drink, through malice or under any other circumstances in any manner disturb any religious meeting, social gathering, school or family, by whooping, shooting fire arms, talking in a loud or boisterous manner, using vulgar, obscene or profane language, or in any manner frightening said meeting, gathering, school or family, shall be guilty of disturbing the peace of the Choctaw nation, and shall be

indicted by the grand jury, and on conviction shall be fined not less than twenty–five dollars nor more than one hundred dollars, and in the event of his failure or inability to pay the fine imposed, he shall receive in lieu thereof not less than twenty-five nor more than one hundred lashes on the bare back, one-fourth of said fine to be paid to the complainant and the remainder to the county wherein the offense was committed.

SECTION XXVIII.

APPROVED OCT. 30, 188

SKINNING DEAD ANIMALS ON THE RANGE.

1. Be it enacted by the general council of the Choctaw nation assembled : It shall not be lawful for any person to skin any animal, the property of another, found dead on the range without the written permission of the owner thereof, and any person so offending, shall be deemed guilty of a felony ; and any person found with the hide of any animal in the mark or brand of another person, or which hide or hides have the marks or brands disfigured without the owner's written authority, shall be deemed guilty of petit larceny, and on conviction shall be punished with not more than thirty-nine lashes on the bare back in each case.

SECTION XXIX.
APPROVED OCT. 30, 1888.

HUNTING AND TRAPPING BY NON-CITIZEN INDIANS AND WHITE MEN.

1. Be it enacted by the general council of the Choctaw nation assembled : Any Indian not a citizen of the Choctaw nation, who shall be found guilty of hunting, trapping or taking and destroying any peltries, or game in this nation, shall be held to be a trespasser, and it shall be the duty of the judge of the county to issue a writ for the apprehension of the offender, wherein the

trespass was committed, to the sheriff of that county, to arrest such offender, and hold him in custody until the next regular term of the circuit court for that district or bind him over in a bond of two hundred and fifty dollars with good and sufficient securities for his appearance at the next regular term of said court to answer the charge preferred under this act. At each term of the circuit courts, the circuit judges shall charge the grand juries of their respective districts, to enquire into and for body of their respective districts for any violations of this act, present a true bill against such trespasser or trespassers: and upon fair and impartial trial in the district wherein such trespass or trespasses have been committed, and upon conviction they shall be fined twenty-five dollars for each offense.

2. One half of fines thus collected shall be divided equally between the sheriff and prosecuting attorney, and the other half shall be paid into the national treasury for the benefit of the school funds; and any property found in the possession of such trespasser or trespassers in the way of a horse, camp equipage, guns, ammunition, peltries, furs, or such as is usually found under such circumstances, shall be seized by the sheriff and held, to be applied to the payment of fines and cost of writ imposed and assessed by the circuit court having jurisdiction thereof.

3. Any citizens inviting others not citizens of this nation, to hunt upon the lands of said nation with guns of all kinds, dogs, hounds, etc., shall be made to suffer the penalty as an accessory.

4. A white man or white men not citizens of the Choctaw nation, who may be found hunting game, trapping, etc., within the limits of said nation shall be arrested by the sheriff of the county wherein such white man or white men are found hunting, trapping, etc., as afore-

said; being violators of the statutes of the United States, *provided*, for such cases; and turn them over to the United States authorities to be dealt with as the laws of said United States may direct.

SECTION XXX.   APPROVED OCT. 30, 1888.

PULLING DOWN FENCES.

1. Be it enacted by the general council of the Choctaw nation assembled: Any person or persons who shall be convicted of the crime or misdemeanor of pulling and leaving down any person's field or farm fence, shall be compelled to pay such a fine as the court may estimate the damage done to the owner of the farm.

SECTION XXXI.   APPROVED OCT. 30, 1888

CUTTING DOWN HICKORY OR PECAN TREES.

1. Be it enacted by the general council of the Choctaw nation assembled: No person or persons shall cut down hickory or pecan trees for nuts in this nation; and the persons so offending shall be liable to a fine of two dollars per tree, and one-half of said fine shall go to the informer and the other half shall be as county funds.

SECTION XXXII.   APPROVED OCT. 30, 1888

BURNING PRAIRIES AND WOODS.

1. Be it enacted by the general council of the Choctaw nation assembled: It shall not be lawful at any time for any person to set the prairies or woods on fire, except in the period of time between the 15th day of March and the 15th day of April each year; and any person or persons violating the provisions of this act, shall on conviction before the circuit judge, forfeit and pay the sum of twenty-five dollars, one-half to the use

of the county, and the other half to the person suing for the same.

2. If any person should be convicted of setting the woods or prairies on fire, and if the fire should destroy any stock, fences, or other articles of any persons, the offender shall be liable for all such damages and injuries done, and the court shall award judgment for the same, to be collected as other fines and forfeitures are collected. And any person or persons having knowledge of any person violating this section, and concealing or withholding the same, or refusing to give evidence against such offending person in any court having jurisdiction thereof, shall upon conviction be fined by the court having jurisdiction any sum not exceeding fifty dollars and not less than five dollars. The person suing such person or persons concealing or withholding the knowledge of the violation of this section shall be entitled to receive as a compensation one-half of the fine, and the other half to go to the county, in which the offense is committed, for county purposes.

APPROVED OCT. 30, 1868.

SECTION XXXIII.

SELLING GOODS ON SUNDAY.

1. Be it enacted by the general council of the Choctaw nation assembled: Any person or persons who shall expose goods, wares or merchandise on Sunday, shall be fined ten dollars with cost of prosecution for every such offense, before the proper court having jurisdiction thereof, and all fines when collected shall be paid into the treasury of the county, where the offense was committed, for county purposes; but this act shall not be so construed as to prevent the sale of medicine, burial clothes or provisions to the traveling community.

SECTION XXXIV.

RACING HORSES OR PLAYING BALL ON SUNDAY.

1. Be it enacted by the general council of the Choctaw nation assembled: Any person or persons making up ball plays or racing horses for bets or amusements on Sunday, shall be indicted before any circuit court in this nation, and shall be fined ten dollars; and fines thus imposed under this law, shall go to the county funds.

SECTION XXXV. APPROVED OCT. 30, 1888.

ACCESSORIES.

1. Be it enacted by the general council of the Choctaw nation assembled. All persons aiding and abetting in the commission of any crime, or being accessories before or after the commission of any crime, shall be held and liable to answer the law as the principal, and the committal and trial of the principal shall be no relief to the accessory; and he or she shall be tried as though they were principal.

APPROVED OCT. 30, 10

SECTION XXXVI.

HUNTING ON SUNDAY.

1. Be it enacted by the general council of the Choctaw nation assembled: It shall not be lawful for any person to hunt any kind of game in the Choctaw nation on Sunday with dog or gun. It shall be the duty of the circuit court of the district in which violations of this act occur to impose a fine of $10 to $2 for each offense if the offender is a citizen of the nation, but if a noncitizen the circuit judge shall report him to the principal chief, who will demand his removal. All fines accruing under this act to be devoted to county uses.

CITIZENSHIP.

SECTION I.

INTER-MARRIAGE.

1. Be it enacted by the general council of the Choctaw nation assembled : Any white man, or citizen of the United States, or of any foreign government, desiring to marry a Choctaw woman, citizen of the Choctaw nation, shall be and is hereby required, to obtain a license for the same, from one of the circuit clerks or judges, of a court of record, and make oath or satisfactory showing to such clerk or judge, that he has not a surviving wife from whom he has not been lawfully divorced; and unless such information be freely furnished, to the satisfaction of the clerk or judge, no license shall issue; and every white man or person applying for a license as provided herein, shall, before obtaining the same, be required to present to the said clerk or judge, a certificate of good moral character, signed by at least ten respectable Choctaw citizens by blood, who shall have been acquainted with him at least twelve months immediately preceding the signing of such certificate ; and before any license, as herein provided, shall be issued, the person applying, shall be and is hereby required to pay to the clerk or judge the sum of twenty-five dollars ; and be also required to take the following oath : "I do solemnly swear that I will honor, defend, and submit to the constitution and laws of the Choctaw nation, and will neither claim nor seek from the United States government or from the judicial tribunals thereof, any protection privilege, or redress incompatible with the same as guaranteed to the Choctaw nation by the

treaty stipulations entered into between them, so help me God."

2. Marriages contracted under the provisions of this act, shall be solemnized as provided by the laws of this nation, or otherwise null and void.

3. No marriage between a citizen of the United States, or any foreign nation, and a female citizen of this nation, entered into within the limits of this nation, except as hereinbefore authorized and provided, shall be legal, and every person who shall engage and assist in solemnizing such marriage shall upon conviction be fined fifty dollars, and it shall be the duty of the district at-torney in whose district such person resides to prosecute such person before the circuit court, and one-half of all fines arising under this act, shall be equally divided between the sheriff and the district attorney.

4. Every person performing the marriage ceremony under the authority of a license provided for herein shall be required to attach a certificate of marriage to the back of the license and return it to the person in whose behalf it was issued, who shall, within thirty days therefrom, place the same in the hands of the circuit clerk, whose duty it shall be to record the same and return it to the owner.

5. Should any man or woman, a citizen of the United States, or of any foreign country, become a citizen of the Choctaw nation by inter marriage, as herein provided, and be left a widow or widower, he or she shall continue to enjoy the rights of citizenship; unless he or she shall marry a white man or woman or person as the case may be, having no rights of Choctaw citizenship by blood; in that case all his or her rights acquired under the provisions of this act shall cease.

6. Every person who shall lawfully marry, under the provision of this act, and afterwards abandon his wife

or her husband shall forfeit every right of citizenship, and shall be considered an intruder and removed from this nation, by order of the principal chief.

SECTION II. APPROVED OCT. 30, 1888.

CHOCTAW TRIBUNAL FOR CITIZENSHIP.

1. Be it enacted by the general council of the Choctaw nation assembled : Any person who is not now recognized as a citizen of this nation, or of Choctaw descent, and claiming to be a citizen, or of Choctaw descent, shall petition to the general council, during the regular session thereof, for the rights and privileges of citizenship of the Choctaw nation. Such petitioner shall prove his or her blood, or other means by which they claim citizenship, by not less than two good, respectable Choctaws, disinterested persons, before a proper committee, or the chairman thereof ; and the chairman or secretary of the committee shall have power to administer any and all oaths that may be necessry in conducting the investigation. The committee aforesaid to be appointed by the general council, and to report to the body, by act or resolution, or otherwise, in reference to the petition, or petitions of the person or persons claiming to be citizens, or of Choctaw blood or descent, and in the event of the adoption of such report of the committee, then such person or persons shall thereafter be deemed and considered to be *bona fide* citizens of the Choctaw nation. Any and all persons who make the attempt, under the provisions of this act, to establish their rights, and fail in establishing the same, shall be reported immediately to the principal chief, by the president of the senate, and the principal chief shall forthwith proceed to remove them as other intruders.

2. It is hereby made the duty of the sheriff of each county in this nation to ascertain the number and names

of persons, or parties in their respective counties, who claim Choctaw rights, by blood or otherwise, and who have never established the same in accordance with the laws of this nation, and report the same to the principal chief immediately. Every such person living in this nation and claiming to be a citizen by blood or otherwise, and who shall fail to comply with the provisions of this act, after having been duly notified thereof by the sheriff, or other authorized person, shall be deemed and considered an intruder, and shall be removed be- yond the limits of the nation forthwith, by the principal chief.

3. All expenses incurred on the part of the officers of this nation in carrying out the provisions of this act, be and the same shall be paid by the parties wish- ing to establish citizenship; *provided, however*, that the cost shall be made out by the principal chief and pre- sented to the committee for collection, previous to said committee's proceeding to act upon the case before them; said cost, collected under the provisions of this act, to be, by the chairman of the committee, paid into the national treasury, for national purposes.

APPROVED CCT. CO, 1888.

ROADS AND RAILROADS.

SECTION I.

ROADS.

1. Be it enacted by the general council of the Choctaw nation assembled : Each county judge shall have the right to appoint two competent citizens of their own county whose duty it shall be to attend to and mark out the way for any road that it may be necessary to make in that county.

2. County judges are hereby authorized to require the people of their respective counties to work on the roads ; *provided*, that only males between the ages of eighteen and fifty years shall be subject to the provisions of this act.

3. Said county judges shall appoint and commission road-overseers, and notify them through the sheriffs, and make assignments of all persons living in certain localities and neighborhoods to certain overseers to work on certain roads, and also give notice of the same through the sheriffs. Road overseers, shall cause to be notified all his hands to meet at a certain time and place to work on their respective roads, by one of his road hands, and such road hand shall be credited with a day's work for every day so engaged ; said road hands to be notified at least five days before the time for working on the roads, who with their hoes, axes, and other utensils that may be necessary for the work, shall meet as directed and work. Said road overseers may work their divisions of roads at any time of the year which best suits the convenience of their respective communities ;

provided, the full time of six days for each hand be put in.

4. Any person or persons liable to road duty who are duly notified, and shall fail or refuse to work on the public roads, he or they shall be fined not less than one dollar and fifty cents per day, for every day they are required to work, and the county judge shall order the sheriff to collect such fine and shall turn the same over to the county treasurer for county purposes; *provided*, any person or persons on showing a good and satisfactory excuse to the county judge for not complying with such notification, he or they shall be exempt from such fine.

5. If any of the county judges shall wilfully neglect to comply with the provisions of this act, he shall be liable to a fine of fifty dollars and cost, before the circuit court of the district wherein he lives; to be collected by the sheriff of the county, who shall turn the same over to the county treasury for county purposes; *provided*, that if the county judge can show good cause for not complying with the provisions of this act, to the satisfaction of the circuit judge having jurisdiction, he shall be exempt from such fine.

6. Those persons who are citizens of the United States, and are residing in this nation, as mechanics, merchants, or in any business, and have received a permit or license to remain, shall be subject to the provisions of this section, but in case he or they refuse to comply with this law, they shall be reported to the proper authority ; *provided, however, Be it further enacted*, that the school teachers, farmers, that belong to the different institutions of learning of this nation, students of the different schools, and doctors shall be exempt from working on the roads.

7. If any person or persons shall obstruct, stop or shut up any public roads in any way whatever, or road leading to church or school, either by throwing trees across them or by making fields over them, or by fence of any kind whatever, he or they shall be compelled by the county court in which such obstruction is made, to remove the obstruction or make another good, substantial road around such obstruction or fences as good as the former, or make a lane, or make gates at the point where the original road comes in and out, for the free and ready ingress and egress through such obstruction, fence or fences. If the person or persons who have obstructed or shut up the roads as aforesaid, fail or neglect to obey the order of the court, he or they shall be fined by the county court in the sum of twenty-five dollars in cash, with which sum to cause a good road to be made around, to make a lane through, or to put gates, to allow free passage through such fence or fences, or other obstruction. But should any other person or persons open such obstruction he or they shall receive the fine.

APPROVED OCT. 30, 1888.

SECTION II.

RAILROADS.

1. Be it enacted by the general council of the Choctaw nation assembled: No citizen of this nation shall have the right to grant a right of way to any railroad company or corporate community, for any branch railroad within the limits of this nation, except by the assent of the general council, and that any person, as aforesaid, shall be found violating this act, such person so offending shall be liable to be indicted by the grand jury of the district wherein the offense was committed; shall on conviction in the circuit court, receive two hundred lashes, during two days, well laid on the bare back, and

fined not less than one thousand dollars nor more than two thousand dollars, at the discretion of the court; and upon conviction of any person so offending, the clerk of said court shall issue a writ of attachment to the sheriff of the county, commanding him to collect such fine and deliver the same to the treasurer of the county to be used for county purposes.

2. No railroad or railroad's branch to any coal mine, pinery or other place, shall be built in the Choctaw nation without a charter shall first be granted by the general council; and all persons violating this act shall, on conviction thereof before the circuit courts having jurisdiction, be fined not less than fifteen hundred nor more than twenty thousand dollars, at the discretion of the court, which fine shall be collected by the sheriff of the county where the offense was committed, who shall be allowed to retain ten per cent thereof for his services, and shall turn one-half of the remainder over to the national treasurer for national purposes, and the other half to the county treasury for county purposes.

APPROVED OCT. 30, 1888.

DOMESTIC RELATIONS.

SECTION I.

MARRIAGE.

1. Be it enacted by the general council of the Choctaw nation assembled: Every male who shall have arrived at the full age of eighteen years, and every female who shall have arrived at the full age sixteen years, shall be capable in law of contracting marriage, provided no other legal prohibition exists. But if under these ages their marriage shall be void, unless free consent by the parents and relations or guardian have been first obtained. Whoever shall contract marriage in fact, contrary to the prohibition of this section; and whoever shall knowingly solemnize the same, shall be both deemed guilty, one or both, of high misdemeanor, and shall upon conviction thereof, be fined or imprisoned at the discretion of the court. It shall be lawful for all the judges of this nation and preachers of the gospel to solemnize the rites of matrimony and issue certificates thereof, if requested, and be allowed and receive for every such service two dollars, to be paid by the parties so joined together. All marriages which are prohibited by law, on account of consanguinity between the parties, or on account of either of them having a former husband or wife then living, shall, if solemnized within this nation, be absolutely void, without any decree of divorce, or other legal proceedings.

APPROVED OCT. 30, 1888.

SECTION II.

DIVORCE AND ALIMONY.

1. Be it enacted by the general council of the Choctaw nation assembled: The circuit court in the district

where the plaintiff resides, has jurisdiction of all cases of divorce and alimony, and of guardianship connected therewith. The petition of divorce, in addition to the facts on account of which the plaintiff claims the relief sought, must state that he or she has been, for the last six months, a resident of the county, and that the application is not made through fear or restraint, or out of any levity or collusion with the defendant, but in sincerity and truth for the purpose set forth in the petition; it must also be sworn to by the plaintiff.

2. Divorce from the bonds of matrimony may be decreed against the husband in the following cases only: First, If the defendant was impotent at the time of his marriage; Second, When he has committed adultery subsequent to his marriage; Third, When he is guilty of such inhuman treatment towards his wife as to endanger her life, and these facts must first be proven by at least two witnesses; and the husband may obtain a divorce from his wife for like causes. If the defendant does not appear and answer the petition at the proper time, the court, if satisfied that the complainant is the injured party, may decree a dissolution of the marriage contract; or when the defendant can be found, it may, in its discretion, bring him or her in by attachment and compel him or her to answer. When a divorce is decreed, the court may make such order, in relation to the children and property of the parties and the maintenance of the wife, as shall be right and proper; subsequent changes may be made by the court in these respects, where circumstances render them expedient. But the parties shall have the right to divide such property equally that may have been jointly accumulated while living together.

3. No decree of divorce shall affect the legitimacy of any child begotten within the bonds of lawful wedlock.

APPROVED OCT. 20, 1888.

SECTION III.

MISSIONARIES.

1. Be it enacted by the general council of the Choctaw nation assembled: All non-citizens who desire to preach the gospel and be missionaries among the Choctaw people shall procure authority to preach from some missionary board, association, conference or other ecclesiastical body, and if such authority shall be recognized and approved by those who are already recognized and received as missionaries, and the applicants be recommended by those who are already recognized and received as missionaries, to the general council for its permission for said applicants to preach, and whenever the general council shall be fully satisfied from such recognition and recommendation as above provided for, it shall authorize such persons to be missionaries and to preach in the Choctaw nation, and then only so long as they shall strictly confine themselves to the sacred office of ministers; *provided*, if such persons shall not confine themselves strictly to said office and pursuit of minister or missionary, they shall be subject to the same pains, penalties, laws, rules and regulations, as other non-citizens, and all privileges herein granted shall be cancelled; and all non-citizens claiming missionary benefits without the consent of the general council of the Choctaw nation shall be notified by the principal chief to appear before the United States Indian agent on the same footing as persons of disputed citizenship; and if they fail to prove their missionaryship they shall be immediately removed out of the Choctaw nation as intruders.

SECTION IV.

APPROVED Oct. 30, 1888.

THE PRACTICE OF MEDICINE.

1. Be it enacted by the general council of the Choctaw nation assembled: The principal chief is author-

ized and required to appoint a board of physicians to consist of three persons, citizens of the Choctaw nation, who are regular graduates of some well known medical college, and residents of said nation, whose duty it shall be to examine all persons not citizens of this nation, who have located or may locate hereafter within the limits of said nation for the purpose of practicing medicine.

2. Any person desiring to come before the board for examination, shall make application in writing to said board, and shall accompany such application with sufficient reference of his or her moral character, by four or more citizens of the nation of good standing, to whom the applicant is known. The fee for examination of each applicant shall be twenty five dollars, and in default of the payment of which in advance, the board are not required to make the examination.

3. If an applicant shall stand a satisfactory examination, or shall hold a diploma such as may be satisfactory to said board, they shall grant said applicant a certificate upon which the principal chief shall authorize the judges of the county courts to grant a permit to such applicant to practice medicine ; and without the authority of the principal chief as above mentioned, the county judge is hereby prohibited from granting the same.

4. Any person, not a citizen, who shall practice medicine in this nation in violation of the provisions of this act, shall be held to be an intruder and dealt with accordingly.

APPROVED OCT. 30, 1888.

PERMITS,

SECTION I.

LICENSED TRADERS.

1. Be it enacted by the general council of the Choctaw nation assembled: Before any person or persons, non-citizens of Choctaw or Chickasaw nations, shall be permitted to expose any goods, wares, merchandise, or drugs for sale within the limits of the Choctaw nation, he, she or they shall be required to obtain a permit from the principal chief of the Choctaw nation; which permit shall be granted by the principal chief on the following terms and conditions only: Person or persons wishing to obtain such permit, shall make application in writing to the principal chief, setting forth the county and place therein in which they desire to carry on their business, and the probable amount of capital to be employed therein; such application shall be signed by five citizens of the county in which the person or persons applying propose to do business, and thereupon the principal chief shall issue to such applicant or applicants, under his hand and the seal of the nation, a permit authorizing such person or persons to carry on their business at the place mentioned in the application, and for the period of one year from the date of such permit; *provided, however*, that the principal chief may renew such permit from year to year, by endorsement thereon under his hand; and such renewal shall have the same force and effect as the original permit. Any person or persons obtaining such permit who shall expose any goods, wares, merchandise or drugs for sale in the Choctaw nation shall, during the succeeding quarter pay to the district

collector of the district in which the business is located, a compensation for the privileges granted in the permit, of one and one-half per centum on the original cost and value of all such goods introduced for sale, for and during the quarter next preceding, which inventory of the actual amount of goods introduced, and the accuracy and correctness thereof, shall be verified by the affidavit of the party in whose favor the permit was issued, before the said district collector; and such inventory shall form the basis by which said district collector shall be governed in collecting the compensation above mentioned; and the district collector in collecting the compensation mentioned above from any merchant, trader or druggist shall receive, if tendered to him, national warrants.

SECTION II.   **APPROVED C͞T. ℧℧, 1888.**

FARMERS OR RENTERS.

1.   Be it enacted by the general council of the Choctaw nation assembled: Every citizen who desires to employ a non-citizen as a farmer or renter, (and a farmer, or renter, by this act, is one who furnishes any or all the teams or utensils used in farming and who receives a part of the crop, or its cash value, for his services) is hereby required to obtain a permit for every farmer, or renter, so employed.   The citizen or his agent desiring to employ such non citizen, shall make application in writing, signed by four responsible householders of the county, one of whom shall be the citizen or his agent, on whose farm the farmer or renter is to labor, to the county judge who shall grant the application, if there are no good reasons for not doing so, and direct the county clerk to make out the permit under his hand and seal ; which permit shall not be for a greater or less period than one year; and give it to the sheriff, who shall deliver it to the said citizen or his agent, on whose farm

the farmer or renter proposes to labor, upon the receipt
of five dollars; one dollar of which shall go to the sheriff
for his services, and fifty cents to the county clerk. After
the expiration of the permits provided for in this paragraph, the dates of which the sheriffs must preserve, and
unless they be renewed, which renewal may be by endorsement of the county judge, and re-seal of the county
clerk, and payment to the sheriff of five dollars, by the
said citizen or his agent on whose farm the farmer or
renter is to labor, such farmers or renters shall be deemed intruders, and the sheriffs shall report them accordingly to the principal chief; *provided, however*, that the
sheriffs and county clerks shall be allowed the same pay
as the original permit.

APPROVED OCT. 30, 1888.

SECTION III.

PROFESSIONALISTS AND TRADESMEN.

1.   Be it enacted by the general council of the Choctaw nation assembled : Before any lawyer, editor, clerk,
artist, barber and such like professionals, shall be allowed to pursue his profession or calling, shall make application in writing to the judge of the county; which
application must be signed by five responsible householders of the county; and the applicant shall state his
calling or profession, and where he wishes to pursue the
same, in his application; and if the judge is satisfied, he
shall direct the clerk to issue his permit, under his hand
and the county seal, and give it to the sheriff, who shall
deliver it to the applicant only on receipt of ten dollars;
sheriffs and clerks to receive the same fees, or pay, as
under the second section of this chapter, and the permit
shall be renewed yearly, by endorsement of the county
judge, and re-seal of the county clerk.

2.   Before any carpenter, wagon maker, blacksmith,
wheelwright, millwright, tailor, shoemaker, miller, ma-

chinist, sawyer, tanner, teamster, (i. e., one owning and running, or hiring his team) or any other such like man or tradesman—all non citizens—shall engage in their respective callings or trades, in this nation, they shall make application to the county judge of the county wherein they propose to practice their respective callings or trades; which application must be signed by five responsible householders of the county, and set forth that the applicant will obey all the laws of the Choctaw nation, and especially the one in regard to stock, approved November 15, 1880; and that they will engage in no business other than the one for which the application is made. If the county judge is satisfied with the application, he shall direct his clerk to issue the permit, under his hand and the county seal, and give it to the sheriff, who will deliver it to the applicant only on the receipt of five dollars; sheriffs and clerks to receive the same fees, or pay, as under the second section of this chapter. The persons mentioned in this paragraph must get a new permit each year.

APPROVED OCT. 20, 188

SECTION IV.

COMMON LABORERS.

1. Be it enacted by the general council of the Choctaw nation assembled: Any person wishing to employ a non-citizen to work for him as a servant (a servant, by this act, is one who is hired by the month or day, for wages), or common laborer, shall report the name of such servant, or common laborer, to the county judge, who shall direct the county clerk, if there are no charges against such servant or common laborer, to record the name of such citizen, and the number and names of his servants, in a book kept for that purpose; *provided*, the citizen shall pay the clerk ten cents for each name recorded; and the clerk shall furnish a list of such serv-

ants to the sheriff, who shall collect two dollars and fifty cents from such citizen for every non-citizen so employed as a servant. The sheriff shall give the citizen a receipt for the money paid on each of said non-citizens, which receipt shall entitle said non-citizen to remain in the Choctaw nation twelve months from the time he went into the employ of the citizen who registered him. The sheriffs shall be allowed to retain ten per cent. of all money collected under this paragraph, the remainder to go into their respective county treasuries for county purposes.

————— APPROVED OCT. 30, 1888.

SECTION V.

MISCELLANEOUS EMPLOYES.

1. Be it enacted by the general council of the Choctaw nation assembled; All licensed traders, persons or companies working coal mines or running saw mills, superintendents of boarding schools, or doing any other kind of business under contract with any of the national authorities, shall pay to the district collectors of their respective districts, the same permit tax on their employes as is imposed by the provision of this chapter on non-citizens of like employment under individual contracts with citizens; *provided, however*, they shall not be required to obtain permits for their employes from the county officers. That all non citizens who may be desirous of carrying on their respective professions, as liverymen, hotel keepers and butchers, shall first apply to the principal chief for license, the application to be signed by at least ten Choctaw citizens; and if the license be granted by the principal chief, it shall be the duty of the district collectors of their respective districts, wherein such business is carried on, to collect from the parties above mentioned the sum of twenty-five dollars; and all non citizens who may be desirous

of carrying on their profession as gamblers, within the limits of the Choctaw nation, shall make application to the principal chief, the said application to be signed by at least twenty citizens ; and if the license be granted, the district collectors of the respective districts shall collect from said professionals the sum of one hundred dollars; and the district collectors shall be allowed to retain ten per cent. of all money collected by them under this section, and the remainder to be reported and returned by them quarterly to the national treasurer for national purposes.

APPROVED OCT. 20, 1888.

SECTION VI.

PUNITORY PROVISION.

1. Be it enacted by the general council of the Choctaw nation assembled : One month shall be allowed all persons having non-citizens in their employ in which to make application, or a permit, or recordation ; and the sheriff or any other person seeing such non-citizen at work on the citizen's place, shall be *prima facia** evidence that such citizen is hiring in violation of this chapter, and he shall be indicted accordingly. Any person who shall employ any non-citizen in any other manner than as provided for in this chapter shall be deemed guilty of a misdemeanor, and, on conviction thereof, shall be fined if a citizen in any sum not less than fifty nor more than one hundred dollars ; and if a non-citizen reported to the principal chief for removal; and any judge, clerk, sheriff or district collector failing in any of his duties herein set forth, shall, on information of three disinterested persons, be suspended by the principal chief from further exercise of his official duties.

APPROVED OCT. 20, 1888.

MILITIA.

SECTION I.

1. Be it enacted by the general council of the Choctaw nation assembled: For the better securing to the citizens of this nation their rights of person and property under the law, and for a speedy apprehension of murderers, robbers, thieves, and any other criminals and felons within the jurisdiction of this nation and bringing them to trial before the courts, there shall be immediately organized under the principal chief a force of three companies of militia—one from each district and each to be composed of fifty members, inclusive of officers—the captains to be appointed by the principal chief, first and second lieutenants to be elected by their respective companies, the captains to select the other members of their companies out of those Choctaw citizens of their respective districts between the ages of eighteen and fifty years, except civil officers; and appoint the non-commissioned officers of their respective companies; all of the officers to take the oath of office before some officer authorized to administer oaths, and the captains to muster in their respective companies.

2. The principal chief may call out said militia, one or more companies or parts of companies whenever the condition of any locality may seem to require it, in pursuance of this act, by giving notice to the captains of twenty days both as to time and place of rendezvous. Captains shall select two faithful men as couriers, and through them notify the other members of their companies of the time and place of meeting. All militia men selected under the provisions of this act shall hold themselves

in readiness to move in obedience to orders from their respective captains, and shall furnish their own equipment, and for every day's actual service captains shall be entitled to two dollars and fifty cents per day; lieutenants, two dollars; non commissioned officers, one dollar and seventy-five cents, and privates, one dollar and fifty cents. The pay of the captains to be drawn under certificates of the principal chief, and that of the lieutenants, non-commissioned officers and privates to be drawn upon certificates of their respective captains.

3. The rank of the captains shall be fixed by the principal chief, and the companies to be known as "A," "B," and "C," and the lieutenants to take rank in the same order as their respective captains; captains or other officers in command of companies or detachments of companies shall preserve the usual military order and discipline in their respective commands, under such rules and regulations as may be prescribed by the principal chief.

APPROVED OCT. 30, 1888.

ROYALTIES.

SECTION I.

1. Be it enacted by the general council of the Choctaw nation assembled: All of the royalty arising and accruing in the Choctaw nation in pursuance of its laws shall be due and payable to the Choctaw nation.

2. Any citizen of this nation, or person under legal permit within the same, shall be allowed to cut, ship and sell prairie or wild grass from the common domain of this nation, upon his notifying the sheriff of his county of his intention, and executing to said sheriff a bond in an amount sufficient to secure the payment of all royalties due the nation on the amount proposed to be cut, to pay to him when cut, fifty cents for each and every ton of hay cut, as aforesaid, for the purpose of being carried and sold beyond the limits of the Choctaw nation.

3. Any citizen failing to notify the sheriff of his county, and executing the bond as aforesaid, shipping any hay or grass from the limits of this nation, shall be guilty of a misdemeanor and shall be fined by the circuit court of his county, if a citizen, fifty dollars, and be collected as other fines are collected; and if a non-citizen, he shall be, by the sheriff, reported to the chief, who shall at once report him to the United States agent and ask his removal from the nation.

4. The royalty collected, as aforesaid, by the sheriffs of the several counties, shall be by them then turned over to the national treasurer for common national purposes, deducting therefrom ten per cent for his fees and services.

5. For royalty on coal, stone, salt, lumber, telegraph poles, railroad cross ties, railroad switch ties, tanbark, cord-wood, shingles and timber of all kinds, see paragraph 2, section 7.

6. All timber or wood growing out of the soil (except such as has been planted and fostered by the hand of man) and all stone and minerals or ore and medicinal water existing in its natural state within the limits of the Choctaw nation is the property of the Choctaw and Chickasaw people, and subject to the control of the Choctaw council.

APPROVED OCT. 30, 1888.

CLAIMS AND IMPROVEMENTS.

SECTION I.

1. Be it enacted by the general council of the Choctaw nation assembled: An improvement in a condition to return to the owner thereof, an annual income in money or property of any kind, shall constitute a claim; *provided, however,* such income be not realized exclusively from the sale of timber or other natural appurtenances on such claim ; and no citizen or citizens of this nation shall have the right to cut or otherwise destroy any timber within the limits of any other citizen's improvement as prescribed in this paragraph without such other citizen's consent, under the penalty of a fine of double the value of such timber so cut or destroyed to be paid to the owner of such claim, to be recovered before the court of the district having jurisdiction thereof, together with the cost of recovery. No citizen or citizens of this nation shall be allowed to settle on unimproved lands within four hundred and forty yards, on a direct line, from the exterior boundary of a former settler's improvements without his or her consent.

2. Any citizen or citizens violating this section shall be subject to removal to the distance from the former settler as specified in the above paragraph by the sheriff of the proper county, and shall pay the cost incurred by the sheriff in such removal ; and moreover, shall pay damages to the former settler, to be determined by three discreet persons, citizens of the county, and shall pay all costs incurred therein ; *provided* such former settler's improvements be not within the limits of an acknowledged town or village.

APPROVED OCT. 30, 1888.

SECTION II.

LEASING LANDS.

1.   Be it enacted by the general council of the Choctaw nation assembled :   The leasing of lands by citizens
to non-citizens is hereby expressly prohibited, and all
offenders against this section shall be fined in any sum
not less than two hundred and fifty dollars nor more
than one thousand dollars and all costs, for each offense
according to the discretion of the court ; one-half of the
fines to go to the county treasury and the other half to
the national treasury.   **APPROVED OCT. 30, 1888.**

SECTION III.

NON CITIZEN IMPROVEMENT.

1.   Be it enacted by the general council of the Choctaw nation assembled :   All non-citizens not in the employ of a citizen of the Choctaw nation, and not authorized to live in the Choctaw nation under the provisions
of existing treaty stipulations, who have made or bought
improvements in said nation are hereby notified that
they are allowed to sell their so-called improvements to
citizens, and if such non-citizens fail to comply with this
section then it shall be the duty of the sheriffs of the
counties in which such improvements may be located to
advertise the same for sale in thirty days; and sell the
same at the appointed time to the highest Choctaw citizen bidder for cash; one-half of which shall be paid into
their respective treasuries, and the other half into the
national treasury, *provided, however*, that if any such
non-citizen fail or refuse to deliver the possession of
such an improvement he shall be reported by the sheriff
of that county to the principal chief, and by said chief
to the United States Indian agent to take the proper
steps for the removal and prosecution of such offender

under section 2118 of the revised statutes of the United
States; *provided further*, that a notice of sale shall be
posted by the sheriff in three public places in his county, which shall be legal notice to all persons against
whom this law may operate.

2. Any citizen who shall attempt to protect or
screen any non-citizen under the pretence of ownership,
or any other false pretence, from the operation of the
preceding paragraph to defeat the same, he shall incur
a penalty of not less than one hundred dollars nor more
than two hundred and fifty dollars to be recovered by
action in the circuit court for the district in which the
improvement is located; the amount of such penalty to
be determined by the circuit judge of said court; and it
shall be the duty of the circuit judges of this nation at
each term of their respective courts, to call the attention
of the grand juries to the provisions of this section, and
instruct them to indict all persons violating this section.

APPROVED OCT. 30, 1888.

STOCK LAWS.

SECTION I.

LAWFUL FENCES.

1. Be it enacted by the general council of the Choctaw nation assembled: A fence made of good rails and ten rails high with four inch cracks between each rail, for two and a half feet from the ground shall be considered a lawful fence; and stock breaking into a field having such a fence the owner or owners of such shall be responsible for all the damages sustained thereby, and the courts of the several districts shall have cognizance of such cases; but no person or persons shall be allowed any compensation for any damage that he or they may sustain from stock breaking into his, her or their farm, unless his, her or their fence be lawful. If any one not having a lawful fence should destroy or injure the stock of another for breaking into his or her farm, he or she shall be liable to pay the value of the stock so injured or destroyed.

APPROVED OCT. 30, 188

SECTION II.

NON CITIZEN HERDSMEN.

1. Be it enacted by the general council of the Choctaw nation assembled: It shall not be lawful for any citizen or citizens of this nation to employ a non-citizen or non-citizens to to take charge of his or her cattle, as a herdsman or herdsmen, within the limits of this nation under any consideration whatever; and any person or persons charged with a violation of this act shall, upon conviction in the circuit court having jurisdiction, be

fined in a sum not less than two hundred and fifty nor more than five hundred dollars, in the discretion of the court, one half of which fine shall go to the national treasury for national purposes, and the other half to the informant.

APPROVED OCT. 30, 1888.

SECTION III.

LIMITATION TO NON-CITIZENS.

1. Be it enacted by the general council of the Choctaw nation assembled: No non-citizens shall be allowed to own, control, or hold any stock, of any kind, within the limits of the Choctaw nation, except they may be under permit according to the laws of said nation, and then only so much as may be necessary for their own use and family consumption, not to exceed ten head of cattle in all; team necessary for the cultivation of the land they may have rented, or to carry on their particular business for which they may have permits; and such other stock as may be kept in an enclosure.

2. Any non-citizen who shall not comply with the provisions of this section shall be reported by the sheriff of the county wherein said non-citizen may be located to the principal chief, who shall report the same to the United States Indian agent for violation of section 2117, United States revised statutes, and demand the removal of said non-citizen.

3. Any citizen of this nation who shall evade or attempt to evade or assist any non-citizen to evade this section by sham sale or sale without a valuable consideration, of any stock to be held by any such citizen, for the use and benefit of such non-citizen within the limits of said nation, shall be deemed guilty of a misdemeanor (section 7, laws of 1882), and the sheriffs of the several counties are hereby directed to make diligent inquiries

in their respective counties and report all citizens whom they believe to be holding stock for non-citizens, to the district attorney, who shall forthwith take steps to have such parties indicted and tried for every such false holding. Any person convicted of falsely holding stock in this nation shall receive thirty-nine lashes on his bare back and be fined not less than one hundred dollars nor more than five hundred dollars, in the discretion of the circuit court, to go into the national treasury for school purposes. No sale or conveyance of stock of any kind over fifty dollars by a non-citizen to a citizen shall be valid except it be recorded in the county record book of the county wherein the transaction shall occur.

SECTION IV

APPROVED OCT. C3, 1

WIRE FENCES.

1. Be it enacted by the general council of the Choctaw nation assembled : Citizens of the Choctaw nation are allowed to inclose for any purpose, an area of land not to exceed one mile square, with wire fence; *provided*, that rails or boards be firmly fastened to the top of the fence-posts, or said fence be staked and ridered ; *and provided also*, that no person shall have more than one such fence-pasture in any one county. (For fine see law of November 6th, 1883, Sec. 1.) Not applicable to present law.

2. The owners of wire fence pastures shall be liable for all damages done to stock, by reason of their running against the wires, and cutting, tearing or otherwise injuring themselves ; said damages to be assessed by the circuit courts having jurisdiction, in any sum not more than fifty dollars to the head—having due regard to the amount of damages actually sustained.

3. All persons having wire fence pastures, shall put up a good and convenient gate on every side of the pas-

ture, on every string of the fence, to each half mile of
the same, for the convenience of persons who may desire
to pass in and through ; and for the failure of persons
owning wire fence pastures to comply with this paragraph of this section, the circuit court shall impose a fine
of five dollars for each gate not so put in ; said fine to be
renewed each year of such failure.

4. For the protection of owners of all pastures, any
one leaving a gate open, letting out stock of the owners,
without their permission, or doing other damage to their
pastures or stock, shall be liable for damages to the
owners, in any just sum, to be determined by the circuit
courts.

SECTION V.

APPROVED OCT. 22, 1888.

MARKS AND BRANDS.

1, Be it enacted by the general council of the Choctaw nation assembled : 'All persons and guardians of
minor children having a brand or mark, or both, shall
furnish the ranger of the county in which they reside a
true statement of the same, to be recorded by said ranger. And all persons or guardians refusing or neglecting to do so, within six months after the passage of this
act, shall be fined five dollars by the judge of the circuit
court of the county in which such offender may reside,
which fine shall be collected by the sheriff, by order of
the judge imposing the fine. And each and every person and guardian, upon having their mark or brand recorded, shall pay twelve and a half cents therefor, to said
ranger. Should there be any change or alteration in the
mark or brand, or any new mark or brand adopted by
any one, he or she shall inform the ranger of their county of the same, and have the same recorded in the manner above provided, for which he shall pay the same

amount to the ranger. But should any person refuse or neglect to furnish the ranger with such change or alteration, within six months, he or she shall be subject to the same fine as above provided; *provided, however,* that if said refusal or neglect in either case, be from sickness or other lawful excuse, such person shall be exempt from paying any fine.

APPROVED OCT. 23, 1888.

SECTION VI.

STRAYS.

1. Be it enacted by the general council of the Choctaw nation assembled: All stray property, the owner of which is unknown, shall be taken and posted as follows: That when any person shall take up any stray horse or horses, he shall be required to give public notice, and if the owner of such stray does not appear within three months from the time that such beast was taken up, then the one that took it up shall take such stray before the county juudge; then it shall be the duty of the judge to authorize two or more persons to appraise the same, and the discription and value taken down in writing, and a copy of the discription and valuation shall be furnished to the ranger; then it shall be the duty of the ranger to have the same advertised in one or more public places in his own county. And if the owner of such beast do not appear within twelve months, after which time the property shall be sold to the highest bidder by the ranger, by first giving at least twenty days' notice of the sale; and one-half of the proceeds shall go to the one that took it up, who shall pay the ranger one dollar and a half, and the other half of the proceeds shall go to the county in which such stray may be sold; but should the owner appear before the expiration of twelve months, and prove his or her property before said judge

he or she shall be entitled to the same, by paying one dollar and a half each to the ranger and the one that took up. No one shall ever be allowed to take or ride any stray horse beyond the limits of the Choctaw nation; and anyone so offending shall pay the value thereof to the county and to the owner of said stray, if said stray should be lost in any way, or should be taken from him by fraud.

2. Every person who shall take up stray cattle shall be required to give public notice of the same, and if the owner of which do not appear within six months from the time that such stray was taken, then the one that took up shall notify the county judge of such stray property ; then it shall be the duty of the judge to authorize two or more persons to appraise the same, and also state the age, brand, mark and color, in writing, and a copy of the same shall be furnished the ranger ; then it shall be the duty of the ranger to advertise the same in one or more public places in his county, and if the owner of such animal does not appear within twelve months, after which time the property shall be sold to the highest bidder by the ranger, by first giving at least twenty days' notice of the sale, and one-half of the proceeds shall go to the one that took up ; then he shall pay the ranger one dollar per head, and the other half of the proceeds shall go to the county in which such sale may take place; but if the owner of such animal should appear before the expiration of twelve months, and prove his or her property before said judge, he or she shall be entitled to the same by paying twenty-five cents per head each, to the ranger and the one that took up. All unmarked cattle two years old and upwards running with the cattle of any person in their range shall be posted as other strays.

3. Every person who shall take up stray hogs or sheep shall be required to give public notice of such

strays, and if the owner of said stray does not appear within six months from the time such stray property was taken up, then the one that took up shall notify the county judge of such stray property; then it shall be the duty of the judge to authorize two or more persons to appraise the same, and state the color and ear-marks of each stray, in writing, and a copy of the same shall be furnished the ranger, and whose duty it shall be to advertise the same in one or more public places in his own county. And if the owner of such property should not appear within twelve months, after which time the property shall be sold to the highest bidder by the ranger, by first giving at least twenty days' notice of the sale, and one-half of the proceeds shall go to the one that took up, then he shall pay the ranger twenty-cents per head; but should the owner appear before the expiration of the twelve months, and prove his or her property before said judge, he or she shall be entitled to the same, by paying twelve and a half cents per head each to the ranger and the one that took up.

4. Should the owner or owners of stray stock find it within twelve months after it was sold, he, she or they shall have the right to the amount that was deposited in the county funds arising from the sales of such strays; *provided*, it is satisfactorily proven to the county judge.

5. No person shall take up any stray unless the same be found on his or her plantation, or running with his or her stock.

6. Every person who shall take up any stray animal, and abuse the said animal so as to cause its death, shall pay the value of the stray to the owner and to the county, as may be determined by any court having jurisdiction thereof.

APPROVED OCT. 30, 1888.

SECTION VI.

DROVERS.

1. Be it enacted by the general council of the Choctaw nation assembled: No person or persons shall be allowed to drive horses, mules, cattle, hogs, or sheep, from the range to which the same may belong; but it shall be the duty of every person or persons who may be driving horses, mules, cattle, hogs, or sheep, if any such stock not belonging to his or her drove, should join the drove, he or she who may be driving shall halt the drove at some convenient place and separate all such stock as do not belong to his or her drove, or to the person or persons for whom they may be employed to collect or drive stock; and if any person or persons shall violate the provisions of this paragraph, shall pay a fine and damages according to the decision of the district court where such offense may be committed, for the use and benefit of the person or persons suing for the same.

2. Every person, except citizens of the Choctaw nation, who may wish to drive stock through the nation, may do so by paying to any of the sheriffs of the nation, or their deputies, the following tax, viz: For beef, work and stock cattle, except sucking calves, ten cents each, loose horses, mules, jacks and jennies, ten cents each, except sucking colts; sheep, hogs and goats, two cents each, except sucking pigs, lambs and kids. And every person, not a citizen of this nation, engaged in driving stock through the nation as above provided, who shall keep such stock in the nation a longer time than is necessary to pass through the nation, shall pay an additional tax, at the rates fixed above, for every day they stop within the limits of the nation. The term "driving stock through this nation" shall be deemed to mean traveling through the nation on a direct traveled route toward the point of destination, at a rate not less than

fifteen miles per day for horses, mules, jacks and jennets; ten miles per day for beef, work and stock cattle, and five miles per day for hogs, sheep and goats; *provided*, that unavoidable detention by high water shall not be construed as a violation of the provisions of this act; and, *provided further*, that families moving through this nation with less than twenty head of stock cattle or mixed stock, shall be exempt from the provisions of this act. But persons driving stock into the nation for the purpose of feeding the same through the winter, shall be liable for the tax thereon, at the same rates fixed for persons driving stock through the same.

3. In all cases where a sheriff, or other person acting under lawful authority, has reason to believe that efforts are being made to evade the provisions of this act by collusion of some citizen of the nation with the owner of such stock, such citizen claiming to be the owner, such sheriffs or other person, shall require the claimant to exhibit his bills of purchase, or establish by witnesses how he came into possession of the stock in question. If deemed necessary, to arrive at the facts, he may put such claimant, or any other person supposed to be cognizant of the facts in the premises, upon oath and question him or them as to the *bona fide* ownership of such stock, and in all such cases if it appear that there has been fraud attempted for the purpose of evading the revenue laws of this nation, then, and in that case, there shall be levied double the amount of tax which would otherwise have been done, and any cost which may attach to the investigation. And every citizen of this nation who shall be cited to answer, on oath, questions as to the ownership of stock passing through the nation, who shall refuse to answer, shall be indicted for a violation of this act, and upon conviction thereof before the circuit court be deemed guilty of a felony, and shall re-

ceive thirty nine lashes on his bare back and be fined in any sum, at the discretion of the court, not less than twenty dollars and not exceeding one hundred dollars, payable one-half to the person prosecuting and recover ing the same, and the residue as hereinafter directed.

4. Every sheriff or deputy, levying and receiving tax of drovers, shall keep correct account of, and report the number and kind of stock taxed; and shall receipt such drover for the amount received, and such receipt shall be a passport through this nation for such stock upon which tax has been paid. And all moneys collected under this section by sheriffs, less ten per cent. for their services, shall go into the national treasury for school purposes.

5. In case any of the drovers refuse to pay the tax required by this section, the sheriff or his deputy shall at once take such steps as necessary to enforce the collection of such tax, and if deemed necessary he shall request the Indian police to assist him in attaching and holding the drove at the expense of the owner of the same, and sell so much thereof as shall make the amount of tax assessed. And the principal chief is hereby requested to send a copy of this act to the United States Indian agent and ask his co-operation in carrying out its provisions.

APPROVED OCT. 30, 1888.

SECTION VIII.

STOCK KILLING ONE ANOTHER.

1. Be it enacted by the general council of the Choctaw nation assembled : All property consisting of horses, cattle, jacks, jennies, mules, hogs, sheep, goats and dogs, that may kill each other, the animal that was killed shall be valued by three disinterested persons, and the person whose beast was killed shall receive half the

amount of his valuation from the owner of the beast that
did the damage, to be collected by the sheriff.

SECTION IX.   APPROVED OCT. 30, 188.

CASTRATION OR INTRUDING STOCK.

1. Be it enacted by the general council of the Choctaw nation assembled : If any stud horse, juck or jackmule is found with any person's horse or horses, and
the owner be known, he shall be notified to take him
away, and should he refuse or neglect to do so, in due
time, or in case the owner of such beast or beasts be unknown, he shall be taken to the nearest person who un-
derstands castrating and have him altered, and should
such a horse, jack or jackmule recover, the owner shall
pay to the taker up, and the person who castrated him,
one dollar each. But should the owner refuse to pay
such fine, the amount may be collected by the sheriff,
who shall have one additional dollar for his trouble. But
should the horse, jack or jackmule die from castration,
the owner will not be required to pay anything.

APPROVED OCT. 30, 1888.

Acts of 1886.

AN ACT to increase the salary of the superintendent of public schools.

Be it enacted by the general council of the Choctaw nation assembled: That the act providing the salary of the superintendent of public schools is hereby amended and changed so that said salary shall be four hundred dollars per annum, and this act shall take effect and be in force from and after its passage.

Approved, this 12th day of October, 1886.

T. McKINNEY,
P. C. C. N.

BILL II.

AN ACT to prohibit the sale or manufacture of Choctaw beer, cider or any other kind of malt, fermented, distilled or any other kind of intoxicating liquor or beverage.

Be it enacted by the general council of the Choctaw nation assembled: That the sale or manufacture of Choctaw beer, cider or any kind of malt, fermented or distilled liquors or beverage or intoxicant of any kind whatsoever in the Choctaw nation is hereby prohibited and the same authority is given to the officers to suppress it and the same pains and penalties to violators of this law as if they were engaged in the sale or manufacture of whisky and this act shall take effect and be in force from and after its passage.

Approved October 18, 1886.

T. McKINNEY,
P. C. C. N.

BILL III.

AN ACT establishing Jackson county.

Be it enacted by the general council of the Choctaw nation assembled: That a county to be called Jackson county is hereby created out of a portion of Kiamitia, Blue and Atoka counties. The following shall be the boundary lines of said county to-wit:

Beginning at the mouth of Boggy; thence up to Boggy to the forks of Muddy and Clear Boggies; thence up Muddy Boggy to the Thompson Wesley Ford; thence by the old Atoka place at the edge of the bottom then on the new blazed road to Hettie Carne's of Clear Boggy; thence down the Caddo road to Wilson Jone's pasture; thence along the eastern string of said pasture to the old Boggy Depot road; thence down said road to Jack Risner's, leaving Jack Risner's place 250 yards within the limits of Jacksan county, thence down the Phelin Wahle branch to Blue river; thence down Blue river to Red river; thence down Red river to the mouth of Boggy the beginning.

Approved, October 21, 1886.

T. McKINNEY,
P. C. C. N.

BILL IV.

AN ACT to appoint two additional inspectors.

Be it enacted by the general council of the Choctaw nation assembled. That the principal chief is hereby authorized to appoint two additional inspectors to operate on the St. Louis and San Francisco Railroad. One inspector to work from Ft. Smith, Arkansas, to Tushka Homma, C. N., and from Tushka Homma, C. N., to Red River, C. N. Said inspectors to be citizens of the Choctaw nation.

SEC. 2. Be it further enacted that the said inspectors shall be appointed in accordance with the law passed and approved at the October, 1883, session of the general council.

SEC. 3. Be it further enacted, that the office of inspector provided for in the act of November 6, 1883, be confined to the M., K. & T. Railroad and its branches in the Choctaw nation, and this act take effect and be in force from and after its passage.

Approved, October 22, 1886.

THOMPSON McKINNEY,
P. C. C. N.

BILL V.

AN ACT giving Jackson county one representative.

Be it enacted by the general council of the Choctaw nation assembled: That hereafter Jackson county shall be entitled to one representative, to be elected by the qualified voters of said county, and that this act take effect and be in force from and after its passage.

Approved, October 29, 1886.

T. McKINNEY,
P. C. C. N.

BILL VI.

AN ACT creating a senatorial district in Pushmataha district.

Be it enacted by the general council of the Choctaw nation assembled: That from and after the passage of this act the counties of Blue and Jackson shall compose one senatorial district and they shall be entitled to one senator in the general council.

Be it further enacted, that this act take effect and be in force from and after August 1st, 1886.

Approved, October 29, 1886.

T. McKINNEY,
P. C. C. N.

BILL VII.

A resolution respecting suits now pending in the third district:

Be it enacted by the general council of the Choctaw nation assembled: That all suits of whatever nature now pending in the county courts of Blue, Atoka and Kiamitia counties wherein the plaintiff and defendant are both residents of Jackson county, and shall be transferred to the county court of Jackson county, and it is hereby made the duty of the judge of Jackson county when organized to demand and receipt for, of the respective clerks of the counties above named, all the papers in said suit, but if both plaintiff and defendant are not residents of Jackson county, then the suits to remain for adjudication in the courts where they were brought and that this resolution take effect and be in force from and after Febuary 1, 1886.

Approved October 29, 1886.

THOMPSON McKINNEY,
P. C. C. N.

BILL VIII.

An Act amending an act relative to deputy sheriffs.

Be it enacted by the general council of the Choctaw nation assembled: That Blue county shall be entitled to four deputy sheriffs and the counties of Atoka, Kiamitia, Jacksfork and Jackson shall each be entitled to four deputy sheriffs and all deputies appointed under

this act, and no more shall be allowed a salary of fifty
dollars to be paid out of the national treasury on the
certificate of the principal sheriffs, and that this act take
effect and be in force from and after Eebruary 1, 1887.
Approved October 30, 1886.
THOMPSON McKINNEY,
P. C. C. N.

BILL IX.

AN ACT amending an act relative to jurors in third judicial district.

Be it enacted by the general council of the Choctaw
nation assembled: That the jury of the circuit court in
the third district, at the August term thereof, 1887, and
at each succeeding term shall be selected as follows to-
wit: Blue county shall have eight jurors, Atoka county
shall have eight jurors, Jacksfork county shall have
eight jurors, Kiamitia county and Jackson county shall
have eight jurors, and be it further enacted that all acts
or parts of acts heretofore passed coming in any manner
in conflict with this act, be and the same is hereby repealed and that this act take effect and be in force from
and after March 1, 1887.
Approved October 30, 1886.
THOMPSON McKINNEY,
P. C. C. N.

BILL X.

AN ACT entitled an act changing the circuit court, Pushmataha district, Choctaw nation from Atoka county
to Jackson county, Choctaw nation.

Be it enacted by the general council of the Choctaw
nation assembled: That the circuit court of Pushmataha district is hereby removed from Tiak Heli in Atoka
county, to Tiak Heli in Jackson county, C. N., and the

February 1887 term and all future terms of the circuit court of Pushmataha district shall be held at Tiak Heli in Jackson county, C. N., and this act be in force from and after its passage.

Approved, November 1, 1886.

THOMPSON McKINNEY,
P. C. C. N.

BILL XI.

An Act authorizing the sheriff of Jackson county to act as sheriff of the circutt court in Pushmataha district.

Be it enacted by the general council of the Choctaw nation assembled: That the sheriff of Jackson county is hereby empowered and authorized to act as sheriff of the circuit court in Pushmataha district to serve and execute all legal process that may eminate from said court and demand, receive and receipt from the former sheriff of said court all papers and process for execution that may be in his hands, and all laws coming in any manner in conflict with the provisions of this act are hereby repealed, and that this act take effect and be in force from and after February 1, 1887.

Approved, November 1, 1886.

THOMPSON McKINNEY,
P. C. C. N.

BILL XII.

An Act entitled an act defining the quantity of blood necessary for citizenship.

Section 1. Be it enacted by the general council of the Choctaw nation assembled: That hereafter all persons non citizens of the Choctaw nation making, or presenting to the general council, petitions for rights of Choctaws in this nation shall be required to have one-eighth Choctaw blood and shall be required to prove the same by competent testimony.

SEC. 2. Be it enacted that all applicants for rights in this nation shall prove their mixture of blood to be white and Indian.

SEC. 3. Be it further enacted that no persons convicted of any felony or high crime shall be admitted to the rights of citizenship within this nation.

SEC. 4. Be it further enacted that this act shall not be construed to effect persons within the limits of the Choctaw nation now enjoying the rights of citizenship.

SEC. 5. Be it further enacted that this act take effect and be in force from and after its passage.

BILL XIII.

AN ACT allowing the ranger a salary of fifty dollars.

Be it enacted by the general council of the Choctaw nation assembled: That the several rangers of the counties of this nation in addition to the fees already allowed them by law, be paid the sum of fifty dollars out of the national treasury, on the certificate of the county clerk, said salary to be paid quarterly, and this act take effect and be in force from and after its passage.

Approved, November 5, 1886.

THOMPSON McKINNEY,
P. C. C. N.

BILL XIV.

SECTION 1. Be it enacted by the general council of the Choctaw nation assembled: That it shall not be lawful for any non-citizen of this nation, whether under a traders' permit or any other permit, to reside or do business in the nation to enclose for his own use and benefit any more lands than sufficient to build a tenement or business house upon, and if a merchant to build a business house not to exceed, in a town or village, more than two town lots of usual size.

SEC. 2. Non citizens who own houses and buildings for the purpose of renting them, and are renting them, shall within sixty days from the passage of this act dispose of same, or be dealt with in the same manner as provided for in the sale of non citizens' improvements in the law of October 30, 1887 in reference thereto.

SEC. 3. All enclosures or pastures owned by noncitizens shall be sold to citizens within sixty days from passage of this act, or they shall be removed by the sheriff of the county where said enclosure or pasture are located or opened up for common pasturage purpose to citizens of the nation.

SEC. 4. Non-citizens failing or refusing to comply with the requirements of the first section of this act shall be deemed and held as forfeiting their permits and shall be further held to be intruders and their removal shall be demanded by the principal chief, and this act take effect and be in force from and after its passage.

Approved, October 28, 1887.

THOMPSON McKINNEY,
P. C. C. N.

BILL XV.

AN ACT to define the duties of the officers of the Choctaw nation who deal with intruders.

Be it enacted by the general council of the Choctaw nation assembled: That it shall be the duty of the sheriff to deal with intruders and non-citizens; to make a sworn statement before any judge of this nation; to the principal chief in every case of refusal to take out a permit, or failing to get the necessary signers to his pe-

tition or refusal to leave the nation when notified by the
sheriff or any other officer, authorized by law to deal
with intruders and non-citizens, and it shall be the duty
of the principal chief to forthwith report all intruders to
the United States Indian Agent, when reported to him in
accordance with this act, and ask their removal.

SEC. 2. If any sheriff shall fail, neglect or refuse to
carry out this act, he shall be deemed and held to be
guilty of a misdemeanor, and shall be prosecuted against,
to the circuit court and shall be fined not less than fifty
dollars nor more than one hundred dollars in every case
of failure, neglect, or refusal, and this act take effect and
be in force from and after its passage.

Approved, November 14, 1887.

THOMPSON McKINNEY,
P. C. C. N.

BILL XVI.

AN ACT defining the duties of the national auditor.

SEC. 1. Be it enacted by the general council of the
Choctaw nation assembled : That it shall not be lawful
for the national auditor to issue a warrant on the national treasury in any manner other than hereinafter provided.

SEC. 2. Be it further enacted, that it shall be the
duty of the auditor on and during the first part of the
month of every succeeding quarter to make out a warrant in favor of every officer in this nation, whose salary
is payable by law out of the national treasury for the
amount that is due him as his salary for that quarter.
The auditor shall forward the warrants in favor of the
national and district officers direct to such officers. The
salaries of all other officers shall be forwarded to the
county judge of each county, who shall deliver them to
each officer for the purpose of this act. It shall be the

duty of the national secretary to file with the national auditor a list of the dates and duration of every commission issued by him.

The sheriff of the circuit courts shall send to the auditor the names and dates of appointment of his regular deputies.

SEC. 3. Be it further enacted, that every officer in this nation who collects or superintends the collection of public monies, shall make a report at the end of each month to the national auditor of the amount of such collection ; how, and on what they are made. On the basis of such reports the auditor shall issue his warrant in favor of the officer for the amount that is due him.

SEC. 4. Be it further enacted, that all expenses of the courts of this nation payable by law, and out of the national treasury, shall be by allowance of the judge, and under the hand and seal of the clerk. A certified list of all such expenses and the date of the law under which they are paid, shall be forwarded by the clerk within one day after adjournment of each court to the national auditor.

SEC. 5. Be it further enacted, that this act take effect and be in force from and after February 1, 1888.

Approved, November 7, 1887.

T. McKINNEY,
P. C. C. N.

BILL XVII.

Supplementary to an act in relation to wire fences.

PASTURES,

Be it enacted by the general council of the Choctaw nation assembled. That no person or citizen shall be allowed to connect his pasture with that of another. There shall be a passage way or lane left between all of such enclosures not less than twenty-five feet wide. In all cases of violations of this act the county judge is hereby authorized to have such fences cut down by the sheriff and the passage way kept clear, and this act to take effect and be in force from and after its passage.

Approved November 8th, 1887.

T McKINNEY,
P. C. C. N.

BILL XVIII.

An Act defining the manner of trying impeachment cases.

Section 1. Be it enacted by the general council of the Choctaw nation assembled: That any three citizens of the Choctaw nation may, at any time, present charges to the principal chief against any national or district officer of the Choctaw nation, except himself, for any misdemeanor in office, and they may also in the same manner, and for the same reasons, prefer charges against the principal chief to the general council and file the same with the national secretary.

Sec. 2. Said charges must be sworn to before some judge of this nation, and must be accompanied with full specification of the misdemeanor charged, and must be supported by at least two respectable witnesses and the principal chief is hereby authorized to administer all oaths necessary to the discharge of the trust imposed upon him by this act.

Sec. 3. If in the judgment of the principal chief, such charges are of such a nature as to endanger the public good by allowing the officer against whom such are made to continue in the exercise of his office, he shall notify such officer to appear before him at some place and time, giving at least ten days' notice, and show cause, if any he can, why he should not be suspended from exercising the duties of his office. In case said officer should fail to appear without giving a lawful excuse, the principal chief shall proceed with the examination, the same as if said officer was present. After the principal chief has heard all of the evidence on both sides, if he is of the opinion that such officer should not exercise the duties of his office he shall suspend him from office. But in no case shall the principal chief suspend any officer except in pursuance of law.

SEC. 4. In all cases arising hereunder, the principal chief shall forward to the national secretary the charges, specifications, evidence and his deposition of the case, who shall deliver all such papers to the speaker of the house of representatives at the next ensuing session of the general council.

SEC. 5. When the house of representatives is satisfied that there is good cause to impeach an officer, they shall make an article of impeachment against such officer and transmit the same to the senate, and the house shall proceed, as soon as practicable, to elect managers to conduct the impeachment trial, and appoint a day for the appearance of the accused, and cause summons to be issued for him, signed by the president of the senate and countersigned by the secretary, with a copy of the articles of impeachment annexed, requiring the accused to appear on the day appointed for the purpose, and be ready to answer the charges preferred against him. Said summons shall be served on the accused personally if he can be found, but if not, then by leaving a copy of the summons and articles of impeachment at the residence of the accused with some person over sixteen years old.

SEC. 6. For the purpose of this act the sergeant-at-arms, with such number of deputies as may be certified to be necessary by the president of the senate, shall execute all process of the court of impeachment; provided, however that said deputies may be relieved at the dis- cretion of such president, who is sitting as a court of im- peachment. The senate shall exercise all powers neces- sary to a full jurisdiction, and final determination of the case before them, but if the accused fails to appear, after being notified, or after appearing fails to answer, the senate may proceed EX PARTE.

SEC. 7. Before proceeding with the trial, the presi- dent of the senate shall administer to all of its members, and the secretary to the president, an oath to try and determine the charges and specification, and to do jus- tice according to law and evidence and all being sworn the senate shall proceed to hear, try and determine. Any case of impeachment may adjourn a trial to any other time, consulting the public good, and shall be the Sole Judge of all questions of law arising during the trial, the advisability of testimony, the competency of witnesses and any other question incident to its jurisdiction; and exercise all needful authority to enforce order and re- spect in as full a manner as a regular court of law could do, provided however that all votes given on any ques- tion whatever shall be VIVA VOCE, and entered on the minutes of said court of impeachment.

SEC. 8. Whenever articles of impeachment are pending against the principal chief, he shall be disqual- ified from holding the office, and the chief or other jus- tice of the supreme court shall preside.

SEC. 9. The secretary of the senate shall make out a certified transcript of the proceedings had on any im- peachment trial, and deposit the same in the office of Na- tional Secretary for future reference, and this act shall take effect and be in force from and after its passage.

Approved November 8, 1887.

T. McKINNEY,
P. C. C. N.

BILL NO. XIX.

AN ACT entitled an act prohibiting a citizen or citizens to employ non-citizens to take charge of stock of any kind as herdsmen.

Be it enacted by the general council of the Choctaw nation assembled: That it shall not be lawful for any citizen or citizens of this nation to employ a non-citizen or non-citizens to take charge of his or her cattle, horses, mules, sheep, goats or hogs, or stock of any kind, and to hunt or gather stock of any kind running on the range within the limits of this nation, under consideration that this act is not to be construed to prevent citizens from employing non citizens to take charge of stock, to feed in pen or pasture; and any person or persons charged with the violation of this act shall, upon conviction in the circuit conrt having jurisdiction, be fined in a sum not less than two hundred and fifty dollars nor more than five hundred dollars, in the discretion of the court, one-half of which fine shall go to the national treasury for national purposes, and the other half to the informant. Be it further enacted that any act or part of any act in anywise coming in conflict with the provisions of this act is hereby repealed, and this act shall take effect and be in force from and after its passage.

Passed over veto of principal chief November 9, 1887.

BILL NO. XX.

AN ACT to provide for the security of the national treasurer.

SEC. 1. Be it enacted by the general council of the Choctaw nation assembled: That the sum of four hundred dollars is hereby annually appropriated as a contingent fund for the use of the national treasurer, to defray the contingent expenses of the office, and to pay the board and lodging of the highthorse when acting as a body guard for the national treasurer; provided the national treasurer shall make a detailed statement annually to the general council of his expenditure of the fund herein provided. For the purpose of this act the principal chief shall immediately on the passage appoint, on the recommendation of the national treasurer, two lighthorsemen to be subject to the order of said treasurer, and shall revoke the commission of the two lighthorse now on the force, unless the said treasurer should recommend them, or either of them, and this act shall take effect and be in force from and after its passage.

Approved, November 9, 1887.

THOMPSON McKINNEY,
P. C. C. N.

An Act construing the treaty of 1866, in reference to missionaries.

Be it enacted by the general council of the Choctaw nation assembled: That the scheme of changing the tenure of lands by the Choctaws and Chickataws, as inaugurated by the eleventh article of the treaty of 1866, having failed, all of the conditions and contingencies connected with and dependent upon the change also failed; that all of those published articles of said treaty contemplating such a change are void, and missionaries, or any other class of persons mentioned therein, have no rights thereunder, and this act shall take effect and be in force from and after its passage.

Approved November 9, 1887.

T. McKINNEY,
P. C. C. N.

BILL NO. XXII.

An Act amendatory of the law of November 1, 1882, in reference to wild or prairie hay.

Be it enacted by the general council of the Choctaw nation assembled : That all that part of the law of November 1, 1882, which allows non-citizens or persons under legal permit, to cut, ship and sell prairie or wild grass from the common or public domain of this nation, is hereby repealed, and it is hereby further provided that non citizens or persons under legal permit shall only obtain what prairie or wild grass or hay they want from citizens, and then only what is necessary for their own use. All violations of this act will subject the offender to removal from the nation, and this act shall take effect and be in force from and after its passage.

Approved November 10, 1887.

THOMPSON McKINNEY,

P. C. C. N.

BILL NO. XXIII

An Act for the protection of the public buildings.

Be it enacted by the general council of the Choctaw nation assembled : That any person who shall deface, injure or destroy any public building of this nation, shall, for each offense, be indicted by the grand jury of the district where the offense was committed and fined not less than fifty nor more than one hundred dollars, and shall also pay all damages done said building ; and in case of his, her or their inability to pay said fine and damages, he, she or they shall receive not less than fifty nor more than one hundred lashes on the bare back, and this act shall take effect and be in force from and after its passage.

Approved, November 10, 1887.

THOMPSON McKINMEY,

P. C. C. N.

BILL NO. XXIV.

AN ACT amendatory of the act of Nov. 9, 1875, in reference to inter-marriage.

Be it enacted by the general council of the Choctaw nation assembled: That the act of Nov. 9, 1875, in regard to the inter-marriage of white men with the Choctaw women is hereby so amended, that county clerks only shall issue license for such marriage, and instead of the white man paying twenty-five dollars they shall pay one hundred dollars and the county clerks receiving said one hundred dollars and issuing the license, shall be allowed to retain two and 50-100 dollars of the same as their fees, and the remainder they shall turn into the county treasuries of their respective counties. In all other respects the laws of Nov. 9, 1875, shall be complied with and this act shall take effect and be in force from and after its passage.

Approved Nov. 10, 1887.

THOMPSON McKINNEY,

P. C. C. N.

BILL NO. XXV.

AN ACT declaiming the late compilation, translation and publication of the Choctaw laws to be laws of the Choctaw nation, in force at the time of their publication.

WHEREAS, by an act of the general council approved November 3, 1885, provision was made for the publication of the laws of the Choctaw nation, and a committee was constituted and consisted of the principal chief, national secretary and national attorney, to award contracts for the compilation, translation and publication, and required bonds for their faithful performance of the work to be done under those contracts, and

WHEREAS, said committee did award said contracts,
receive the work done under them, issue certificates to
the various parties for their pay, and the work has all
been paid for.

Therefore the following shall be the enacting clause
of said publication:

Be it enacted by the general council of the Choctaw
nation assembled, that the said publication is hereby
declared to contain the laws of the Choctaw nation at
the time of said publication, and they shall be obeyed
and respected accordingly; and this act shall take effect
and be in force from and after its passage.

Approved, October 30, 1888.

B. F. SMALLWOOD,
P. C. C. N.

BILL XXVI.

AN ACT declaiming the time when officers shall qualify.

Be it enacted by the general council of the Choctaw
nation assembled: That all district and county officers
who receive their certificates of election from the supreme judges, shall take the oath of office and enter
upon the discharge of their duties on the 1st day of
October next succeeding the election at which they are
chosen, and shall hold office for two years unless removed for cause.

Be it further enacted, that all officers who are elected
by the joint ballot of the senate and house of representatives, together with all officers appointed by the chief
by and with the advice and consent of the senate, shall
qualify and enter upon the discharge of their duties on
the 1st day of November succeeding their election or
appointment.

Be it further enacted, that all officers now holding
shall continue in office, if they are elected by the people,

until October 1, 1890, and those elected by the council or appointed by the chief until November 1, 1890.

Be it further enacted, that this act shall not apply to senators or representatives, principal chief or any member of his cabinet, circuit and supreme judges, and that this act shall be in force from and after its passage.

Approved, November 6, 1888.

B. F. SMALLWOOD,
P. C. C. N.

BILL XXVII.

An Act in reference to pay of witnesses.

Be it enacted by the general council of the Choctaw nation assembled: That in addition to the fees and mileage already allowed witnesses by the law of October 26, 1883, to be paid in county script, they shall be allowed one dollar per day while attending circuit court on behalf of the nation, until discharged, in all criminal cases, and in civil cases where the nation is a party in interest, to be paid out of the national treasury, on the certificates of the judges of the courts and attested by the clerks, with the seals of the courts attached; provided, that in no case the costs in a civil suit between individuals are to be paid out of the national treasury, and provided further, that no officer, prisoner or other person, whose business takes him or her to court without a summons, or who happens to be present, not having been summoned, shall be allowed the above per diem for simply testifying in a case.

The act of November 7, 1887, is hereby repealed, and this act shall take effect and be in force from and after its passage.

Approved, November 6, 1888.

B. F. SMALLWOOD,
P. C. C. F.

BILL XXVIII.

AN ACT providing for three more students to be sent to school in the states.

Be it enacted by the general council of the Choctaw nation assembled: That paragraph six of the law in reference to students to be sent to the states to school, on page 61 of the late compilation and revision of the Choctaw laws is hereby stricken out, and the following substituted in its stead: The superintendent of public schools is hereby authorized and instructed to select fifteen boys and twelve girls to be sent to school in the states, the same to be divided according to sex, equally among the several districts of the Choctaw nation, and this act shall take effect from and after its passage.

Approved November 1, 1888.

B. F. SMALLWOOD,
P. C. C. N.

BILL XXIX.

AN ACT in reference to permits.

Be it enacted by the general council of the Choctaw nation assembled: That no permit shall be issued to any one keeping saloons, billiard halls or tables. Pool rooms or tables, or any kind of gambling, in the Choctaw nation is hereby prohibited, and that no non-citizen shall have the right to take out a permit for another non-citizen, and all laws or parts of laws in conflict with this act are hereby repealed, and this act shall take effect and be in force from and after its passage.

Approved November 6, 1888.

B. F. SMALLWOOD,
P. C. C. N.

BILL XXX.

AN ACT to prevent hunting, gathering or running cattle on Sunday.

Be it enacted by the general council of the Choctaw nation assembled: That the law in reference to hunting on Sunday, found on page 170, section 36, of the new compilation and revision of the Choctaw laws, is hereby amended by adding the following language to line two: Or to hunt, gather or run cattle on Sunday; *provided, however*, this act shall not be so construed as to prevent watching and caring for stock already under 'herd when overtaken by a Sunday, and this act shall take effect and be in force from and after its passage.

Approved November 2, 1888.

B. F. SMALLWOOD,
P. C. C. N.

BILL XXXII.

AN ACT to prohibit the leasing or renting pastures.

SECTION 1. Be it enacted by the general council of the Choctaw nation assembled: That it shall not be lawful for any person to rent or to lease a pasture to any other person for the purpose of grazing or pasturing cattle or stock of any kind.

SEC. 2. Any person violating this act, shall on conviction be fined in any sum not less than two hundred and fifty dollars ($250), nor more than five hundred dollars ($500), to be paid into the national treasury for general purposes and the pasture so rented or leased be sold to satisfy said fine and cost if the person be unable otherwise to satisfy the same.

SEC. 3. That this act shall take effect and be in force from and after its passage.

Approved October 26, 1888.

B. F. SMALLWOOD,
P. C. C, N.

BILL XXXIII.

AN ACT to provide interpreters for both houses of the general council.

Be it enacted by the general council of the Choctaw nation assembled: That the senate and house of representatives shall each be entitled to an interpreter to be elected by their respective houses as the door keeper and other officers, who shall take an oath of office which shall be administered by the presiding officer of the house, to which he is elected and who shall receive the same per diem as the members of their respective houses· It shall be the duty of said interpreters to be on hand at all sessions or meetings of their respective houses and do all interpreting required by any member thereof, and this act shall take effect and be in force from and after its passage.

Approved October 26, 1888.

B. F. SMALLWOOD,
P. C. C. N.

BILL XXXIV.

AN ACT amendatory of an act to provide for the security of the national treasury.

Be it enacted by the general council of the Choctaw nation assembled: That Section 2 of an act to provide for the security of the national treasury approved November 9, 1887, is hereby amended so that the two lighthorsemen to be subject to the order of the treasurer, shall be in addition to the nine lighthorsemen formerly provided for, and this act shall take effect and be in force from and after its passage.

Approved October 16, 1888.

B. F. SMALLWOOD,
P. C. C. N.

BILL XXXV.

An Act amendatory of an act of November 6, 1880, in reference to the time coal contracts shall run.

Be it enacted by the general council of the Choctaw nation assembled: That on page 85 of the late compilation of the Choctaw Laws, in the eighth line and immediately after the words, "Mining Coal" there shall be inserted the words: "and quarrying stone" so that when amended the law should read. (All contracts made hereunder shall expire on the 31st day of December of each year, except for mining coal and quarrying stone, which shall cover a period of six years, and all royalty accruing under the same shall be due and payable monthly, and this act so amended shall take effect and be in force from and after its passage.)

Approved, October 15, 1888.

B. F. SMALLWOOD,
P. C. C. N.

BILL XXXVI.

An Act establishing election precinct in Atoka county, C. N.

Be it enacted by the general council of the Choctaw nation assembled: That an election precinct is hereby established in Atoka county at a point about forty miles from the town of Atoka, a little west of north and about one mile south of Austin Weaver's, which shall be called and known as Red Oak Hill precinct, and this act shall take effect and be in force from and after its passage.

Approved, October 22, 1888.

B. F. SMALLWOOD,
P. C. C. N.

BILL XXXVII.

An Act establishing an election precinct in Atoka county, C. N.

Be it enacted by the general council of the Choctaw nation assembled: That an election precinct is hereby established in Atoka county, Choctaw Nation, about twenty-seven miles northeast of Atoka, at a school house, about five miles west of Kiowa, known as Little Boggy school house, about one hundred yards from George Lowry's residence, and said precinct shall be called and known as Little Boggy precinct, and this act shall take effect and be in force from and after its passage.

Approved, October 26, 1888.

B. F. SMALLWOOD,
P. C. C. N.

BILL XXXVIII.

An Act for the benefit of crippled, blind and idiotic.

Be it enacted by the general council of the Choctaw nation assembled: That each person, citizens of the Choctaw nation, so crippled as to be unable to keep themselves and having no property, blind or idiotic, shall be entitled to fifty dollars payable out of the national treasury, on the certificate (under the direction and di scretion) of their respective county judges, who are hereby authorized and required to see that the money is used for the beneficiaries under this act, and all laws or parts of laws heretofore passed conflicting with this act are hereby repealed, and this act take effect and be in force from and after its passage.

Approved, November 7, 1888.

B. F. SMALLWOOD,
P. C. C. N.

BILL XXXIX.

AN ACT suspending the militia law.

Be it enacted by the general council of the Choctaw nation assembled : That the law passed and approved November 1, 1883, creating the militia for the Choctaw nation be and the same is hereby suspended, and that this act take effect and be in force from and after its passage.

Approved November 28, 1888.

B. F. SMALLWOOD,
P. C. C. N.

BILL XL.

AN ACT requiring the manner of application for citizenship.

Be it enacted by the general council of the Choctaw nation assembled: That hereafter all claimants for citizenship in the Choctaw nation shall pay into the national treasury the sum of one hundred dollars for each person asked to be adopted, and that no petition shall be entertained by the committee for citizenship unless accompanied by the national treasurer's receipt as above required, and that this act shall take effect and be in force from and after its passage.

Approved, November 6, 1888.

B. F. SMALLWOOD,
P. C. C. N.

BILL XLI.

AN ACT requiring the M., K. & T. Ry. Co. to reduce the rates of mileage on their line of railroad through the Indian Territory.

WHEREAS, the Gulf, Colorado & Santa Fe Railroad and St. Louis & San Francisco line of railroad have been required by the congress of the United States to charge only three cents per mile as rates of mileage through the Indian Territory, and

WHEREAS, the M., K. & T. Ry. Co. has been (since it constructed said line of railroad through the Indian Territory), charging the rates of five cents per mile, and should be required by an act of the general council, to be approved by the interior department, to reduce the rates from five cents per mile to that of three cents per mile, as required of other lines of railroads through the Choctaw nation, therefore

SEC. 1. Be it enacted by the general council of the Choctaw nation assembled: That the M., K. & T. Ry. Co. be and it is hereby required to reduce the rates of fare from five cents per mile as charged heretofore, to three cents per mile, as are required by other companies operating lines of railway through the Choctaw nation.

SEC. 2. Be it further enacted, that a certified copy of this act be forwarded by the national secretary to the Hon. Secretary of the Interior for his approval.

SEC. 3. Be it further enacted, that this act shall take effect and be in force from and after its passage.

Approved October 23, 1889.

BILL NO. XLII.

AN ACT changing an election precinct in Kiamichi county, Choctaw nation.

SEC. 1. Be it enacted by the general council of the Choctaw nation assembled: That an election precinct in Kiamichi county, heretofore known as Clear Spring election precinct, is hereby changed and removed to Good Land station in said county, to be called and known hereafter as Good Land precinct.

SEC 2. Be it further enacted, that the first election held at said Good Land precinct shall be on the first Wednesday in August, 1890, and thereafter, and that this act shall take effect and be in force from and after its passage.

Approved October 28, 1889.

BILL XLIII.

AN ACT changing Clear Springs court ground in Kiamichi county, Choctaw nation.

SEC. 1. Be it enacted by the general council of the Choctaw nation assembled: That Clear Springs court ground in Kiamichi county be and is hereby changed and removed to Good Land station on the St. Louis & San Francisco railway, in said county, to be hereafter called and known as Good Land court ground.

SEC. 2. Be it further enacted, That in holding the first court at the said Good Land court ground it shall begin on the first Monday in January, 1890, and the first Monday in each month thereafter the year round.

SEC. 3. Be it further enacted, That the county judge of said county is hereby authorized and required to appoint two or more competent persons to sell the former court house at Clear Springs, who shall first give public notice thirty days previous to the sale, in at least three public places in the county, and that the proceeds of such sale shall be set apart for the building of a new court house at Good Land, above mentioned.

SEC. 4. Be it further enacted, That this act shall take effect and be in force from and after its passage.

Approved Occober 28, 1889.

BILL XLIV.

AN ACT to appeal the act of citizenship, approved Octotober 1, 1892.

Be it enacted by the general council of the Choctaw nation assembled: That the decision of the general council, on the application for citizenship by any person claiming the right of citizenship, shall be final, and that the act approved October 21, 1882, is hereby repealed in whole, and this act shall take effect and be in force from and after its passage.

Approved October 30, 1889.

BILL XLV.

AN ACT suspending an act making distribution of the net proceed money.

SECTION 1. Be it enacted by the general council of the Choctaw nation assembled : That the law passed and approved November 6, 1888, creating a commission for the distribution of the net proceeds money; also, an act amendatory to an act approved January 18, 1889, be and the same is hereby suspended.

SEC. 2. Be it further enacted, That the said net proceeds commission is by this act required to file with the national secretary all the books, records, dockets and all other papers belonging to said commission's office for the inspection of the general council, and that this act take effect and be in force from and after its passage.

Approved October 30, 1889.

BILL XLVI.

Joint resolution of the Choctaw general council.

WHEREAS, It has been reported to this body from reliable sources, and has been publicly announced in the newspapers upon the authority of the officers of the St. Louis & San Francisco Railway, that the said Company has prepared a bill to be presented to the next session of the congress of the United States, asking that rights of way through the Indian Territory be granted by the said congress to a corporation known as the California & St. Louis Railway, said corporation being owned and controlled by the said St. Louis & San Francisco company system.

WHEREAS, The rights of way asked for aggregate more than two thousand miles and cover every section of the Indian Territory available for railway purposes, also paralleling rights of way already granted by congress and lines of railway now building or in progress of construction, and practically constitute a monopoly of the railway business in the said Indian Territory, and grants the same to California & St. Louis & San Francisco railway, otherwise known as the St. Louis & San Francisco railway, to the exclusion of all competitors and to the consequent injury of citizens of the said Indian territory; and

WHEREAS, By the terms of the treaty made by the United States with the five Indian tribes in the year 1866, which provided that one right of way should be granted for a railway north and south through the said Indian Territory, and one right of way east and west through the said Indian Territory; and

WHEREAS, The north and south right of way has been taken by the Missouri, Kansas & Texas railway, a line of railway constructed thereon, and a line of railway east and west has been taken by the Choctaw Coal and railway company, which said company is constructing a line of railway thereon; and

WHEREAS, In addition to these railways provided for in the treaty of 1866, the congress of the United States

19

has granted to other railways at different times, right of way through the said Indian Territory, some of which have actually been built upon and others are now building, and

WHEREAS, The public policy demands that the business of this territory shall be given to no one corporation to the exclusion of all others and the territory obligations of the United States having been violated by the giving of other rights of railway than those provided for in the treaty of 1866; now, therefore

Be it resolved by the general council of the Choctaw nation in joint session assembled; That we hereby solemnly protest against the granting of the right of way asked for by the said California & St. Louis Railway, otherwise known as the St. Louis & San Francisco Railway Company, as being a subversion of all the rights of Indian citizens and as having a tendency to destroy that competition which has been inaugurated by the granting of the rights of way to others than those provided for in the treaty.

And we desire to respectfully represent to the congress of the United States that if the St. Louis & San Francisco Railway, otherwise known as the California & St. Louis Railway, be granted the rights asked for it will practically end railway building outside of that company in the territory, and leave the citizens of the five nations at the mercy of one corporation in all future railway developments.

And we further declare that in our opinion, based upon the record of the St. Louis & San Francisco Railway in this territory in the past, that the said railways for which the rights of way are to be asked in the proposed bill, and that the corporation is asking for the same for the purpose of intimidating other corporations seeking to do business in the territory and to retard the development of competitive systems.

And we further respectfully represent to the congress of the United States that the said St. Louis & San Francisco Railway has held over twenty years right of way through this territory upon which it has never built and is not now engaged in building.

Be it further resolved, that a certified copy of this joint resolution be forwarded by the national secretary of the Choctaw nation to the president of the United States, to the honorable secretary of the interior, to the president of the senate and speaker of the house of representatives of the United States of America.

Be it further resolved, that this resolution shall take effect and be in force from and after its passage.

Approved, November 5, 1889.

BILL XLVIII.

An Act repealing a portion of the preamble of "An act authorizing the appointment of three commissioners to treat with the U. S. commissioners in reference to the leased district," and for other purposes, approved Nov. 5, 1889.

Be it enacted by the general council of the Choctaw nation assembled: That all that portion of the preamble of the act authorizing the appointment of the commissioners to treat with the U. S. commissioners in reference to the leased district, and for other purposes, approved Nov. 5, 1889, which reads, "And whereas, the Choctaws, by treaty of 1837, sold to the Chickasaws a one-fourth interest in all of their lands" be and the same is hereby repealed, and this act shall take effect and be in force from and after its passage.

Approved, November 9, 1889.

BILL XLIX.

AN ACT entitled an act repealing an act to prohibit introducing steer cattle in the Choctaw nation.

Be it enacted by the general council of the Choctaw nation assembled: That an act heretofore passed and became a law by its own limitation on the 30th of October, 1888, to prohibit introducing steer cattle in the Choctaw nation, except in the months of November and December, is hereby repealed, and that this act shall take effect and be in force from and after its passage.

Approved, November 13, 1889.

BILL L.

AN ACT changing the county court ground of Wade county.

Be it enacted by the general council of the Choctaw nation assembled: That the county court ground of Wade county is hereby removed from what is known as Kochot owa Kah court grounds to Tvli Hina, and it shall be called and known as Tvli Hina court ground.

The county court of Wade county shall hold its first session at Tvli Hina court ground on the first Monday in January, 1890, and this act shall take effect and be in force from and after the 31st day of December, 1889.

Approved, November 13, 1889.

BILL LII.

AN ACT to provide for protection of the rights of the Choctaw nation and her citizens against increased encroachments by U. S. courts.

WHEREAS, In pursuance of a custom long established among the Choctaws and of the 38th article of the treaty of 1866, white persons who intermarry with Choctaw citizens became entitled to all the rights and privil-

eges of citizenship in the Choctaw nation, to vote and
hold office, to sue and be sued in the Choctaw courts, to
be tried for offenses and punished in all respects as
though they were native born Choctaws; and whereas,
Stephen Belvin, a Choctaw citizen by blood, being
charged with the killing of one A. E. Powell, a white
man, and citizen of the Choctaw nation by intermarriage,
and had been arrested by the Choctaw authorities and
held for his appearance at the regular February term of
the circuit court of the third district of the Choctaw nation for trial; and whereas, the said Stephen Belvin has
been arrested for the same offense and held for trial by
the district court of the U. S., holding session at Paris,
in disregard of the said 38th article of the treaty of 1866,
and disregard of the rights of the said Belvin and of the
Choctaws; and

Whereas, A case of a precisely similar nature has
been taken into the U. S. courts at Paris, Texas, against
Captain Joe Everidge, Turner Everidge, and Martin Everidge, charged with the killing of one Luther, a white
man, but a citizen by intermarriage, and the defendants
are held there under bond; and whereas, in pursuance of
the laws of the Choctaw nation of October 30, 1877, and
October 28, 1887, Joe Nale, sheriff of Tobucksy county,
in pursuance of his duties under said laws, and in pursuance of instructions of the U. S. Indian agent, sold
some houses in the town of Krebs, C. N., the property of
non-citizens- intruders—and disposed of them, they being illegally there and pursuing an illegitimate business
in them, and whereas, in consequence suit has been
brought in the U. S. court at Muskogee against the said
Joe Nale for the value of the houses sold, and damages,
by the non-citizens; and

Whereas, Suit has been brought in the court at
Muskogee against Adolphus Riddle, administrator of the

estate of Mick Nichols, deceased, of Jacks Fork county, and a citizen of the Choctaw nation, by intermarriage, at the instance of one Huggins, a citizen of the state of Arkansas, and the property of said estate has been attached by said court and the property taken from the custody of the said Adolphus Riddle and ordered to be sold at auction to the highest bidder for cash, to the great detriment of the interest of said estate and in utter disregard of the jurisdiction of the Choctaw courts; and whereas, Sam Harris, a registered freedman of the Choctaw nation, became involved in a difficulty with and killed Sam Brown, also a registered freedman of the Choctaw nation, both being residents of Towson county, and the case clearly coming within the jurisdiction of the courts of the Choctaw nation, as in such cases decided by Judge Parker, of the Fort Smith court, in the case of Morris Green et al., from Gaines county; and whereas, the said Sam Harris is held for trial by the United States court at Paris, Texas; therefore,

Be it enacted by the general council of the Choctaw nation assembled: That the principal chief of the Choctaw nation is hereby authorized to employ the firm of Guthridge, Fleming & Co., of Paris, Texas, to appear in said courts and represent the interest of the Choctaw nation by pleading to jurisdiction of said courts in all such cases, or to take such course as may be necessary in the defense of the treaty and other rights of the Choctaw nation and her citizens, and for their services they shall receive the sum of fifteen hundred dollars, to be paid on the certificate of the principal chief whenever it shall have been satisfactorily proven to him to be justly due. The said amount of money to be paid out of any money in the treasury not otherwise appropriated, and this act shall take effect and be in force from and after its passage.

Approved November 14, 1889.

BILL LIII.

An Act to increase the pay of county officers.

Be it enacted by the general council of the Choctaw nation assembled: That the pay of the county officers of the Choctaw nation is increased as follows:

County judges,	$100 00
County clerks,	50 00
Sheriffs and their deputies, each	50 00

These amounts to be in addition to what is already allowed them, and this act shall take effect and be in force from and after its passage.

Approved November 14, 1889.

BILL LVI.

An Act changing an election precinct in Kiamitia county.

Be it enacted by the general council of the Choctaw nation assembled: That the election precinct known as Lockston precinct in Kiamitia county, is hereby discontinued, and instead there is hereby established one-half mile south of the said Lockston precinct, at what is known as Saw Mill Church, a precinct which shall be called and known as Saw Mill Church, and this act shall take effect and be in force from and after its passage.

Approved November 20, 1889.

B. F. SMALLWOOD,
P. C. C. N.

BILL LV.

An Act amending an act in reference to the scholars attending boarding schools.

Section 1. Be it enacted by the general council of the Choctaw nation assembled: That the act of November 1842, as found in paragraph 4, section 5, chapter 1, at the top of page 67 of the late compilation of Choctaw laws, and which reads as follows:

"No family shall be allowed to have more than one scholar in the boarding schools of the Choctaw nation," shall be and is hereby amended to read as follows:

No family shall be allowed to have more than one scholar at schools in the states or in the boarding schools of the Choctaw nation

SEC. 2.   In all cases wherein any family may have more than one scholar at school in the states, or in a boarding school of the nation, the superintendent of public schools shall revoke the certificate of all but one, and proceed at once to fill any vacancies created thereby. This act shall take effect from and after the first day of August, 1890, and be in force thereafter

B. F. SMALLWOOD,
P. C. C. N.

BILL LVI.

AN ACT to provide for further development of the mineral resources of the Choctaw nation.

WHEREAS, There is a growing necessity for increase of the funds of the Choctaw nation to meet the demands for education and all elevating agencies ; and whereas those minerals which are undiscovered in the bowels of the earth can be of no possible benefit to the present or future generations unless they find development and are operated, therefore,

Be it enacted by the general council of the Choctaw nation assembled: That any citizen of the Choctaw nation who shall discover lead, iron or other metal, or mineral other than coal, shall be allowed the exclusive privilege of working the same within a radius of one mile from the point of discovery, provided that he shall duly record the same in the office of the county clerk of the county wherein the same metal or mineral may be located.

Provided, further, that he shall pay a royalty on the same to the Choctaw and Chickasaw nations of 6 per cent., three-fourths to the Choctaw and one fourth to the Chickasaw nation of said 6 per cent., of the value of the metal or mineral when it is prepared for the general market; and provided, further, that he shall be required to enter into contract with the national agent

BILL LVII.

AN ACT relating to citizens of the Choctaw nation taking the oath of allegiance to the United States.

Be it enacted by the general council of the Choctaw nation assembled: That any member of the Choctaw tribe of Indians, either by blood, adoption, or by marriage into said tribe and subject to the government of the Choctaw nation, who has taken or may hereafter take the oath of allegiance to the government of the United States, shall be disqualified to hold any office of trust or profit in the Choctaw nation, and to vote at any election in said nation, and to be impanneled as a juror in any court under the government of said Choctaw nation.

This act shall take effect from and after its passage.

Approved, October 25, 1890.

W. N. JONES,
P. C. C. N.

BILL LXI.

AN ACT relating to the school system of the Choctaw nation.

Be it enacted by the general council of the Choctaw nation assembled:

BOARD OF EDUCATION.

CHAPTER I.

SECTION 1. There is hereby created a board of education of the Choctaw nation, to be composed of the principal chief, who shall be ex officio president of said board, one superintendent of schools, and three (3) district trustees, one from each district. The superintendent of schools and the district trustees shall be elected by both houses of the general council in joint session; shall hold office for the term of two years, and until their successors are qualified, and shall receive for compensation an annual salary as follows: The superintendent, six hundred dollars ($600); each district trustee four hundred dollars ($400), to be paid quarterly out of the general funds of the nation.

SEC. 2. Said superintendent and district trustees shall each, before entering upon the duties of their respective offices, give bond to the Choctaw nation with at least two good sureties, in the sum of five thousand dollars ($5,000), to be approved by the principal chief, conditioned upon the faithful performance of all duties imposed on them by law. They shall each take the usual oath of officers of the Choctaw nation.

SEC. 3. The powers and duties of the board of education shall be as follows, to-wit:

1. To exercise a general supervisory control over the school system of the Choctaw nation.

2. To make all necessary rules and regulations, not inconsistent with this act, for its own government and the government of the various academies, seminaries and neighborhood schools.

3. To examine and appoint all teachers as hereinafter provided.

4. To contract with superintendents of public schools, but no such contract shall be valid unless approved by the principal chief and signed by at least three other members of the board.

5. To revoke the certificate of any teacher for immoral, intemperate or improper conduct.

6. To prescribe the text books to be used in all schools.

7. To suspend any academy or seminary in case of general sickness or epidemic.

8. To discontinue any neighborhood school, should the same in their judgment be expedient.

9. To designate permanent locations for any or all the neighborhood schools, if in their judgment such action would promote the cause of education. Powers in paragraphs 8 and 9 may be delegated to respective district trustees.

10. To prescribe the course of study in the various public schools, and it is made the duty of the board to foster, as far as possible, in the academies, manual training in the mechanical arts and theoretical and practical agriculture.

11. To select scholars to be sent to the states to school at the public expense; such scholars must be selected from those in attendance upon public schools; they shall be selected from the various districts as nearly as may be in proportion to the school population of each, and the number of each sex shall be kept equal. They shall be examined by some competent physician selected by the superintendent of public schools, and if physically disqualified, shall be rejected and others sent in the stead of such as may be rejected.

The board of education shall have a seal with the inscription, "Board of Education, Choctaw Nation." It shall keep a record of its proceedings, and its official acts shall be authenticated by its seal.

SEC. 4. It shall be the duty of the board of education to select one superintendent and at least two teachers for each public school now, or hereafter to be erected in the Choctaw nation. Advertisements shall be inserted in papers in at least three different states and in one paper in the Choctaw nation, setting forth the duties, qualifications and emoluments of such superintendents and teachers, other things being equal, preference shall be given to applicants professing Christianity. The teachers shall have at least ten years' experience in their profession, and must bring ample testimonials as to competency and morality. The male teachers must be graduates of some college of established reputation and capable of giving instruction in Greek, Latin, German and French. The females must be graduates of some higher institution of learning or some reputable normal school, and capable of instructing in two modern languages other than English. Upon the approval of this act, it shall be the duty of the superintendent of schools at once to notify the superintendent of public schools in writing, that the Choctaw nation elect to cancel all existing contracts at the expiration of the current scholastic year. He shall then begin to negotiate for new contracts. As to academies, seminaries or high schools hereafter to be established, contracts will be made in accordance with the first paragraph of this section and section 5 of this chapter.

Paragraph 2, as to public schools now in existence; The board of education may in its discretion, make contracts as heretofore, subject to the general provisions of this act, with boards of home missions, in which latter event, however, paragraph 1 of this section and section 5 of this chapter shall not apply, nor will the nation engage to pay the salaries of superintendents or teachers in such schools. Such contracts shall also contain a clause authorizing either party to rescind the same upon six months' notice in writing to the other, and the absence of such stipulations shall render such contract void *ab initio.*

SEC. 5. The superintendent of each of the public schools shall receive an annual salary of $1,200, to be paid in equal quarterly installments out of the general funds of the Choctaw nation. The teachers in said public schools shall receive each an annual salary of not less than $750 and not more than $1,200, to be paid in like manner and out of said general funds. The superintendents shall hold their positions for six years, and the board is authorized to make written contracts to that effect. Any superintendent or teacher may, however, be discharged upon charges sustained by the board; but said charges must be in writing; must be heard by the full board. The party charged must have written notice of the time and place of investigation and give full opportunity to be heard in his or her own defense, and at least four members of the board must concur in sustaining the charge and charges.

SEC. 6. All sums appropriated for the support and maintenance of the public schools shall be paid out to the respective superintendents in equal installments on the first Mondays in September, November, February and May of each year. The superintendent of schools shall make his requisition for such sums, under direction of the board, upon the national auditor, who shall thereupon issue his warrant for the same, said warrants shall be paid out of the respective appropriations by the national treasurer, any surplus remaining over at the expiration of the scolastic year, shall be returned by the superindent in whose schools such surplus shall exist, to the national treasurer, and by him converted into the treasury. This section shall apply to all new contracts whatever with superintendents of public schools.

SEC. 7. The board of education shall examine all applicants for the position of teacher in the neighborhood schools, but for this purpose the principal chief and each district trustee'may each select a proxy to rep- resent him at such examination. Such proxies need not be citizens of the Choctaw nation, but must be com- petent to conduct such examination. The applicants shall be examined in reading, writing, spelling and gram mar of the English language, in geography and history, particularly of the United States ; a fair knowledge of the constitution of the United States and of the Choctaw nation shall also be required. It is particularly enjoined upon the board, in selecting teachers, that regard can be had to the disposition of applicants as far as the same can be determined by personal observation at the time of such examination. Upon the conclusion of the exami- nations in each district, each successful candidate shall be required to enter according to merit into one of the three grades to be known as "First," "Second" and "Third" Grades, the first being the highest. Each successful candidate shall receive a certificate from the board, specifying his or her grade. Teachers shall be assigned by the board, as near as may be, to the neigh- borhood school whence they are sent by the respective local trustees ; but if any local trustee fails to send a candidate, or having sent one, such candidate fails to secure a certificate, then the board shall send some other competent person to such neighborhood. The foregoing examination shall be conducted at least once in each district annually, and for their services in this behalf the members of the board doing the actual labor shall receive each the sum of $5.00 per day and mileage at the rate of five (5) cents per mile for each mile actually traveled. Such examinations shall not be held more than five (5) days each year in each district. The times and places of such examinations shall be fixed previously by the board, and at least three months' notice given thereof by advertisement in one newspaper published in the nation, the expense to be paid out of the contingent fund of the superintendent of schools.

SEC. 8. The scholastic year of the public schools shall begin on the first Monday of September of each year, and shall close between the 10th and 30th of June. The superintendent of schools and three district trustees shall attend the annual examination of each of said schools; and to this end the board of education shall, by regulation, fix the dates of the closing thereof in such wise as to enable said superintendent and district trustees to be personally present at all of said examinations.

SEC. 9. The superintendent of schools shall have an annual contingent fund of $450, and each district trustee of $750, for the expenditure of which they must account to the full board of education at its annual meeting. All minor expenses not herein specifically provided for shall be paid out of the respective contingent funds.

SEC. 10. The full board of education shall meet at least once in every year in regular annual session. This meeting shall be at Tushka Humma, and shall begin during the first week of the regular annual session of the general council; at such meeting the board shall make up its annual report to said council. Such report shall contain an itemized account of all expenditures on account of schools by said board, or any of its members. It shall also contain a general review of the last scholastic year, the condition, progress and attendance at all schools, and such recommendations as to legislation as the board may deem expedient or necessary. The board shall transmit with its own report the reports of the various superintendents of public schools.

SEC. 11. The president may call special sessions of the board whenever he shall deem it necessary, to be held at such places as he may designate.

SUPERINTENDENT OF SCHOOLS.

CHAPTER II.

SECTION 1. The superintendent of schools shall be the executive officer of the board of education, and is charged with carrying into effect all orders, rules and regulations of said board.

SEC. 2. He shall correspond with the principals of schools outside of the nation, at which Choctaw pupils are attending, at the public expense, and with the scholars themselves, in order to acquaint himself with the progress and needs of such scholars.

DISTRICT TRUSTEE.

CHAPTER III.

SECTION 1. Each district trustee shall have a seal of office, which shall bear on the outer edge the words, "District Trustee Choctaw nation," and within the circle the Choctaw name of his district, followed by the word, "District." As soon as qualified, each district trustee shall write his signature in a book to be kept by the national treasurer for that purpose. All certificates required by law to be made by a district trustee shall be signed in person and his seal of office affixed to the same.

SEC. 2. The teachers of neighborhood schools shall be paid by the national treasurer, upon monthly certificates of the district trustee of the district in which such shall be located. Such certificate shall be made out upon the monthly report of each teacher when certified to by the local trustee. Each district trustee shall file all certified teachers' reports and present the same to the board at its annual meeting, with his district report.

SEC. 3. The district trustees shall also report to the board, at its regular annual meeting, the names of all the scholars as reported to them by the local trustees.

SEC. 4. Each district trustee shall have power to suspend any neighborhood school in the district in time of general sickness or epidemic in the neighborhood.

SEC. 5. The district trustee shall, each in his own district at once upon the receipt by him of any charges against any teacher in the district, to investigate the same, and if the charges are sustained to suspend the delinquent and appoint as a substitute any available person holding a certificate from the board of education.

LOCAL TRUSTEES.

CHAPTER IV.

SECTION 1. There shall be a local trustree in each neighborhood, who shall be the head of a family; shall be appointed by the district trustee of his district; shall hold office for one scholastic year.

SEC. 2. It shall be the duty of the local trustee to select one competent person in his neighborhood who may be a non-citizen and send him or her to the annual teachers' examination in this district. He shall visit his school at least once a month, and at the end of each month he shall examine the teacher's report and account, and if the same be correct, he shall so certify. Such account and certificate shall be sent by the teacher to the district trustee. He shall report to the district trustee

20

any improper conduct on the part of the teacher for investigation as provided in the act.

It shall be the duty of all local trustees to uphold teachers in enforcing proper discipline in the neighborhood school, and to enjoin upon pupils the necessity of showing due respect to the teacher.

SEC. 3. Local trustees shall receive no compensation for their services.

SEC. 4. Local trustees shall enroll all children in their respective neighborhoods between the ages of seven and eighteen, and report the same to the proper district trustee at the end of each scholastic year.

NEIGHBORHOOD SCHOOLS.

CHAPTER V.

SECTION 1. Any neighborhood that can employ a teacher shall be entitled to a neighborhood school; provided, however, that such schools shall not be nearer to each other than three miles, measured along the most direct traveled wagon road; and provided further, that this limitation as to distance shall not apply to acknowledged towns. The provisions of this section are subject to the powers conferred upon the board of education by section 3, paragraph 8 and 9, chapter I, of this act.

SEC. 2. Neighborhood schools shall be taught at least six (6) hours daily, Saturdays and Sundays excepted, during the term, and shall have regular hours of opening and closing. They shall open for the term on the first Monday of September and close on the last day of May of each year; but the district trustee shall have power to grant short vacations and holidays at stated times during the term.

SEC. 3. The benefits of a free neighborhood school shall extend only to such Choctaw children as attend the schools within the Choctaw nation established; and it is hereby made the duty of all Choctaw parents or guardians to send their children to school.

SEC. 4. The parents or guardians of all enrolled children who fail to send them to school shall be fined ten cents per day for each child enrolled who shall fail in attendance (not, however to exceed $2.00 per child per month), except in cases of sickness, bad weather, or other casualty. The money shall be collected as provided in section 5, chapter VI., of this act (but in no case shall any sum be paid out of the county treasury on this account), shall be paid into the contingent fund of the district trustee of that district. In case of necessity or other good cause shown to the district trustee, he may excuse any child from attendance upon the neighborhood schools for reasonable periods of time.

SEC. 5. Teachers in neighborhood schools shall be entitled to two dollars ($2.00) per month for each scholar in attendance, when such scholar has attended more than twenty days in the month. But where the attendance has been less than twenty (20) days, then such teacher shall receive 10 cents for each day of attendance; provided, however, that teachers of the first grade shall not receive over forty-five dollars ($45) in any one month; those of the second grade not over thirty dollars ($30), and those of the third grade not over twenty dollars ($20.)

SEC. 6. A scholastic month shall be taken and held to extend from a day of one calendar month to the corresponding day of the succeeding calendar month.

BOARDING SCHOOLS.

CHAPTER VI.

SCTION 1. The superintendent of each boarding school in the nation shall give a bond with at least two sureties, payable to the principal chief, and to be approved by him; in the sum of five thousand dollars ($5,000), conditioned upon the faithful performance of his duties as imposed by law, and observance of his contract with the board of education.

SEC. 2. The superintendents shall take charge of their respective schools, and conduct the same under the supervision of the board of education. They shall make full reports to the board at the end of each scholastic year, which reports shall embody the names and ages of all scholars, with their percentage in each study, the attendance, and other matters connected with their progress and the internal discipline of the schools, together with an itemized statement of all moneys received and expended, accompanied with proper vouchers.

SEC. 3. The number of scholars at each of these schools shall be one hundred; at Spencer Academy they shall be boys, and at New Hope Seminary they shall be girls. One of each sex shall be chosen from the Choctaws residing in the Chickasaw country, ninety nine of each sex shall be apportioned among the various counties in the Choctaw nation by the board of education in proportion to the school population of said counties. The board shall notify the county judge of each county at least thirty days before the beginning of each scholastic year, how many pupils of each sex his county is entitled to; each county judge shall then select his county's quota from the neighborhood schools and give each person so selected, or to his or her parents or guardian, a certificate of such selection.

SEC. 4. Before admission each scholar shall be re quired to pass a creditable physical examination before some competent physician selected by the superintendent of schools, and also a mental examination, the standard of which shall be fixed by the board. There shall be no limit as to age, though a regular course shall be held to be five years, but any pupil may be retained longer or sooner discharged by the board upon recommendation by the superintendent of either school.

SEC. 5. Upon selecting the scholars from his county each judge shall forthwith notify the proper superintendent of public schools of names and postoffice address of such scholar, and also the name and address of the sheriff of his county. If any pupil to whom a certificate has been issued shall fail for ten (10) days after the opening of school, or, when the certificate was issued after the opening of school, for ten days after the proper superintendent has been notified to report to his or her school, it shall be the duty of the superintendent of such school to notify the proper sheriff of such failure. The sheriff shall at once investigate the case, and if the pupil was not detained by high water, or sickness of self or family, then he shall take such pupil within five days to the proper school at the expense of parent or guardian. For this duty he shall be allowed $2 per day and five cents per mile for each mile actually traveled by each student and by himself by the usual traveled route. The sheriff's account must be verified under oath and if, on demand, the parent or guardian refuse to pay the same, the sheriff may take summary judgment in the circuit court of his district, upon a satisfactory showing to the judge thereof, that the expenses were lawfully incurred, for the amount of his bill and costs, without further notice or demand against such parent or guardian. Upon such judgment execution shall issue forthwith. If such execution cannot be satisfied, then the sheriff shall be paid out of the county treasury where such execution debtor resides, upon the county judge being satisfied of the correctness of the account. The county paying the account shall be subrogated to the sheriff's rights under the execution. If there shall be more than one delinquent pupil in the same county, it shall be the duty of the sheriff to take all such in one trip, and the circuit court shall not give judgment in any case where this provision appears not to have been complied with.

SEC. 6. No family shall have more than one scholar at any one time at the boarding schools of this nation, nor in the states at the expense of this nation.

ORPHAN SCHOOLS.

CHAPTER VII.

SECTION 1. There shall be fifty (50) orphan boys at Armstrong academy and fifty girls at Wheelock seminary. During vacation such as have no relatives or proper friends to visit, shall be cared for by the respective superintendents.

SEC. 2. There shall be no restriction as to age. The regular course shall be five years; but the board in its discretion may, in particular cases, order the retention or discharge of any pupil. No pupil shall be discharged except upon the order of the board.

SEC. 3. The county judge shall select the pupils, apportionment having been made by the board of education as provided for in the case of boarding shools. Regard shall be had in selections to the most needy, and more than one pupil may be sent from the same family.

SEC. 4. Each sheriff shall collect all pupils and take them in one trip to the proper school. He shall be allowed $2.00 per day and actual necessary expenses, to be paid out of the respective county treasuries upon properly certified accounts.

SEC. 5. The superintendents of orphan schools shall give a similar bond and shall report in like manner to the board as prescribed in this act for superintendents of boarding schools.

This act shall take effect from and after its passage and approval, and all other acts and parts of acts on the subject of schools are hereby repealed.

Approved, October 31, 1890.

W. N. JONES,
P. C. C. N.

BILL LVIII.

Amendment to section 2 of the act of November 1, 1892, in regard to shipping hay.

Be it enacted by the general council of the Choctaw nation assembled: That from and after the passage of this act a royalty of fifty cents per ton is hereafter levied on all prairie or wild grass cut for sale or barter, whether upon a public domain or within citizens' enclosures.

The sheriff of each county shall collect said royalty and pay the same, less ten per cent. for his services, to the county treasurer for county purposes of the county in which such grass shall have been cut.

Nothing herein contained as to impose a royalty on grass cut by any citizen for his own use, and this act take effect from and after its passage.

Approved, October 30, 1890.

W. N. JONES,
P. C. C. N.

BILL LIX.

An Act to abolish Good Spring and Cole Spring precincts in Blue county and to establish Jones' precinct instead.

Be it enacted by the general council of the Choctaw nation assembled: That Good Spring precinct and Cole

Spring precinct, located in Blue county, be and the same are hereby abolished.

Be it further enacted, That an election precinct is hereby established at Cornelius Jones' house, in Blue county, and shall be called and known as Jones' precinct, and voters may vote at said precinct. And this act shall take effect and be in force from and after its passage.

Approved October 30, 1890.

W. N. JONES,
P. C. C. N.

BILL LX.

AN ACT changing boundary lines of certain counties.

Be it enacted by the general council of the Choctaw nation assembled: That the boundary line of Wade county shall be as follows, to-wit: Beginning on the top of the dividing ridge where the dividing line of Mosholattubbee district strikes the boundary line of the state of Arkansas, running thence along the top of the dividing ridge westward to where the road leading from Horse prairie to Fort Smith crosses the same; thence along said road to Jack's Fork, to its junction with Kiamitia; thence down Kiamitia to the narrows, one mile above Hoteka's place; thence on a straight line to a spring on the Kiamitia mountain, known as Okchaga's place; thence following a line on the top of the main Kiamitia mountain, eastwardly, to the Arkansas line; thence along said line northwardly to the beginning.

SEC. 2. Be it further enacted, That the boundary lines of Cedar county are hereby changed, so that it will follow up Ward's creek to its junction with Little river to the source of said Ward's creek; thence in a northwardly direction on a straight line to the top of the main

Kiamitia mountain to a junction with Wade county un der the old boundary east of Ward's creek, and the line from its source to the top of Kiamitia mountain is here by declared a part of Nashoba county, and all that portion on the west of said Ward's creek and the line is hereby declared a part of Cedar county.

SEC. 3. Be it enacted, That all former laws are hereby repealed, and this act take effect and be in force from and after its passage.

Approved October 31, 1890

W. N. JONES,
P. C. C. N.

BILL LXII.

AN ACT to punish official corruption and the bribery of voters.

SECTION 1. Be it enacted by the general council of the Choctaw nation assembled: Any Choctaw citizen holding any office of honor, trust or profit, under the Choctaw government, and any witness or juror in any Choctaw courts who shall corruptly take or accept any money, valuable thing or consideration whatever, either before or after such officer, witness or juror has qualified, offered him or her by any other person with intent to influence the official action or duty of such officer, witness or juror, shall be deemed guilty of a felony, and upon indictment and conviction thereof, shall be pun ished by a fine of not less than one hundred dollars, and in default of the payment of such fine for one day, shall receive not less than thirty nine (39) nor more than one hundred (100) lashes well laid on the bare back.

SEC. 2. Any person who shall corruptly offer, or attempt to offer to any qualified voter of the Choctaw nation at any general or special election held under the Choctaw laws, any intoxicating liquor, money or valuable thing whatever, as a consideration for the suffrage of said voter, or with intent to influence said voter, as to his vote, or to subvert his free choice, shall be deemed guilty of a felony, and upon indictment and conviction, shall be punished as provided in section 1 of this act.

This act shall take effect from and after its passage and approval.

Approved, November 3, 1890.

W. N. JONES,
P. C. C. N.

BILL LXIII.

An Act to facilitate the detection of larceny of cattle in the Choctaw nation.

Be it enacted by the general council of the Choctaw nation assembled: That every butcher doing business in this nation shall keep a written record of the marks and brands of all cattle and hogs purchased for slaughter and from whom purchased; at the end of each month he shall file the same with the clerk of the county court in the county in which such butcher does business.

Sec. 2. It shall be the duty of each county clerk to safely preserve such record so filed and to freely permit the public to inspect the same.

Sec. 3. The violation of any of the provisions of this act shall constitute a misdemeanor, and shall be punished by a fine of not less than $5 nor more than $25. In case the offender be a non-citizen his license as butcher permit shall be revoked.

Sec. 4. This act shall take effect from and after its passage and approval.

Approved November 13, 1890.

W. N. JONES,
P. C. C. N.

No. 16.

AN ACT recognizing the citizenship of certain Mississippi Choctaws.

Be it enacted by the general council of the Choctaw nation assembled: That the following Mississippi Choctaws, late arrival to-wit: 1 Cornelius Hickman, 2 Eliza Ann Hickman, 3 Jeff Hickman, 4 Presley Isham, 5 Ellen Isham, 6 William Isham, 7 Nat Sakki, 8 Dixon Ripley, 9 Taylor Bell, 10 Alex Sakki, 11 Jane Sakki, 12 Lee Nobbe, 13, Henson Haltenstyle, 14 Phœbe Haltenstyle, 15 Milton Haltenstyle, 16 Jesse Haltenstyle, 17 Fall Haltenstyle are hereby recognized as citizens of this nation ane are entitled to all the rights, privileges and immunities of other citizens of this nation; and this act take effect and be in force from and after its passage.

Approved April 9, 1891.

W. N. JONES,
P. C. C. N.

No. 25.

AN ACT changing an election precinct in San Bois county.

Be it enacted by the general council of the Choctaw nation assembled: That the election precinct in San Bois county, known as Kulli Chito precinct, be and the same is hereby removed and located at Jerry Folsom's place, two miles south, and to be called and known as Oak Hill election precinct; and all future elections shall be held there; and this act shall take effect and be in force from and after its passage.

Approved April 10, 1891.

W. N. JONES,
P. C. C. N.

No. 27.

AN ACT granting to John E. McBrayer a ferry on the Arkansas river.

Be it enacted by the general council of the Choctaw nation assembled: That John E. McBrayer, a citizen of the Choctaw nation, residing at Tamaha in San Bois county, is hereby authorized and permitted to establish and operate a ferry at Pleasant Bluff, on the Arkansas river, the said McBrayer being the owner of the premises on the Choctaw side adjoining the landing. This privilege shall continue for the period of ten years, extend up and down the river for the distance of one mile each way. Said McBrayer to keep the banks and approaches to the ferry, and his ferry boats in good condition, and the Choctaw nation to be in no way responsible or liable to any party for loss or damage by reason of said ferry. Said McBrayer shall have the right to charge for vehicles drawn by more than two horses, mules or oxen, seventy-five cents; for vehicles drawn by two horses, mules or oxen, fifty cents; for vehicles drawn by a single animal, thirty-five cents; for each animal, horses, mules or cattle, besides those drawing vehicles, ten cents; for each person on horseback, twenty-five cents; for each person on foot, ten cents; for each hog or sheep, five cents, and this act shall take effect and be in force from and after its passage.

Approved April 11, 1891.

W. N. JONES,
P. C. C. N.

No. 29.

AN ACT for the protection of the interest of orphans in the money arising from the sale of the leased district under act of congress, approved March 3, 1891.

SECTION 1. Be it enacted by the general council of the Choctaw nation assembled: That the gross amount ascertained to be due the orphans now at Armstrong and Wheelock, arising under *per capita* distribution of the leased district money, under act of congress, approved March 3, 1891, shall be covered into the national treas- ury and so entered on the books thereof, and shall draw interest at the rate of four per cent. per annum.

SEC. 2. That a list of said orphans shall be filed in the auditor and treasurer's office, with the age of each orphan, and upon becoming of age of any orphan herein provided for, it shall be the duty of the national auditor, without further action of the general council, upon proper application, to issue his warrant on the treasurer for the said orphan's prorata of said sum with the ac- crued interest thereon.

SEC. 3. That this act take effect and be in force from and after its passage.

Approved, April 11, 1891.

W. N. JONES,
P. C. C. N.

No. 3.

AN ACT repealing an act in reference to licensed traders, approved November 4, 1890.

SECTION 1. Be it enacted by special session of the general council of the Choctaw nation assembled: That an act in reference to licensed traders, approved Nov. 4, 1890, be and the same is hereby repealed.

SEC. 2. Be it further enacted, that the act of Nov- ember 1, 1883, in reference to licensed traders be and the same is hereby re-enacted and declared to be in force, and this act shall take effect and be in force from and after its passage.

Approved, April 6, 1891.

W. N. JONES,
P. C. C. N.

No. 4.

AN ACT requiring national contractors to furnish transportation for inspectors.

WHEREAS, It is necessary that the inspector for the Choctaw nation be present when every inspection of ties and measurement of lumber and all kinds of timber is had, and

WHEREAS, Great numbers of ties and other timbers are brought to the track at points where there is no station, and

WHEREAS, It is a source of great inconvenience to said inspectors on all the lines of railroads in this nation to devise means for attending said inspections, therefore,

SECTION 1. Be it enacted by the general council of the Choctaw nation assembled: That the contractors for furnishing ties and timbers of all kinds to the several railroads running through this nation are hereby required to furnish transportation for the several inspectors on the several railroads in this nation in going to and from places of inspection.

SEC. 2. Be it further enacted, that all contractors for furnishing ties and timber of all kinds to the said railroads who shall fail or refuse to furnish said transportation for inspectors shall forfeit their contracts ; and this act shall take effect and be in force from and after its passage.

Approved, April 6, 1891.

W. N. JONES.
P. C. C. F.

NO. 7.

SECTION 1. Be it enacted by the general council of the Choctaw nation assembled: That the privilege is

hereby granted to Walter Patterson to turnpike and establish a toll-gate at a point on the Fort Smith and Mc-
Alister road, where said road crosses Gaines creek, in
Gaines county, upon the following terms and conditions:
That if said Walter Patterson turnpikes by grading the
earth and leveling with stones the said road from where
it crosses Gaines creek westward to a distance of five
miles he shall be entitled to demand and receive therefor, from all persons on the same, except citizens of this
nation, the rates of toll, to-wit: For each four wheel
wagon, or other vehicle, drawn by four or more horses,
mules or oxen, with driver, the sum of 50 cents; for each
four wheel wagon or other vehicle drawn by one or two
horses, mules or oxen, with driver, 25 cents; for man and
horse, 10 cents; each person on foot, 5 cents; for each
animal in every drove of cattle, horses, mules, hogs or
sheep, 1 cent.

SEC. 2. Be it further enacted, That privilege to receive toll herein given shall not take effect until said
turnpike is completed, and shall continue in full force
for the period of ten years, provided said turnpike shall
be kept in good order and repairs; and all other persons
are hereby prohibited from making any road across said
creek for a distance of a mile up or down said creek.

SEC. 3. Be it further enacted, That if any person or
persons, not citizens of this nation, refuse to pay the
aforesaid toll upon application, with proper proof being
made to the United States Indian agent for the Choctaw
and Chickasaw, he shall take such steps as may be necessary to secure and collect the same.

SEC. 4. Be it further enacted, That this act shall
take effect and be in force from and after its passage.

Approved April 8, 1891.

W. N. JONES,
P. C. C. N.

No. 8.

AN ACT admitting certain Mississippi Indians to citizenship.

Be it enacted by the general council of the Choctaw nation assembled: That Mrs. Anna Boyd, Mrs. Lenas Southerland, Mrs. Ozie Travis, Mrs. M. William, Choctaws lately from the state of Mississippi—and full sister of C. A. Bilbo who has been heretofore admitted—and their descendants be and they are hereby declared citizens of the Choctaw nation.

Be it further enacted that this act take effect and be in force from and after its passage.

W. N. JONES,
P. C. C. N.

No. 9.

AN ACT in relation to peddlers and other traders herein mentioned,

SECTION 1. Be it enacted by the general council of the Choctaw nation assembled: That all non-citizens who desire to engage in the following businesses shall pay to the sheriff of the county wherein they propose to trade as follows, to-wit: Ice cream and lemonade stands at picnic, $5 per day; ice cream and lemonade stands in towns, $25 per year. Peddlers who travel in a wagon $25 per year, and pack peddlers $10 per year.

SEC. 2. Be it further enacted, that all non-citizens proposing to engage in such business, as above stated, shall first present a petition to the principal chief, signed by five responsible citizens of this nation. When he shall have obtained the permit he shall pay to the sheriff of the county wherein he proposes to trade the sum above stated, to be by him placed in the national treasury for national purposes. The said sheriff shall be entitled to 10 per cent of all money collected by him under this law; and this act shall take effect and be in force from and after its passage.

Approved April 8, 1891.

W. N. JONES,

P. C. C. N.

No. 13.

An Act entitled an act regulating the time and manner of sheriff's making reports to their respective county treasurers, and for other purposes.

Be it enacted by the general council of the Choctaw nation assembled: That each and every sheriff of this nation is hereby required to make quarterly reports to their respective county treasurer, exhibiting for his inspection all papers, permits, executions and other documents of whatsoever character remaining in his hands uncollected or served, and then and there turn over all funds belonging to his county to said treasurer; and all funds due to the officers or other persons, such as fees, judgments, etc., taking their respective receipts. And failure on the part of any sheriff of this nation, or refusal to comply with the foregoing, or attempt to withhold any funds the county official or person to whom, by law the same is due, shall be construed as sufficient grounds for the vacation of his commission as sheriff by the principal chief, who shall at once vacate the same upon the sworn statement of any county treasurer, setting forth the facts that such sheriff refuses, fails, or neglects to comply wity the terms of this act.

Sec. 2. Be it further enacted that it shall be the duty of each county treasurer of this nation to carefully examine all papers, permits, executions and other documents in the hands of the sheriffs of their respective counties quarterly, when presented to him by said sheriff,

21

in compliance with section 1 of this act, and if it should be found, after examination, that said sheriff has fairly exhibited all papers in his office and duly turned over and accounted for all funds due the county of which he is sheriff, he shall so certify in writing to that effect, and it shall be a receipt to the sheriff for that quarter; *provided, however*, that the sheriff's report and examination of the papers in his office, together with the delivery of the county funds by said sheriff to his respective county treasurer shall be made in open county court and under the supervision of the county judge, and the result of such examination, etc., be spread upon the minutes of said court to be approved by said judge. And provided further, that should the treasurer find upon examination of any sheriff's office that he is withholding funds due the county of which he may be sheriff, it shall be his duty to so state to the principal chief, under oath, setting forth the facts and amount of such shortage.

SEC. 3. Be it further enacted, that from and after the passage of this act it shall be unlawful for any sheriff of this nation to receive money and receipt for the same in lieu of a permit in any case before such permit shall have been applied for and issued. Every sheriff violating this section shall be fined not less than twenty dollars for each and every offense upon conviction in the circuit court of his district. And such receipt or sworn testimony of the party to whom it was given shall be conclusive evidence against him.

SEC. 4. Be it further enacted, that the fees allowed by law to the county clerks for the issuing of permits be and the same is hereby made payable out of the county treasury of their respective counties; and all acts and parts of acts heretofore enacted, coming in contact with

this act, are hereby repealed, and that this act take effect from and after its passage.

Approved April 8, 1891.

W. N. JONES,
P. C. C. N.

No 15.

AN ACT admitting certain Choctaws from Mississippi to
citizenship in the Choctaw nation.

Be it enacted by the general council of the Choctaw
nation assembled: That Joe Willis and his children,
Nancy Selan, and Frank Willis and his sister Liney
Willis, and Billy Willis and his children Lee and Serena
Willis, Thompson Barnett, James Sakki and Thomas
Sakki, and Wallace Sam and his wife Fannie Sam and
their children Milley, Jeruzy, Luke, Silley, Lizzie, Liza
and Era Sam, all having just come from the old nation
in Mississippi, are hereby admitted to all of the rights
and privileges of citizenship in the Choctaw nation, and
this act shall take effect and be in force from and after
its passage.

Approved April 8, 1891.

W. N. JONES,
P. C. C. N.

No. 6.

AN ACT establishing an additional election precinct
in San Bois county.

Be it enacted by the general council of the Choctaw
nation assembled: That an additional precinct is hereby
established at the place known as Iron Bridge, in San
Bois county, and called and known as Iron Bridge precinct, and all the citizens of San Bois county are privileged to vote at said precinct in all special and general

elections; and this act shall take effect and be in force from and after its passage.

Approved, October 15, 1891.

J. H. BRYANT,
Acting P. C. C. N.

No. 8.

AN ACT establishing a precinct in Cedar county.

SECTION 1. Be it enacted by the general council of the Choctaw nation assembled : That an election precinct is hereby established at or near the Gilbert Cooper place, in Cedar county, to be called and known hereafter as Lick precinct.

SEC. 2. Be it further enacted, that the first election held at said Lick precinct shall be on the first Wednesday in August, 1892, and thereafter ; and this act shall take effect and be in force from and after its passage.

Approved, October 15, 1891.

J. H. BRYANT.
Acting P. C. C. N.

No. 9.

AN ACT establishing a precinct in Gains county.

SECTION 1. Be it enacted by the general council of the Choctaw nation assembled : That an election precinct is hereby established at or near James Leflore's place, in Gains county, to be called and known hereafter as Leflore's precinct.

SEC. 2. Be it further enacted, that the first election held at said Leflore precinct shall be on the first Wednesday in August, 1892, and thereafter ; and that this act shall take effect and be in force from and after its passage.

Approved, October 15, 1891.

J. H. BRYANT,
Acting P. C. C. N.

No. 11.

i n ACT granting to Moses Wooldridge the privilege to grade and work the Fort Smith and Eufala road a certain distance in San Bois county.

Be it enacted by the general council of the Choctaw nation assembled:

SECTION 1. That the privilege is hereby granted to Moses Wooldridge to establish a toll gate at a place on the Fort Smith and Eufala road between Emachia's creek and Broken Town, in San Bois county, upon the following conditions: If the said Moses Wooldridge shall, by grading the earth and removing the rocks, make a good traveled road or highway from Emachia's creek to Broken Town, a distance of twelve miles, he shall be entitled to demand and receive toll from all persons, except citizens passing over said road, as follows: For each four wheeled wagon or vehicles drawn by four or more animals, fifty-five cents; drawn by two animals, twenty-five cents; drawn by one animal, ten cents; two wheeled carts or buckboards, ten cents; men on horseback, ten cents; each head of grown stock, one cent; each man on foot, five cents; sheep or hogs, one cent each.

SEC. 2. The privilege herein given shall not take effect until said Moses Wooldridge shall complete and fix said road to the satisfaction of the road overseer of that division, and shall continue for the term of ten years, or so long as the road is kept in good condition.

SEC. 3. If any non-citizen shall refuse to pay the toll as aforesaid, he shall be reported to the United States Indian agent for his action in the matter.

SEC. 4. That an act approved Nov. 3, 1890, granting similar privileges to Moses Wooldridge, is hereby repealed; and this act to take effect and be in force from and after its passage.

Approved Oct. 20, 1891.

J. H. BRYANT,
Acting P. C. C. N.

AN ACT governing district collectors and inspectors.

SECTION 1. Be it enacted by the general council of the Choctaw nation assembled : The district collectors and inspectors shall make, at the end of each quarter, a report of all monies due from contractors or licensed traders, or any other person under their supervision, to the national auditor and treasurer, and upon such statement the auditor shall issue a warrant to such collector or inspector for his services ; provided, in no event shall a collector or inspector receive any money from any person, but the same shall be paid direct to the treasurer.

SEC. 2. The collectors and inspectors shall take sworn statements, before the county judge of the county where the trader or contractor resides, as to the amount of taxes due by them, and shall send same to the national treasurer with his report.

SEC. 3. The first report under the provision of this act shall be made on the first day of November, A. D. 1891, and every three months thereafter. The county judge, on said first day, shall be at the court ground for the purpose of administering oaths, or in the absence of the collector or inspector, the parties knowing themselves to be indebted to the nation may go before the county judge at the term of his court and make affidavit as to the amount due, read such statement to the collector or inspector. The judge shall receive no fee for adminstering such oaths.

SEC. 4. This act shall take effect and be in force from and after its passage.

Approved, October 20, 1891.

J. H. BRYANT,
Acting P. C. C. N.

No. 16.

AN ACT granting to Robert Benton a ferry on Poteau river.

SECTION 1. Be it enacted by the general council of the Choctaw nation assembled: That Robert Benton, a citizen of the Choctaw nation and a resident of Sugar Loaf county, Choctaw nation, is hereby authorized and permitted to establish and operate a ferry boat on Poteau river, at the mouth of Caston creek, the said Robert Benton being the owner of the premises on the Robert Benton side adjoining the landing. This privilege shall continue for the period of ten years; said Robert Benton is to keep the banks and approaches to the ferry and his ferry boat in good condition and that the Choctaw nation to be in no way responsible or liable to any party for loss or damage by reason of said ferry and that the said Robert Benton shall have the right to charge and collect the following rates of ferriage at said ferry. For wagons or vehicles drawn by more than two horses, mules or oxen, fifty cents; for wagon or vehicle drawn by two horses, mules or oxen, twenty-five cents; wagon or other vehicle drawn by one horse, mule or other animal, twenty-five cents; for each animal, horse, mule or cattle besides those drawing wagons or other vehicles, ten cents; for each person on horseback twenty-five cents; for each person on foot, ten cents; and this act to take effect and be in force from and after its passage.

Approved Oct. 22, 1891.

W. N. JONES,

P. C. C. N.

No. 18.

AN ACT creating the office of inspector of the St. Louis and San Francisco railroad and Choctaw road.

SECTION 1. Be it enacted by the general council of the Choctaw nation assembled: That the principal chief is hereby authorized to appoint two competent persons, citizens of the Choctaw nation, to be inspectors of the St. Louis and San Francisco railroad and one on the Choctaw coal railroad.

SEC. 2. Persons so appointed shall give bond, take the oath and discharge the duties of his office, as provided in the compiled laws section 8, page 87.

SEC. 3. That all acts or parts of acts in conflict herewith are hereby repealed, and this act take effect and be in force from and after its passage.

Approved Oct. 22, 1891.

W. N. JONES,

P. C. C. N.

No. 19.

AN ACT relating to district judges.

SECTION 1. Be it enacted by the general council of the Chectaw nation assembled: That no district judge of this nation shall practice law in any court in his district while in office, or counsel aid, or advise in any suit that may be pending in any of the courts, district or county, in his district, during his term of office.

SEC. 2. Be it further enacted, that any judge guilty of violating the above section shall be declared guilty of a misdemeanor in office, and removed from office, as the law in such cases prescribes, and this act shall take and be in force from and after its passage.

Approved Oct. 22, 1891.

W. N. JONES,
P. C. C. N.

AN ACT establishing an additional election precinct in Nashoba county.

Be it enacted by the general council of the Choctaw nation assembled : That an additional election precinct is hereby established at Second District court ground, in Nashoba county, and shall be called and known as Alikchi precinct, and all the citizens of Nashoba county are privileged to vote at said precinct in all elections.

And that this act take effect and be in force from and after its passage.

Approved, October 27, 1891.

W. N. JONES,
P. C. C. N.

AN ACT conferring citizenship on Henry Lewis, Mississippi Choctaw.

Be it enacted by the general council of the Choctaw nation assembled: That one Henry Lewis, late of the state of Mississippi, is hereby recognized as a citizen of this nation, and entitled to all the rights, privileges and immunities of a citizen of this nation, and this act shall take effect and be in force from and after its passage.

Approved, October 27, 1891.

W. N. JONES,
P. C. C. N.

An Act to establish an additional election precinct in Jack's Fork county.

Section 1. Be it enacted by the general council of the Choctaw nation assembled : That there be an additional election precinct in Jack's Fork county, about one mile east of Graham Anderson, and to be called and known as Big Cane precinct, and all the voters in Jack's Fork county shall have the right to vote at said precinct, and this act shall take effect and be in force from and after its passage.

Approved, October 28, 1891.

W. N. JONES,
P. C. C. N.

An Act granting to Maurice Cass the privilege to turnpike the Nanili-itte-tekili Gap, and establish a toll gate thereon.

Be it enacted by the general council of the Choctaw natioe assembled: That the privilege is hereby granted to Maurice Cass and Solomon Folsom to establish a toll gate at a place on the public road in San Bois county, Choctaw nation, leading from Fort Smith to the mouth of Canadian river, through the Garland settlement, known as the Nanili-itte tekili Gap, upon the following conditions and terms: That if the said Maurice Cass shall turnpike, grading the earth and leveling with stone and earth the said place called Nanili-itte-tekili Gap, he shall be entitled to demand and receive therefor from all persons passing on the same, except from citizens of the nation, the rates, to-wit: For each four wheel wagon or other vehicle, drawn by four or more horses, mules or oxen, with driver, the sum of fifty cents; for each four wheel wagon or other vehicle, drawn by one or two horses, mules or oxen, with driver, the sum of twenty–five cents; for man and horse, ten cents; each person on foot, the sum of five cents; for each animal in every drove of cattle horses, hogs, goats and sheep, the sum of one cent per head.

SEC. 2. Be it further enacted, That the privilege to receive toll herein granted shall not take effect till said turnpike is completed, and shall continue in full force for the period of ten years; provided said turnpike shall be kept in good order and repair.

SEC. 3. Be it further enacted, That if any person or persons, not citizens of this nation, refuse to pay the toll aforesaid upon application, with proper proof being made to the United States Indian Agent, he shall take such steps as may be necessary to receive and collect the same.

SEC. 4. Be it further enacted, That this act take effect and be in force from and after its passage.

Approved Oct. 29, 1891.

W. N. JONES,
P. C. C. N.

An Act in relation to the scholars at the public schools.

SECTION 1. Be it enacted by the general council of the Choctaw nation assembled: That the board of education shall not allow more scholars at any of the public schools of this nation than is specified by law, and this act to take effect and be in force from and after its passage.

Approved Oct. 29, 1891.

W. N. JONES,
P. C. C. N.

An Act to change an election precinct in Jackson county.

Be it enacted by the general council of the Choctaw nation assembled: That the election precinct in Jack-

son county known as Luk-Fappa precinct, is hereby removed to a point formerly known as Itakshish Church
Ground, about five miles distant, and shall be known as
Itakshish election precinct, and all elections, special and
general, shall hereafter be held there, and all acts or
parts of acts coming in conflict with the provisions of
this act are hereby repealed, and this act shall take
effect and be in force from and after its passage.

Approved, December 3, 1891.

W. N. JONES,
P. C. C. N.

An Act to establish an additional precinct in Sugar
Loaf county.

Be it enacted by the general council of the Choctaw
nation assembled : That an additional election precinct,
to be called and known as Black Fork election precinct,
is hereby located in Sugar Loaf county, at Black Fork,
in said county, and shall hold an election on the first
Wednesday in August, A. D. 1892, and this act shall
take effect and be in force from and after its passage.

Approved, December 3, 1891.

W. N. JONES,
P. C. C. N.

An Act changing the court ground of Cedar county.

Be it enacted by the general council of the Choctaw
nation assembled: That the county court ground of
Cedar county is hereby removed from Pine Hill court
ground to Sulphur Spring, and it shall be called and
known as Sulphur Spring court ground. The county
court of Cedar county shall hold its first session at Sulphur Spring court ground on the first Monday in Jan-

uary, 1892, and this act shall take effect and be in force from and after its passage.

Approved, December 3, 1891.

W. N. JONES,
P. C. C. N.

An Act changing the court ground of Gaines county.

Be it enacted by the general council of the Choctaw nation assembled: That the county court ground of Gaines county is hereby removed from Boiling Spring court ground to Hartshorne, and it shall be called and known as Hartshorne court ground. The county court of Gaines county shall hold its first session at Hartshorne court ground on the first Monday in January, 1892, and this act shall take effect and be in force from and after its passage.

Approved, December 3, 1891.

W. N. JONES,
P. C. C. N.

An Act changing the election precinct of Gaines county.

Be it enacted by the general council of the Choctaw nation assembled: That the election precinct of Gaines county is hereby removed from Freeney precinct to Hartshorne, and it shall be known as Hartshorne precinct. The first election shall be on the first Wednesday in August, 1892, and this act shall take effect and be in force from and after its passage.

Approved December 3, 1891.

W. N. JONES,
P. C. C. N.

AN ACT for the protection of public moneys.

Be it enacted by the general council of the Choctaw nation assembled.

SECTION 1. That the national auditor shall issue no warrant on the national treasury, except in consequence of an appropriation made by the general council, and that the national treasurer is hereby instructed to pay no warrants unless issued in conformity with this act.

Be it further enacted, that this act shall take effect and be in force from and after its passage.

Approved December 5, 1891.

W .N. JONES,
P. C. C. N.

AN ACT to authorize the board of education to let contracts for conducting the several new academies and naming the same.

SECTION 1. Be it enacted by the general council of the Choctaw nation assembled: That the academy located near Hartshorne shall be known as Jones academy; that the academy located near Tushka Homa shall be known as Tushka Homa Female Institute; that the academy lately provided for Choctaw freedmen shall be known as Tushka Lusa Institute.

SEC. 2. Be it further enacted, that the board of education shall be authorized to let contracts for carrying on the school at Jones Institute with one hundred boys; at Tuska Homa Female Institute with one hundred girls; at Tushka Lusa Institute with thirty students, in proportion prescribed by law.

SEC. 3. Be it further enacted, that the board of education in letting said contracts shall be governed by the school law of the Choctaw nation, approved October 31, 1890, said contracts to be for the opening of each institution on the first Monday in September, 1892.

Sec. 4. Be it further enacted, that this act shall take effect and be in force from and after its passage.

Approved December 5, 1891.

W. N. JONES,

P. C. C. N.

Section 1. Be it enacted by the general council of the Choctaw nation assembled : That all persons of African descent, resident in the Choctaw nation at the date of the treaty of Fort Smith, September 13th, 1865, and their descendants formerly held in slavery by the Choctaws or Chickasaws, are hereby declared to be entitled to, and invested with all the rights, privileges and immunities, including the rights of suffrage, of citizens of the Choctaw nation, except in the annuity moneys and the public domain of the nation.

Sec. 2. Be it further enacted : That all said persons of African descent, as aforesaid, and their descendants, shall be allowed the same rights of process, civil and criminal, in the several courts of this nation, as are allowed to Choctaws, and full protection of person and property is hereby granted to all such persons.

Sec. 3. Be it further enacted : That all said persons are hereby declared to be entitled to forty acres each of the lands of the nation, to be selected and held upon the same terms as the Choctaws.

Sec. 4. Be it further enacted, that all said persons aforesaid are hereby declared to be entitled to equal educational privileges and facilities with Choctaws, so far as neighborhood schools are concerned.

Sec. 5. Be it further enacted, that all said persons that shall elect to remove and do actually and permanently remove from the nation, are hereby declared to be entitled to one hundred dollars per capita, as provided in said third article of the treaty of 1866.

SEC. 6. Be it futher enacted, that all said persons who shall decline to become citizens of the Choctaw nation and who do not elect to remove permanently from the nation are hereby declared to be intruders on the same footing as other citizens of the United States resident herein, and subject to removal for similar causes.

SEC. 7. Be it further enacted, that intermarriage with such freedmen of African descent, who were formerly held as slaves of the Choctaws, and have become citizens, shall not confer any rights of citizenship in this nation, and all freedmen who have married, or may hereafter marry freedwomen who have become citizens of the Choctaw nation, are subject to the permit laws, and allowed to remain during good behavior only.

SEC. 8. Be it further enacted, That all such persons of African descent, who have become citizens of the Choctaw nation, shall be entitled to hold any office of trust or profit in this nation, except the offices of principal chief and district-chiefs.

SEC. 9. Be it further enacted, That the national secretary shall furnish a certified copy of this act to the secretary of the interior. And this act shall take effect and be in force from and after its passage.

Approved May 21, 1883.

An Act conferring citizenship on certain persons named.

Be it enacted by the general council of the Choctaw nation assembled: That Abbot Leflore, Felicie Landers, Louis C. Leflore, and his three children, Rosa, Michael and Josephine, all late of Mississippi, are hereby recognized as citizens of the Choctaw nation, and entitled to all the rights, privileges, and immunities of citizens of this nation, and this act shall take effect and be in force from and after its passage.

Approved, October 13, 1893.

W. N. JONES,
P. C. C. N.

An Act extending toll bridge privileges over Perryville creek, granted Oct. 31, 1872, to Oct. 31, 1892.

Be it enacted by the general council of the Choctaw nation assembled : That an act granting a toll bridge privilege over Perryville creek to James S. Johnson, from October 31, 1872, to October 31, 1882, and subse. quently renewed to October 31, 1892, be and the same is hereby further renewed so as to extend to October 31, 1902, to Annie Keys, formerly a wife of and now legal heir of the said James S. Johnson, in accordance with the conditions of the grant of October 31, 1872.

Sec. 2. Be it further enacted, that in addition to the privileges of the grant of October 31, 1872, the said Annie Keys shall have exclusive bridge privileges one mile in both directions up and down the stream from the said bridge, provided, she does not interfere with the former settler, and this act to take effect and be in force from and after its passage.

Approved October 16, 1893.

W. N. JONES,
P. C. C. N.

An Act prohibiting the floating of timber from the Choc-taw nation.

Section 1. Be it enacted by the general council of the Choctaw nation assembled : That the rafting or floating of timber, or an attempt to raft or float timber of all kinds, within the limits of the Choctaw nation, or

22

from the Choctaw nation, shall be prohibited after January 31st, 1894.

SEC. 2. That any person or persons violating the provisions of this act after the above named date, shall thereby forfeit his or their contract and the national agent shall revoke the same.

SEC. 3. That the national secretary is hereby commanded to publish this law for weeks in the papers of the Choctaw nation, and one of Fort Smith, Ark., and one paper of Paris, Tex.

SEC. 4. That the sheriffs of all the counties shall advise the national agent of all parties violating the provisions of this act, and this act take effect and be in force from and after its passage.

Approved, October 19, 1893.

W. N. JONES,
P. C. C. N.

AN ACT creating the office of delegate to the congress of the United States, prescribing his duties and providing for his compensation.

SECTION 1. Be it enacted by the general council of the Choctaw nation assembled: That the office of delegate to the congress of United States be and the same is hereby created; that said delegate so appointed as herein provided, shall not be less than thirty-five years of age and a Choctaw Indian by blood.

SEC. 2. That said delegate shall be appointed by the principal chief, by and with the consent and approval of the senate. Said delegate shall represent the Choctaw nation in all her interests whatever in congress, and before the departments, and shall keep the principal chief thoroughly advised as to all matters under his charge and supervision, and he shall make an annual report of all matters in his charge to the general council annually, and such matter and other reports as he may be called upon to make from time to time by the principal chief.

SEC. 3. That the term of office of said delegate shall be for four years. He shall be required to reside at Washington, D. C., and shall be present during all sessions of congress, unless otherwise directed by the principal chief.

SEC. 4. That the salary of said delegate shall be five thousand ($5,000) dollars per annum, payable quarterly, upon warrants to be issued by the national auditor, the first quarter's allowance of said delegate to be paid in advance at the time of his appointment.

SEC. 5. That said delegate is authorized and empowered to employ such attorney or attorneys as he may deem advisable, and by and with the advice and consent of the principal chief, on requisition drawn by said delegate and countersigned by the principal chief on the treasurer of the Choctaw nation to disburse and expend not more than two thousand ($2,000) dollars per annum in payment of such attorney or attorneys so employed by said delegate.

SEC. 6. That this act shall take effect and be in force from and after its passage.

Approved October 19th, 1893.

W. N. JONES,
P. C. C. N.

AN ACT abolishing the office of coal weigher.

SECTION 1. Be it enacted by the general council of the Choctaw nation assembled : That the office of national coal weigher created by an act approved November 1, 1882, amended October 26, 1888, is hereby repealed.

Sec. 2. Be it further enacted that this act shall take effect from and after its passage.

Approved, October 20, 1893.

W. N. JONES,
P. C. C. N.

An Act in relation to the boarding schools.

Section 1. Be it enacted by the general council of the Choctaw nation assembled: That the requirements necessary for admission into any of the boarding schools of the Choctaw nation shall not include literary qualifications, but only such other requirements as the school board may see fit to improve from time to time.

Sec. 2. That all acts or parts of acts coming in conflict with the provisions of this act shall be and the same is hereby repealed, and this act to take effect from and after its passage.

Approved, October 21, 1893.

W. N. JONES,
P. C. C. N.

An Act relating to report of Simon McCoy, district collector of the second district, C. N.

We, your committee to whom was referred the report of Simon McCoy, district collector of the second district, have carefully examined the same, and find that he is defaulter to the nation of four hundred and sixty-six dollars and sixty-one cents ($466 61) and therefore would ask the adoption of the following act:

Be it enacted by the general council of the Choctaw nation assembled : That the district attorney of the second district is hereby instructed to proceed at once, by law, against said Simon McCoy, and his sureties on his bond, for the collection of said sum and all proper costs,

and the money so collected be turned into the national
treasury for national purposes, and this act to take effect
and be in force from and after its passage.

Approved, October 25, 1893.

W. N. JONES,
P. C. C. N.

Be it enacted by the general council of the Choctaw
nation assembled: That Greenwood Leflore and his two
children, Nola and Louis Leflore, be adopted as citizens
of this nation, and are hereby declared to be entitled to
all the privileges and rights of such citizens, and this act
take effect from and after its passage.

Approved, October 26, 1893.

W. N. JONES,
P. C. C. N.

AN ACT creating the office of national inspector of coal
companies books.

SECTION 1. Be it enacted by the general council of
the Choctaw nation assembled: That the office of national inspector of coal companies books is hereby created.

SEC. 2. That the duties of the national inspector
shall be to inspect the books of the different coal companies of the Choctaw nation, to make quarterly reports
of the same to the national treasurer, and annually report to the general council at the regular session; said
report to contain the amount of royalty on coal timber
and permits due the Choctaw nation.

SEC. 3. That the office of national inspector shall
be required to take the oath of office prescribed in the
constitution and enter into bond with good and sufficient
sureties in the penal sum of five thousand ($5,000) dol-

lars, payable to the Choctaw nation, conditioned that he will well and truly 'discharge his duties in accordance with the law.

SEC. 4. That the salary of national inspector shall be one thousand (1,000) dollars per annum, payable quarterly, upon a warrant issued by the national auditor upon the national treasurer for the same; and this act shall take effect and be in force from and after its passage.

Approved, October 26, 1893.

W. N. JONES,
P. C. C. N.

AN ACT authorizing the principal chief to have the laws of the Choctaw nation compiled, translated and printed.

Be it enacted by the general council of the Choctaw nation assembled: That the principal chief be and he is hereby authorized to enter into contract with one competent person to compile, translate, print and bind in good substantial leather binding five hundred copies each in English and Choctaw language.

Be it further enacted, that the amount stipulated in the contract above provided for shall not exceed four thousand dollars, and whatever amount may be stipulated in the contract, any part of it is not to be paid until the work has been completed and accepted, and approved.

Be it further enacted, that when the work is completed the compiler shall report it to the principal chief for inspection, and the principal chief shall appoint a committee of three competent persons and they shall investigate the work and report their investigation, and if the work is accepted the principal chief shall issue a certificate to the compiler for the amount under contract, and the national auditor shall issue his warrant for it and the national treasurer pay the same.

Be it further enacted, that the work above provided for must be completed in a reasonable length of time not to exceed four months from the date of the contract. The national secretary is hereby required to furnish the compiler with all laws in his office whatsoever, in bound books, pamphlet, or manuscript, and take receipt for them, and this act shall take effect and be in force from and after its passage.

Approved, October 27, 1893.

W. N. JONES.
P. C. C. F.

Section 1. Be it enacted by the general council of the Choctaw nation assembled : That the judge of each county of the several counties of Mosholetubbee district shall appropriate one hundred dollars each out of their respective treasuries to pay for the circuit court house of Mosholetubbee district.

Sec. 2. It shall be the duty of the circuit judge of Mosholetubbee district to select and locate the circuit court ground and enter into contract with any person he may see proper to contract with for the building of the court house.

Sec. 3 The circuit judge is hereby directed to order the judges of the several counties of the district to forthwith appropiate the amount of money required from each county. The circuit judge be, and he is here·by authorized to take the money so appropriated and pay to the party who contracted to build the courthouse.

Sec. 4. The circuit judge shall be entitled to the sum of fifty dollars, ($50) payable out of any money in

the national treasury not otherwise appropriated, for selecting and locating the circuit court ground and superintending the building of the courthouse.   The national
auditor shall issue his warrant on the national treasurer
for the sum of fifty dollars on the certificate of the circuit judge and the national treasurer shall pay the same,
and this act shall take effect and be in force from and
after its passage.
     Approved.

W. N. JONES,
P. C. C. N

AN ACT disposing of the firearms purchased by the
    Choctaw nation for the Antlers trouble.

    SECTION 1.   Be it enacted by the general council of
the Choctaw nation assembled :   That the captains of
the militia are hereby instructed to collect all firearms
purchased by the Choctaw nation for the use of the
militia and return them to the capitol at Tushka Hum·
ma for storage.   In case, however, should any member
of the militia propose to retain said firearms, then he
shall pay to the captain its value in money, to be turned
into the national treasury to be credited against the
militia account and report by the next general council.

    SEC. 2.   Be it further enacted, that this act be in
force from and after its passage.

    Approved, July 5, 1893.

W. N. JONES,
P. C. C. N.

WEST MIDLANDS EDUCATION AUTHORITIES
EDUCATION SERVICE FOR TRAVELLING CHILDRE

INDEX.

A

PAGE

Amendment to the constitution 30
Attorney at law 185
Arbitration 188
Assault with intent to kill 203
Assault and battery 204
Arson 212
Alteration or destruction of wills . . . . : . 213
Accessories . . . . , ... 224
An act in reference to cases pending in Atoka, Blue and
    Kiamichi counties, etc. 264
An act in reference to compilation of the Choctaw laws . 277
Alikchi precinct in Nashoba county 329
Adoption of freedmen 335
Abbot Leflore, et. al., admitted to citizenship 336

B

Burglary 210
Burning prairies and woods 222
Boarding schools—in reference to 295
Board of education 298
Boundary lines changed in certain counties 312
Bribery of voters— in reference to 313
Benton Robert, granting charter 327
Big Cane precinct in Jacksfork county 330
Blackfork precinct in Sugarloaf county 332
Board of education let contracts for new academies and
    naming same 334
Boarding schools, in relation to 340

C

PAGE.

Constitution . . . . ' 5
Clerk of the supreme court 125
Circuit courts 129
Clerks of the circuit courts 137
County courts and courts of probate 143
Clerks of county courts 155
Cutting down hickory or pecan trees 222
Common laborers 240
Claims and improvements—citizens rights defined . . . 247
Castration of intruding stock 260
Circuit court located in Jackson county 265
Cititizens not allowed to employ non-citizens as herdsmen 274
Coal contracts—in reference to 283
Crippled, blind and idiotic—in reference to 284
Citizenship—manner of applying for 285
Citizenship—act repealed 288
Commissioners—in reference to leased district 291
County officers' pay increased 295
Cass Maurice to establish a toll gate 330
Coal weigher—abolishing office of 339
Coal inspector—office created 341
Compilation, translation and printing of the Choctaw laws 342
Circuit court house in Mosholitubbee district—erection of . 343

D

District boundaries 6
Declaration of rights 7
Distribution of power 11
District chiefs, defining duties of 88
District collectors, defining duties of 111
District attorneys 141
Depositions 187
Disturbance of schools, religious devotions or families, etc. 219
Divorce and alimony 233
Drovers 257
Deputy sheriffs 264
District trustees 304

PAGE.

District collectors and inspectors, in reference to 326
District Judges, an act relating to 328
Delegate to congress, creating office of 338
District collector second district, relating to report . . . 340
Disposal of firearms 344

E

Executive department 18
Exemptions 190
Elections 191
Embezzlement of public money 214

F

Fees of officers of court 178
Fines and bonds 189
Forgery 213
Farmers or renters 238

G

General provisions 22
General council 116
Goodland precinct in Kiamichi county 286
Greenwood LeFlore et al. are made citizens 341

H

Hunting and trapping by non-citizens, Indians and white
    men 220
Hunting on Sunday 224
Hartshorne court ground in Gaines county 333
Hartshorne precinct in Gaines county 333

I

Itakshish precinct, in Jackson county 331
Impeachments 21
Inspector, defining duties of 110
Incest 205
Inter-marriage with negroes 206
Introduction of whisky 215

PAGE.

Inter-marriage 225
Inspectors, two additional 262
Intruders, how to be dealt with 268
Impeachment act 271
Inter-marriage, an act in reference to 277
Interpreters for general council 282
Iron Bridge precinct, in San Bois county 323
Inspector St. Louis & S. F. R. R., creating office of . . . 328

J

Judicial department 14
Juries 174
Jackson county established 262
Jackson county, one representative 263
Jackson and Blue counties compose a senatorial district . 263
Jurors in third district 265
Joint resolution of general council 288
Jones precinct in Blue county 311
John E. McBrayer, charter granted to 316

K

Killing a person for a witch, etc 197
Kidnapping 208
Keys Annie—extending charter 337
Kiamichi county court grounds 287

L

Legislative department 11
Lawful fence—in reference to hogs 198
Larceny 210
Libel and slander 214
Licensed traders 237
Leasing lands 248
Lawful fences—what constitutes 250
Limitation to non-citizens 251
Little Boggy precinct in Atoka county 284
Larceny of cattle—detection of 314
Licensed traders—in reference to 317

PAGE.

Lick precinct in Cedar county 324
Leflore's precinct in Gains county 324
Lewis Henry—conferring citizenship on 329

M

Militia 25
Mode of amending and revising the Constitution 26
Murder 200
Manslaughter 202
Mayhem 208
Malicious mischief 210
Marriage 233
Missionaries 235
Miscellaneous employes 241
Militia, an act creating three companies 243
Marks and brands 253
Missionaries, acts in reference to 275
Militia law suspended 285
M. K. & T. R'y to reduce the rates of mileage 285
Mineral resources, in reference to 296
Mississippi Choctaws, in reference to 315
Mississippi Indians, in reference to 320
Mississippi Choctaws, admitting 323

N

National secretary, defining duties of 90
National treasurer, defining duties of 93
National auditor, defining duties of 99
National attorney, defining duties of 104
National agent, defining duties of 106
National lighthorsemen 113
Non-citizen improvements 248
Non-citizen herdsmen 250
Non-citizen enclosures or pastures, how to be disposed of 267
National auditor's duty defined 269
National treasurer's contingent fund, etc. 274
National treasurer, security of 282
Net proceeds money, distribution of 288
National contractors, in reference to 318

O

PAGE.

Officers—when to qualify 278
Oath of allegience—in reference to 297
Orphans' interest—in reference to 316
Oak Hill precinct in San Bois county 315

P

Public money—protection of 334
Peddlers and other traders—in reference to 320
Patterson Walter turnpike—in reference to 318
Pistols—carrying of 218
Principal chief—defining duties of 85
Punishment for selling the country 198
Polygamy and adultery 205
Poisoning 207
Perjury 212
Pulling down fences 222
Practice of medicine 235
Professionalists and tradesmen 239
Punitary provision 242
Prohibition of the manufacture or sale of any intoxicant . 261
Pastures—an act in relation to 270
Prairie hay—in reference to 276
Public buildings—protection of 276
Permits—in reference to 280
Pastures—in reference to leasing or renting 281
Prairie hay—an act amendatory 311

Q

Quantity of blood necessary for citizenship 266

R

Rangers, defining duties of 181
Respecting wills 197
Repealing certain laws 199
Rape 204
Robbery 209
Racing horses or playing ball on Sunday 224

PAGE.

Roads 229
Railroads 231
Royalties 245
Ranger, increasing salary of 267
Red Oak Hill precinct in Atoka county 283
Records, changing of 213

S

Schedule 27
Sheriffs, defining duties of 164
Supreme court 120
Sentences and executions 186
Sodomy (unnatural intercourse) 206
Skinning dead animals on the range 220
Selling goods on Sunday 223
Strays 254
Stock killing one another 259
Superintendent of public schools, increase of salary . . . 261
Sheriff of Jackson county 266
Students to be sent to the States 280
Sunday, in reference to hunting cattle 281
Steer cattle, in reference to 292
Saw Mill Church precinct, in Kiamichi county 295
School systems, in reference to 297
Superintendents of schools 304
Stock, cruelty to 209
Schools, neighborhood 306
Schools, boarding 307
Schools, orphan 310
Sheriff's reports, time and manner of making 321
Scholars at public schools, in relation to 331
Sulphur Spring precinct, in Cedar county 332

T

Treaty of 1830 31
Treaty of 1837 34
Treaty of 1855 37
Treaty of 1866 49

PAGE.

Treason 200

Tribunal for citizenship . . . . · 227

Trustee, local 305

Timber, prohibiting the floating of 337

U

Unlawful fence (stating damages) 198

U. S. courts—in reference to 292

W

Witnesses 184

Wire fences 252

Witnesses pay—in reference to 279

Wade county court ground 292

Woolridge Moses—granting charter to 325

00074